GIVE ME
LIBERTY

ALSO BY RICHARD BROOKHISER

John Marshall: The Man Who Made the Supreme Court

Founders' Son: A Life of Abraham Lincoln

James Madison

*Right Time, Right Place: Coming of Age with
William F. Buckley Jr. and the Conservative Movement*

George Washington on Leadership

*What Would the Founders Do?:
Our Questions, Their Answers*

*Gentleman Revolutionary: Gouverneur Morris,
the Rake Who Wrote the Constitution*

America's First Dynasty: The Adamses, 1735–1918

Alexander Hamilton, American

Founding Father: Rediscovering George Washington

*The Way of the WASP: How It Made America
and How It Can Save It . . . So to Speak*

*The Outside Story: How Democrats and
Republicans Reelected Reagan*

GIVE ME LIBERTY

LIBERTY

A HISTORY OF AMERICA'S EXCEPTIONAL IDEA

RICHARD BROOKHISER

BASIC BOOKS
New York

Basic Books
Hachette Book Group
1290 Avenue of the Americas, New York, NY 10104
www.basicbooks.com

Printed in the United States of America

First Edition: November 2019

Published by Basic Books, an imprint of Perseus Books, LLC, a subsidiary of Hachette Book Group, Inc. The Basic Books name and logo is a trademark of the Hachette Book Group.

The Hachette Speakers Bureau provides a wide range of authors for speaking events. To find out more, go to www.hachettespeakersbureau.com or call (866) 376-6591.

The publisher is not responsible for websites (or their content) that are not owned by the publisher.

Print book interior design by Amnet Systems.

Library of Congress Control Number: 2019948392

ISBNs: 978-1-5416-9913-7 (hardcover), 978-1-5416-9912-0 (ebook)

LSC-C

10 9 8 7 6 5 4 3 2 1

To the American people

"Give me liberty, or give me death!"
—Patrick Henry

CONTENTS

INTRODUCTION

NATIONALISM IS ALL THE RAGE. IT IS TRUE IN THE world's oldest democracies. Donald Trump has made securing America's borders and protecting its industries top priorities. "From this moment on," he said in his 2017 inaugural address, "it's going to be America first."[1] Half a year earlier, Britain voted to leave the European Union.

It takes sinister forms elsewhere. Narendra Modi conflates Indian nationalism with Hinduism, to the consternation of India's other religions. Vladimir Putin, Viktor Orban, and Recep Tayyip Erdogan invoke nationalism to make their countries one-party states. Xi Jinping invokes it to guarantee his own power for life. Aung San Suu Kyi, winner of the Nobel Peace Prize, invokes it to ethnically cleanse the Muslim minority of Myanmar.

Nationalism is a given in human society. It supplies feelings of belonging, identity, and recognition. It binds us to our neighbors, tells us who we are, and makes others notice us. But it takes different forms from country to country and from era to era.[2]

The unique feature of America's nationalism is its concern for liberty. We have been securing it, defining it, recovering it, and fighting for it for four hundred years. We have been doing it since we were a floundering settlement on a New World river, long before we were a country. We do it now on podiums and battlefields beyond our borders.

Our concern for liberty shapes how we live in society and what we know ourselves to be in the order of things: how we relate to each other and what God has made us. Americans are free and equal men and women, marked for liberty at birth. Ignorance and vice may obscure and sometimes even steal our birthright, but we work, stolidly or heroically, to reclaim it.

American liberty is liberty of the person. If liberty is applied to collections of persons, its meaning changes. When a country liberates itself from a colonial or imperial overlord (as dozens have since we did), it wins independence. When the machinery of the state liberates itself from incompetence or customary restraints, it may achieve efficiency or despotism. When a mob liberates itself from habits of good behavior, it produces chaos. American liberty is about Americans—you, me, her, him.

But this liberty is plural; it cannot be experienced alone. If one person living in a tyrannical state were somehow freed from all its supervision and punishments, he or she would experience the immunity of an alien or practice the duplicity of a spy. That person would not enjoy liberty. My liberty as an American is also yours; ours is others'.

We claim it for no other reason than we are persons, and America recognizes the sovereign importance of this fact. We enjoy liberty not because we are people *and*: people who have the right ancestors, people who practice the approved creed, or people who spend the most money. We enjoy it because we are men and women.

As Americans we claim to have a uniquely clear understanding of human nature and to act in accordance with it. But a desire for liberty asserts itself in other countries, too. The two with which our history is most bound enjoy elements of liberty, as we understand it. We inherited much from our mother country, Britain, and France's revolution and republics have mirrored, and fun house–mirrored, our own. But Britain's liberty is deeply rooted in a mold of custom, while France's is buffeted by storms of passion. Britain still has a crown and classes; France every so often produces a new constitution. This is not a book about almost liberty elsewhere; it is a book about the real thing, here in America.

A complete history of liberty in America would be a complete history of America. This book focuses instead on thirteen documents, from 1619 to 1987, that represent snapshots from the album of our long marriage to liberty. They say what liberty is. They show who asked for it, when, and why. Since no marriage is ever simple, they track its ups and downs. These thirteen liberty documents define America as the country that it is, different from all others.

Six of the liberty documents are speeches or addresses— one delivered in writing, one over the radio, four to live audiences (a courtroom, a political convention, and two outdoor events). Five are collective statements, written by an individual or a committee, but endorsed by a group. One is the minutes of an assembly; one is a poem on a statue.

The documents vary in length: the assembly met over five days, the briefest speech lasted two or three minutes, and the poem is a sonnet. Some of the liberty documents are official pronouncements; others are appeals to, or by, the marginalized. Some are so famous they are ubiquitous; others are little known. Some are clumsy but earnest, others eloquent. All are important. We are what we are because of them, and we made them because of who we are. We stay true to what we are by staying true to them.

All of them are public statements, making a case to the world—the opinion of mankind, as the Declaration of Independence puts it—or to a relevant public official—"Right Honorable," begins the Flushing Remonstrance, addressing Dutch governor-general Peter Stuyvesant. None of them is absorbed with personal details or written in a way that is willfully oblique. But standing alone, they would be naked, so I have clothed them with context: who wrote or spoke them, where, and when. You have to know something about the economy of the late nineteenth century to understand William Jennings Bryan or something about the politics of early eighteenth-century New York to understand the trial of John Peter Zenger.

Something isn't everything. From one document to the next, years, sometimes decades, pass. One speech here was given in Berlin, another in Chicago, the rest on or near the East Coast, but none in California or Hawaii. Whole swaths of the American experience are missing. But I keep a forward momentum.

Two of the liberty documents, and the important part of a third, are about foreign affairs—what America promises, threatens, or fears from other countries. This may seem surprising in a book about liberty, especially in a book about liberty conceived as the essence of our nationalism. But the world is always close at hand. America began as a collection of colonies and won its independence in a revolution against an imperial master. We live among neighbors and wars. Even when we are not interested in them, they may be interested in us.

Several of the liberty documents are accompanied by lists of names—of signers, audiences, or participants; delegates, jurors, or burgesses. Some of the lists are quite long, with many or most of the names obscure. Read them all. Whether these people were already famous, became famous, or are known only for being there at one moment of history, they all contributed to their liberty and ours. Remembering them is a duty and a pleasure. As a witness to one of the liberty documents said, "How sweet it is to speak of good men!"— and women.[3]

Two of my linguistic choices in this book require explanation. I use *America* as a synonym for the United States, even at the risk of confusion when the story overlaps with other countries in the Americas—Mexico, Brazil, Argentina. I do it despite the boisterous stadium chant, *USA! USA!* I use America partly because one-quarter of my story (and more than a quarter of our history) occurs in the seventeenth and early eighteenth centuries, before there was a United States. I do it because every country in this hemisphere, from Canada to Chile, has its own story, with its own America. Let them tell theirs. I will tell ours.

I also use words like *ours, our, we,* and *us* to refer to actions, things, or people that no living American has done, possessed, or known. But that is what a nation is: a many-headed, centuries-old being that embraces the living, the dead, and the still to be born. Before battles, George Washington exhorted his soldiers to fight as if "the fate of unborn millions" depended on their efforts—because it did.[4] As he looked ahead, so we must look behind—and see ourselves.

Where are the dark chapters documenting oppression, brutality, injustice? Americans—we—are human, and the heart—yours and mine—is desperately wicked. There are dark pages aplenty in our story, when the light of liberty was unlit or eagerly blown out. Sometimes liberty's enemies have been foreigners, careless colonizers, or bloody monsters; sometimes they have been all-American. This book is not about them. They loom, of course, since any account of brave men and women—and many of the authors and signers of these documents put their reputations or their lives on the line—must include who and what they struggled against. You cannot read about Abraham Lincoln or John Murray without reading about slavery, about Tobias Feake or Andrew Hamilton without reading about oppression, about Elizabeth Cady Stanton or Rhoda Palmer without reading about inequity. But this book is about what prompted men and women to resist: to think, speak, and sometimes fight for what was right.

My authority for telling this story is my career as a historian and a journalist. For over twenty years, I have been engaged with American lives, particularly those of the founders. I have studied the greatest Americans, describing their achievements (and failures), explaining their beliefs.

I know what they worked for. For fifty years I have been writing about contemporary American politics, covering men and women—usually less great than the founders, though sometimes they hit their mark—writing about how they have maintained, advanced, or manhandled their predecessors' handiwork.

The need for telling this story now is what I see around me. This is the most confused historical moment I have lived in. Between a haggard establishment, a perverse intelligentsia, and an inchoate populist pushback, America's national essence is being ignored, trampled, or distorted. Those who remember the right words and principles repeat them as platitudes; others spurn them or offer substitutes, do-it-yourself or imported from abroad. Because the people offering substitutes are either less intelligent or less virtuous than the authors and original audiences of the liberty documents, their alternatives are worse.

We always have been a free country; our advances are fulfillments of old promises, not lunges in the direction of new ones. This is our nationalism, and we should be proud of it.

The epigraph of this book is a famous exclamation about American liberty. I did not give it a chapter, so let me quickly tell the story here.

British troops occupying Boston, a disorderly colonial city, set out in April 1775 on a police action to round up troublemakers said to be lurking in the countryside nearby. The mission spiraled out of control, however, when one group of locals, then a second, fired back, then swarms of them sniped at the troops as they returned to base.

News of the clashes spread as fast as horses could convey it. In Richmond, hundreds of miles to the south, an extralegal assembly of colonials met in an Anglican church to debate how they should respond. Patrick Henry, a thirty-nine-year-old attorney and planter, was one of those who spoke. He had a reputation for being ambitious, lazy, and vain. He deplored slavery but owned slaves. One modern historian accuses him of self-interest bordering on corruption, opposing political reform because it queered a land deal he was invested in. He was also the best speaker on the continent. Thomas Jefferson, who disliked him, said simply that he spoke as Homer wrote.

Henry's speech was not recorded until 1817, when a biographer printed it, which gave rise to the presumption that the biographer, though he interviewed surviving witnesses, had rewritten it himself. Maybe, maybe not. Many of the biographer's own speeches survive, and they are nothing like this one.

It is short: twelve hundred words, three printed pages. It is urgent: almost a third of its sentences are questions—*Is it? Have we? But when? Shall we?* It is desperate: Americans everywhere had to support the liberty of Americans in Boston or all our liberty would be undone.

"Why stand we here idle? What is it that gentlemen wish? What would they have? Is life so dear, or peace so sweet, as to be purchased at the price of chains, and of slavery? Forbid it, Almighty God!—I know not what course others may take; but as for me, give me liberty, or give me death!"[5]

Read on.

chapter one

MINUTES OF THE JAMESTOWN GENERAL ASSEMBLY

Self-Government

T HEY THOUGHT THEY WERE LOST.

Three ships, the *Susan Constant*, the *Godspeed*, and the *Discovery*, sailed from London on December 20, 1606, carrying 144 passengers and crew, bound for Virginia. After being held off the coast of England for six weeks by contrary winds, they crossed the Atlantic by a southerly route, reprovisioned in the West Indies, then headed north, expecting landfall in the third week of April 1607. Instead they found themselves in a tempest. For four days they sounded, seeking offshore shallows in vain. Then, at four o'clock in the morning of April 26, they saw land. The ships sailed into Chesapeake Bay and found, in the words of one voyager, "fair meddowes and goodly tall Trees, with such fresh waters running through the woods, as I was almost ravished at the first sight thereof."[1] They picked an island in a river for a settlement and named it for their king, James.

The English were latecomers to the New World. Although their sailors had explored the western Atlantic for more than a hundred years, the home country, preoccupied by the upheavals of the Reformation and the feral family politics of the Tudors, had followed none of its discoveries with colonies; efforts to settle Newfoundland and North Carolina sputtered out. (Spain, by contrast, built an empire from its colonies spanning two continents, ornamented with cathedrals and universities.)

At the turn of the seventeenth century, however, England was ready to try colonization in earnest. A group of merchant investors, salted with noblemen, called the London Company received a charter from King James I allowing them to develop a swath of the North American coast named Virginia, after his late unmarried predecessor, Elizabeth I.

The promoters of the scheme expected economic benefits. A transatlantic colony would be a haven and a workshop for England's surplus poor. As Richard Hakluyt, England's premier geographer, put it, "Valiant youths rusting [from] lack of employment" would find it building a life for themselves overseas. The crops they would grow and the items they would make, Hakluyt went on, could be sold back home, "yield[ing] unto us all the commodities of Europe, Africa and Asia"—the entire rest of the world, no less.[2] With luck, the valiant youths might strike it rich. Spain had discovered mother lodes of precious metals in its colonies; why not England? A 1605 comic play, *Eastward Ho!*, described Virginia colonists using golden chamber pots.

God would be served as well as mammon. Spain was shepherding its indigenous overseas populations into Roman Catholicism (hence its colonial cathedrals). England could convert native Virginians to the true—Anglican—faith.

What the Jamestown colonists found, however, was hardship. In their first year, they took their drinking water from the James River, which resulted in many succumbing to typhoid, dysentery, and (since the stream was tidal) salt poisoning. Once they had dug a well, they were able to drink safely, but growing enough edibles was another trial. Modern studies of tree rings preserved in old logs show that during the first seven years of the colony's existence, the Chesapeake Bay area was baked by a drought, making gardening and farming virtually impossible. This left the English dependent on bartering for supplies with local natives, whose own stores were depleted. Settlers who died of starvation or disease had to be replaced by new settlers from England, who arrived once or twice a year (the pioneers had been heavily male, but the newcomers increasingly included women).

The colonists were capable of hard work. One month after landing, they built a palisade to protect themselves from possible attack. Over nineteen hot June days, they cut and split more than six hundred trees weighing four hundred to eight hundred pounds each and set them in a triangular trench three football fields long and two and a half feet deep. Four hundred years later, the makers of a Hollywood film about Jamestown built a replica of the fort in about the same amount of time—using power tools.

But forts were not an exportable product. The settlers found a few semiprecious stones—garnets, amethysts, quartz crystals—but no silver or gold. One resupply ship brought German and Polish glassmakers, meant to generate local manufacturing; most of them ran off to live with the natives.

Relations between the settlers and local natives were the most significant variable in Jamestown's early history. The western Chesapeake was ruled by Wahunsonacock, chief of the Powhatan. He was an expansionist, no less than James I, having brought thirty local tribes under his sway in an empire of fifteen thousand people. Capt. John Smith, one of the early leaders of the Jamestown colony, described Wahunson-acock's royal state: "He sat covered with a great robe, made of raccoon skins, and all the tails hanging by," flanked by "two rows of men, and behind them as many women, with all their heads and shoulders painted red."[3] The settlers hoped to make him a tributary of their king; conversely, Wahun-sonacock hoped to make the settlers his allies. Sometimes they fought (hence the palisade); sometimes they traded. Wahunsonacock wanted the copper the settlers offered in exchange for food, and he very much wanted their swords and firearms: muzzle-loaded long guns, their charges ignited by matchlocks—clumsy and dangerous to use but deadly, especially when fired in volleys.

But when the Powhatan refused to trade for food, Jamestown's colonists died horribly. The winter of 1609 was the "starving time." The colonists ate horses, dogs, vermin, boot leather, even (it was said) corpses. In June 1610 the survivors staggered onto their ships and sailed into the bay, either looking for help or intending to sail home. Help came: the London Company, reorganized as the Virginia Company, had sent three resupply ships from England, which met the despairing colonists in the nick of time.

In a desperate effort to extend the life of the shattered colony, it was put under strict martial law. Men farmed in work parties supervised by overseers, for the common good. Runaways, if captured, were shot, hanged, burned, or beaten to death.

Such a ferocious regime could only be an emergency measure; if word of it got out in England, who would come willingly to live in such a place? Three changes began to improve Jamestown's prospects.

In 1612 the colonists acquired a marketable crop when one of their number, John Rolfe, introduced seeds of *Nicotiana tabacum* from Spain's colonies in South America. The Powhatan smoked a crude local weed, but South American tobacco was sweeter in the mouth; smoking it was already a craze in England. Now the home market would not have to buy from foreigners. By 1620 Jamestown was shipping almost fifty thousand pounds of tobacco across the Atlantic. Fifty years later, Virginia and Maryland, its neighboring colony, would ship fifteen million pounds.

Rolfe gave the colony another benefit—publicity—when he married one of Wahunsonacock's daughters, Matoaka, better known to history by her childhood nickname, Pocahontas (meaning *playful one*). She was captured as a teenager during a bout of native-settler strife. She converted to Christianity, was baptized as Rebecca, and married Rolfe in 1614; two years later, she accompanied her husband to England, where she was depicted in a Virginia Company advertisement and presented to the king. The couple set sail for Virginia in 1617, but Rebecca died, age twenty or twenty-one, before their ship exited the Thames River.

A third substantial change was the introduction and regularization of private property. The colony could not flourish as an agricultural garrison state. Beginning in 1616, settlers who had survived there for seven years or more were awarded fifty acres; newcomers were promised fifty, plus an additional fifty for each additional person they brought with them.

What the colony most needed, though, was stable government. Since its inception it had been ruled by a shifting cast of governors, picked and sent out by the London Company (and later by the Virginia Company). Though the governors were assisted by a council of advisors, their own decisions were final, and they could pick and dismiss the members of their council at will. They were not supposed to do anything contrary to the laws of England, but that left much room for improvisation. Wide powers and uncertain tenure, combined with difficult circumstances, led to disagreement and recrimination. The typical firsthand account of early Jamestown argues that everything would have gone well if everyone besides the author had not done wrong. Acrimony in Virginia was matched by squabbles among the company's investors back in London.

In 1618 a newly dominant faction within the Virginia Company tapped a new governor, George Yeardley, with a mandate for comprehensive reform in the colony. Yeardley was a veteran who had fought against Spain in the Netherlands, survived a shipwreck in Bermuda, and lived at Jamestown for seven years. Before taking up his new job, he had an audience with the king, who knighted him, "to grace him the more."[4] In Virginia he would be assisted by John Pory, a man whose various careers—diplomatic secretary, author, would-be silkworm breeder—included six years' service in Parliament.

Scholars debate whether Yeardley and his council of advisors meant to liberalize the regime of the colony in the interests of the common good or simply to make it more profitable.[5] Their reforms, whether intentional or otherwise, had the former effect.

By 1618 the colony was composed of two dozen settlements spread over seventy miles from the mouth of the James River on Chesapeake Bay to the fall line; Jamestown lay along the north shore about a third of the way in. Under the new dispensation, the colony was divided into four boroughs—an old English unit of government between a town and a county in size—as well as seven plantations, the estates of investors that had been granted quasi-autonomous status (how autonomous was still to be determined). This domain was to be ruled, as before, by the parent company in London, with its day-to-day operations overseen by a governor (now Yeardley).

Yeardley would not rule alone. He was seconded by a Council of State, appointed not by him but by the company. He had another body of helpers too, whose composition marked an epoch in American history.

In June 1619 Yeardley, newly arrived in Virginia from visiting the king, called on the colony's freemen to elect "by a pluralitie of voices" two burgesses from each borough and plantation. They were to join with him and the Council of

State in a "general Assemblie" which would have "free power to treat, consult & conclude . . . all emergent occasions concerning the publique weale."[6]

Since the burgesses would establish such an important precedent, let us record their names.

The four boroughs sent eight burgesses.

(James City, the borough of Jamestown) Capt. William Powell, Ensign William Spense
(Charles City) Samuel Sharpe, Samuel Jordan
(Henricus City) Thomas Dowse, John Polentine
(Kiccowtan) Capt. William Tucker, William Capp

Seven plantations sent fourteen.

(Martin Brandon) Mr. Thomas Davis, Mr. Robert Stacy
(Smythe's Hundred—not a numeral but an English geographical term) Capt. Thomas Graves, Mr. Walter Shelley
(Martin's Hundred) Mr. John Boys, John Jackson
(Argall's Gift) Mr. Pawlett, Mr. Gourgainy
(Flowerdew Hundred) Ensign Roffingham, Mr. Jefferson
(Capt. Lawne's Plantation) Capt. Christopher Lawne, Ensign Washer
(Capt. Warde's Plantation) Capt. John Warde, Lt. Gibbes

The first meeting of the General Assembly convened on July 30, 1619, in Jamestown's church, a wooden building fifty by twenty feet, with plastered walls and a roof of wood or thatch. (Only the foundation survives; the seventeenth-century brick church tower that stands at Jamestown today is the remnant of a later construction.) Yeardley and his Council of State sat in the chancel, the portion of the church nearest the altar. Pory sat in front of them, acting as Speaker or secretary. A sergeant at arms stood by, ready to maintain order. The burgesses sat alongside the chancel in the choir. The Rev. Richard Buck, the cleric who had married Rolfe and Rebecca/Pocahontas, said a prayer (since, as Pory wrote, "men's affaires doe little prosper where God's service is neglected").[7] The burgesses were then asked to step into the nave, or body of the church, to swear their loyalty, one by one, to James I. This done, they returned to their seats in the choir, and the General Assembly turned to business.

The business of the first legislature in America began with disputes over credentials. Capt. John Warde was a burgess from his own plantation, fifteen miles upriver. He had, however, settled in the colony without the permission of the Virginia Company; should he be allowed a role in the deliberations of a body that the company had created? Another controversy concerned the two burgesses representing Martin's Hundred, a plantation ten miles east of Jamestown. But the patent or charter issued to Capt. John Martin, the plantation's absent master, exempted him and his hundred from the colony's laws. Governor Yeardley himself objected to the presence of Martin's burgesses. There was another problem with Martin: a boatload of his men stood accused of stopping Indians in a canoe on the bay and seizing their corn. The settlers had given trinkets in return, but the Indians had not been willing sellers. Relations with the Powhatan had been peaceful since Rolfe's wedding, but this was not the way to maintain them.

The General Assembly seated Captain Warde on the grounds that he had behaved as a model settler, with the understanding that he procure a commission from the company as soon as possible, which he promised to do. A message addressed to "our very loving friend" Captain Martin ordered him to come to Jamestown to explain himself.

The assembly next formed into committees. Pory explained their business. They were to examine all the instructions that the company had sent to the colony and decide which should become laws ("putt on the habite [clothing] of lawes" was how Pory phrased it). They were also to make their own suggestions for legislation ("what lawes might issue out of the private conceipte [thought] of any of the Burgesses").[8]

On July 31 the assembly drew up petitions to send back to the company in London: they wanted more settlers; they wanted a school ("a University and colledge"); they wanted the easternmost borough, Kiccowtan, to change its Indian name to something not "savage" (it would be renamed Elizabeth City); they wanted quit-rents—a fee of twelve pence a year that landowners paid to the company—to be payable in goods, not cash, of which the colonists had little. Most important, they wanted to be sure that any land awarded Governor Yeardley and his councilors as payment for their services not be carved from land that settlers already possessed. "After so much labor and coste, and so many years habitation," wrote Pory, "no man [should] suffer any wrong in this kinde."[9]

They also set the price of tobacco. They summoned Abraham Piersey, keeper of the company's warehouse, and instructed him to pay three shillings a pound for the best quality and half that (eighteen pence a pound) for second best.

Since the next day, August 1, fell on a Sunday, the assembly did not meet. They lost a member: Walter Shelley, burgess from Smith's Hundred, died. The cause of death was not recorded, but the heat, which was intense, may have sped his passing. (What made the heat of a Virginia summer even worse was that the colonists made little effort to adjust their dress to it; they continued to wear padded doublets as if they were in Devon or Kent.[10])

On August 2 Captain Martin appeared. He promised that his sailors on the bay would behave better toward Indians, but he would not surrender the privileges he had been granted in his patent; as a result, his burgesses were refused seats on the assembly. He would not play by the rules, so he lost his say.

A number of the company's instructions were given the form of laws. Colonists were forbidden to provoke the Indians; Indians were allowed to live among them, but no more than six per settlement ("though some amongst them ... may prove good, they are a treacherous people").[11] The cultivation of wheat, mulberry trees, flax, hemp, and vines was encouraged; tobacco was Virginia's bonanza, but the company stubbornly insisted on diversification. Tobacco was subjected to quality control. Any leaves that were brought to the company warehouse damp, and thus liable to rot, were to be "burnt before the owner's face."[12] Contracts made with servants in England were guaranteed in Virginia; the usual form was an indenture, an agreement by one person to serve another for a given time, usually seven years. Crossing the ocean could not cancel an obligation. Idleness, gambling, and drunkenness were penalized.

On August 3, the assembly heard a petition from Capt. William Powell, burgess for Jamestown, complaining of a "lewde and treacherous servante." The man, Thomas Garnett, had "committed wantonness" with another female servant and accused his master of drunkenness and theft.[13] The assembly ruled that Garnett should be whipped and have his ears nailed to the public pillory four days running. (Martial law had been suspended, but ordinary punishments of the seventeenth century were harsh enough.) The assembly also heard a reading of the proposed laws that had issued from the burgesses' thoughts.

On August 4, Governor Yeardley announced that because of the "extream heat," which had made him ill, this would be the final meeting of the session.[14] The assembly approved the laws proposed by the burgesses: Settlers could offer goods to the Indians in trade, except for large hoes, English dogs, and armaments or ammunition of any kind (the penalty for violating the last prohibition was hanging). The secretary of the colony had to be provided with lists of christenings, burials, marriages, and newly arrived servants. Swearing and whoredom were forbidden, as were stealing boats and slaughtering cattle. Church attendance was required. Colonists who wanted to trade in the bay needed a license. Maids and servant girls who wanted to marry needed parental consent.

There was one potentially ominous development: Wahunsonacock, the Powhatan chief, had died the year before. His place in the Indian empire was taken by a brother or half brother, Opechancanough, a wily leader who may have lived among the Spaniards as a young man. The assembly now heard from Robert Poole, an interpreter who dealt directly with the Indians, who accused another interpreter, Capt. Henry Spelman, of bad-mouthing Governor Yeardley to the new Powhatan ruler, bringing him and the colony "in much disrespect."[15] Captain Spelman defended himself grudgingly and angrily, but he was stripped of his rank and sentenced to labor for the company for seven years, though that would not undo the damage he had done.

Pory's record of the proceedings ended with an apology for "break[ing] up so abruptly," which he blamed on the "intemperature of the weather."[16] The next session of the assembly was called for the following March.

Once we get past the premodern language and the odd (and occasionally awful) customs—quit-rents, ear nailing—the deliberations of that first five-day session of the General Assembly have a familiar ring: the sweltering Virginians discussed economic self-interest, regulation of morals, and foreign relations (the Powhatan were an alien state, however near and—for now—friendly). Every legislative body deals with the first two subjects; every national one also considers the third. Anyone who has watched a political convention is familiar with credentials fights.

Familiarity must not blind us to the newness of this happening in North America in 1619. The General Assembly was not a fully formed legislature yet: there was no distribution of power among executives, aristocracy, and people; the governor, his appointed advisors, and elected burgesses sat mixed together. Their deliberations—how to punish Thomas Garnett, for example—were sometimes those of a court rather than a lawmaking body. Sticking the burgesses in the choir, while the governor and his council sat in the center of the chancel, was a spatial mark of subordination. (The business of a church service is not done in the choir; sermons are not preached nor sacraments administered there.)

Still, the General Assembly had some of the most important qualities of a legislature. The model naturally was England's Parliament. Proposed laws were read three times, a parliamentary practice designed to ensure clarity and understanding and to prevent sleight of hand. John Pory was called (likely at his own suggestion) Speaker, the title of the presiding officer of the House of Commons, although he was effectively the assembly's clerk.

The language of the assembly's deliberations was mild, even timid—until you looked closely. Pory inserted into his record of the first day, July 30, a question: Why had the assembly assigned committees to discuss instructions that the Virginia Company "had already resolved to be perfecte, and did expect nothing but our assente thereunto"? The real power in the company was in England, not Virginia; why hadn't the Virginians simply rubber-stamped whatever directions they were given? Pory answered modestly: "We did it not to the ende to correcte or controll anything" but to petition for redress. The Virginians were only asking their transatlantic masters to change their instructions wherever necessary.

But when was change necessary? Pory's instances, mentioned in passing, were quite extensive: the assembly would suggest changing any of the company's instructions that did not "perfectly squar[e] . . . with the state of this Colony" or "any lawe which did presse or binde too harde."[17] In other words, the assembly might ask to change anything that did not fit their assessment of conditions on the ground or that struck them as onerous—which could be almost anything they disagreed with or disliked. The assembly was presuming the principle of local control, or home rule.

Its discussion of tobacco price-setting on July 30 had the same character. Abraham Piersey, warehouse manager, agreed to offer the three shilling/eighteen pence per pound price schedule if "the Governor and Assembly," acting on the instructions of the company, "layd their commandment upon him."[18] The prices had been proposed in London, but it was the government in Jamestown that made them stick.

The last motion of the assembly on August 4 was simultaneously humble and assertive. It was up to the company, the Virginians admitted, "to allowe or to abrogate any lawes which we shall here make." Yet they requested that "these lawes which we have now brought to light . . . be of force" until they learned the company's pleasure.[19] The company could veto, but the assembly legislated. Since the company's disapproval could be rendered and received only after two transatlantic voyages—each perhaps as long as the four months it had taken the first ships to arrive—the assembly was claiming considerable leeway. The company knew it and rejected this request.

Another notable feature of the assembly concerned its decisions. They were to be made the same way the burgesses were picked: by vote. "All matters shall be decided, determined & ordered by the greater part of the voices then present" (the governor was allowed a veto).[20] The governor's council sat in the chancel, the burgesses in the choir. But when it came time to decide, all assemblymen were equal.

Under this new regime, more settlers came—over thirty-five hundred in forty-two ships—between 1619 and 1621. Disease and death decimated them (the winter of 1622 was a second starving time), but still the population grew. Yeardley, who retired from the governorship in 1621, moved to a plantation called Flowerdew, where he built a windmill. A watermill was being built near Jamestown; upriver there was an ironworks. It was all too much for Opechancanough. The Virginians, it seemed to him, were not auxiliary new-comers who might be occasional allies or sources of copper but permanent neighbors bound to become rivals. On March 22, 1622, he launched a massive, well-planned strike on twenty-eight plantations and settlements, killing 347 men, women, and children—a quarter to a third of the colony's population. As the survivors fled outlying settlements, hud-dling together for safety, the Indians destroyed their aban-doned property. William Capp of Elizabeth City had been one of the first burgesses. "God forgive me," he now wrote, "I think the last massacre killed all our Country, besides them they killed, they burst the heart of all the rest."[21]

The colony responded heartlessly. No more biracial wed-dings or hopes of trade and conversion. The settlers' coun-terattack on the Powhatan was sustained and implacable. Technology and discipline overwhelmed numbers. In July 1624, eight hundred Indian warriors risked a two-day battle with sixty well-armed colonists and lost. Twenty years later, Opechancanough, nearly a century old, was captured and shot in the back in a Jamestown jail.

Back in London, the Virginia Company sputtered in wrath at the imprudence of the colonists in allowing themselves to be massacred. But the company itself was on the block for the apparent mismanagement of its colony; a royal commission deemed it "weak and miserable." In 1624 James I dissolved the company. After he died the following year, he was succeeded by his son, Charles I, who announced that the government of Virginia would henceforth "depend upon Our Self."[22]

Charles I was distracted, however, by foreign policy and domestic politics. In the shadow of royal inattention, Virginia's governors continued to convene the General Assembly, including elected burgesses. In 1639 the status quo was formalized in royal instructions. "Once a year or oftner if urgent occasion shall require," governor, council, and burgesses were to meet in a "Grand Assembly . . . to make Acts and laws for the Government" of Virginia.[23]

The paper trail for the first meeting of the General Assembly is fainter than we would like, considering the momentousness of the occasion. A fire in Richmond, Virginia, at the end of the Civil War consumed most of the colonial archives. Patient scholars found copies of documents in British archives and private collections (including Thomas Jefferson's) that restitched the record, but there are still gaps. When Yeardley arrived in Jamestown to become governor, he carried a great charter of instructions from the company; it said nothing about convening a General Assembly, but a separate commission to him, mentioned in a 1621 document, evidently did. (This is the telltale phrase: the governor shall have a veto "att any Generall Assembly according to a former commission granted."[24]) Another 1621 document, *An Ordinance and Constitution for Council and Assembly in Virginia*, describes the election of burgesses. John Pory's official transcript of the first session of the General Assembly is lost; a copy of a report he made based on the official transcript was found in London in the 1850s.[25]

Practice made real what the paper trail sketches. Crises shook the political world on both sides of the Atlantic throughout the seventeenth century. England was wracked by a civil war, in which one king (Charles I) was executed, and a Glorious Revolution, in which another (James II) was deposed. In Virginia an army of frontiersman, led by a disaffected burgess, Nathaniel Bacon, and inflamed by the corruption of a governor and hatred of Indians, burned Jamestown to the ground in 1676. Still, the assembly marched on. In 1643 the House of Burgesses became an independent body, meeting separately from the governor's council. Its meeting place moved inland from the unhealthy coast to Williamsburg in 1699.

Other colonies in British North America, and England's New World empire generally, would have their own assemblies with elected representatives—Bermuda's first met in 1620—but the example of Virginia was important due to its size as well as its seniority: at the time of the American Revolution, one in five Americans was a Virginian.

Representation is a means by which rulers engineer the consensus of the ruled. As the Somers Isles Company, which ran Bermuda, put it, "Every man will more willingly obey laws to which he hath yielded his consent."[26] So it was in the seventeenth century, and so it remains today. But consent inevitably shades into agency. The representatives who do not presume to correct or control eventually—soon—aspire to control quite a bit. If you give men a portion of rule, they will in time rule themselves, and they will see themselves as worthy to do so. The sense of worthiness belongs both to the people's representatives and to those who choose them. Just as all matters in the assembly were decided by the greater part of the voices present, so burgesses were picked by a plurality of voices in the boroughs or plantations they represented. Elections were decided and laws approved by adding votes to votes, because no voter (except the governor wielding his veto) was more important or better than any other.

The burgesses were encased in a world of rank, much of it determined by heredity (the king, the House of Lords). Over time the burgesses themselves would fall prey to disorder, power grabs, corruption—the ills of governments everywhere, with and without legislatures. But the Virginia colony would not be ruled entirely from the imperial metropolis or by its onsite administrators. Self-rule in America began, however haltingly, at Jamestown. So did equality.

chapter two

FLUSHING REMONSTRANCE

Religious Liberty

ENGLAND COLONIZED MORE OF NORTH AMERICA than Jamestown: a second prong of settlers, also with a charter from the Virginia Company, and known to history as the Pilgrims, landed at Plymouth in what is now Massachusetts in 1620. But between these two anchor settlements lay the domain of a rival imperial power—Holland.

Holland itself was a newly independent nation, freed after a decades-long war of independence from Spain. The liberated Dutch quickly became a commercial and naval power, owning a string of outposts from Brazil to the Indian Ocean, and to the Malay Straits.

Holland's colonies were trading posts, designed to extract whatever the locals had to offer. What the Dutch got from North America was furs. Their traders settled as far north as Fort Orange (now Albany, New York), 145 miles up the river explored and later named after Henry Hudson. But the headquarters of their enterprise was the trading post on the island of Manhattan at the river's mouth, New Amsterdam.

Like Jamestown, New Amsterdam was operated by a company—the Dutch West India Company. According to the legendary story of its founding, Manhattan was bought from the Indians for sixty guilders', or twenty-four dollars', worth of trade goods—history's greatest real estate deal. In some versions of the story, the Indians who sold it were just passing through, so there was sharp dealing on both sides. The story in this barebones version is a myth. In fact, no one was cheated; the trade goods were worth considerably more than twenty-four dollars—knives and kettles were valuable prizes on the frontier—and the native sellers expected, and continued, to live and hunt on the island alongside its purchasers for years to come.[1] But like most myths, this one captured a truth: New Amsterdam was, from day one, transactional. It was founded to enrich the company's investors, and they maintained it for that reason. Their agent in charge was a director-general, appointed in Holland. The colony had the polyglot population of a port: Dutch, French, German, and English, and after conquering a smaller Swedish trading post on the Delaware River, it added Swedes and Finns.

Many of New Amsterdam's residents were transients, there to work and move on. One director-general, after a dispute with his employers, hired himself out to rival Sweden. But other New Amsterdamers wanted to put down roots. As at Jamestown, there were reformers who wanted the company to pay attention to the prosperity and good government of its permanent population.

This the company was slow to do. But in 1647, after the disastrous tenure of a director-general who had embroiled the colony in a bloody Indian war, the company sent the colony a new and more effective man: Peter Stuyvesant.

Stuyvesant, the son of a village minister in Holland's bleak northern rim, had attended a Dutch university (hence his use of the Latin form of his given name, Petrus). In his early twenties he went to work for the Dutch West India Company, first in Brazil, then in Curaçao, the headquarters of its Caribbean operations. He showed energy and ambition, and in 1642, at only thirty-two years old, he became acting governor there. He raided the Spaniards on the coast of Venezuela and led an expedition to conquer St. Martin, one of their islands in the Lesser Antilles. That operation marked him for life when, as he was planting the Dutch flag on a rampart, a "rough ball" fired from a Spanish cannon crushed his right leg.[2] The limb was amputated, and he took a furlough home to allow the wound to heal. The company, impressed with his grit, decided to transfer him to New Amsterdam.

Stuyvesant had an aesthetic, even romantic streak. In his new posting, he made sure that he was supplied with parakeets and parrots from Curaçao. He also maintained a years-long correspondence, in verse, with an admiring younger male friend, another company employee.

The company had not sent him to New Amsterdam to cultivate birds or write poetry. They wanted him to bring efficiency and order to their North American settlement. This he did. He improved its infrastructure by transforming the improvised pathways of the town into regular streets and a creek in its center into a canal (naming it the Heere Gracht, or Lords' Canal, after a much grander one in Amsterdam). He attended to health and safety, forbidding householders to build wooden chimneys ("very dangerous," he noted) or to throw "rubbish, filth, ashes, oyster-shells, dead animal[s] or anything like it" into his new thoroughfares.[3] He built public services, including a hospital and a post office, and opened the Heere Gracht to a weekly market where farmers from Long Island could bring their produce. For security against attack, he built a palisade across the island along the town's northern edge (the path of this wall is now Wall Street in New York City). Stuyvesant, in the words of a modern scholar, turned New Amsterdam "from a seedy, beleaguered trading post into a well-run Dutch town."[4]

His vision of a well-run town came at a price. The day he arrived he told the assembled residents who greeted him that he would rule them "like a father over his children."[5] From a combination of military experience and the example of his own father, he was both a martinet and a bigot. He could be patient, even devious, but he meant to keep power firmly in his hands. He believed in the Dutch Reformed Church in which he had been born and raised and was determined to uphold it where he ruled.

The Dutch Reformed Church was the established religion of Holland. A child of Calvin, it was rationalistic and rigorous. All outside its fold, fellow Calvinists excepted, were destined for eternal fire. Yet the Dutch state, perhaps reacting to its long persecution by Catholic Spain and certainly recognizing that money is the same whoever spends it, allowed believers in other faiths to worship as they wished so long as they did so in the privacy of their homes.

Those were the rules in Amsterdam. In New Amsterdam Stuyvesant regularly overstepped them, arresting Lutherans and keeping out Jews. The Dutch Reformed dominie, or pastor of the colony, encouraged him, condemning other sects as "servants of Baal."[6] Whenever the company, which had Lutheran directors and Jewish investors, learned of Stuyvesant's prohibitions, they ordered him to relent; only then did he comply with home country practice. Ten years into his governorship, he was confronted with a new set of believers: Quakers.

During and after the English civil war that toppled Charles I, religious convictions, unorthodox or lunatic, that would once have been quashed luxuriated. Independents advocated a bishopless congregational structure, each church responsible for its own affairs. Baptists maintained that the sacrament of admission to the church should be administered only to willing adults, not infants. Fifth Monarchy Men expected the rule of Christ on Earth to begin in 1666 (the four human monarchies, which His would supersede, had been Babylon, Persia, Macedon, and Rome). John Robins, a farmer, claimed to be the reincarnation of Adam, able to raise the dead; two friends of his, John Reeve and Ludowicke Muggleton, tailors, claimed to be the two witnesses of the eleventh chapter of the book of Revelation, whose curses entailed damnation.

Quakers, simultaneously mystical and activist, claimed that God spoke directly to them; when they preached or exhorted, they urged their listeners to tremble at their words, which were the words of the Lord (hence the term *Quakers*, originally a hostile nickname). Since all believers were equal, they rejected the forms of social hierarchy, such as formal pronouns and doffing hats. Since any one of them, women included, could exhort, they had no clergy. They called themselves Friends, but not surprisingly, given their radicalism, every person was against them except those they won over.

In April 1657, Robert Fowler, a Quaker from the north of England, sailed with a small party of Friends from London across the Atlantic. In an account he wrote of his voyage, he expressed the essence of Quaker immediatism. Whenever he "ent[ered] into reasoning" about his journey, "it brought me as low as the grave, and laid me as one dead." But when he surrendered himself to God's guidance, all went well. At the end of May, his ship landed in New Amsterdam, passing from Long Island Sound into the East River through a channel known, due to its narrowness and rough currents, as Hell Gate. Thus, wrote Fowler, was "the Scripture fulfilled in our eyes, in the figure *Hell's gates* cannot prevail against you."[7] Fowler interpreted a school of fish following his rudder to be another sign of the prayers of Quakers supporting his voyage. God spoke to Quakers in everything, and they were called to speak to everyone.

This enthusiast duly presented himself to Director-General Stuyvesant. In the words of the dominie, "He stood still with his hat firm on his head, as if a goat."[8] Stuyvesant encouraged him to keep voyaging, and Fowler sailed with the next tide back through Hell Gate and down the sound to Rhode Island. He left behind two women in their twenties, Dorothy Waugh and Mary Wetherhead, who, according to the dominie, "began to quake and go into a frenzy and cry out loudly in the middle of the street, that men should

repent, for the day of judgment was at hand."[9] These Stuyvesant arrested, then expelled from the colony.

That summer another young Quaker, Robert Hodgson,
appeared on the western end of Long Island. There, across
the East River from Manhattan, lay four towns belonging to
Stuyvesant's domain: Gravensand (Gravesend), Middleburgh
(Newtown), Vlissingen (Flushing), and Heemstede (Hemp-
stead), to give their Dutch and English names. They bore two
sets of names because although they were ruled by the Dutch
West India Company, they were populated by English settlers,
invited by Stuyvesant's predecessor in the expectation that
they would act as buffers against Indian and pirate attacks.

Heemstede/Hempstead had a Calvinist minister, a Presbyterian who, wrote the dominie, agreed with the Dutch
Reformed Church "in everything."[10] But once Hodgson
began speaking there, he "brought several under his influence."[11] Stuyvesant had Hodgson arrested and brought to
Manhattan, where he was treated far worse than his female
coreligionists. Stuyvesant sentenced him to a hundred-
guilder fine—more than the price of Manhattan—or two
years' labor in a work gang. When Hodgson refused to accept
either punishment, Stuyvesant had him whipped, in private
and in public, for days on end. An anonymous letter writer
appealed to the director-general for mercy, asking whether
it would not be better to send the hapless Quaker to Rhode
Island, "as his labor is hardly worth the cost."[12] What good
could Hodgson do in a work gang if he had been beaten
almost to death? Stuyvesant released him and sent him away.

Stuyvesant had encountered four Quakers and dealt with
them in three different ways: he had let Fowler go, expelled

Waugh and Wetherhead, and brutalized and expelled Hodgson. Now he announced a new policy: keeping Quakers out altogether. Any ships that arrived bearing Quakers would be seized; anyone hosting them would be fined. Since there were no Quaker directors or investors in the company, who would rebuke him?

Rebuke came at the end of the year from his own people. On December 27, 1657, thirty inhabitants of Vlissingen/ Flushing signed a remonstrance deploring his new orders.

The source was not surprising. Founded thirteen years earlier by English families, Flushing had strayed from the Calvinist path. The town's Presbyterian minister had left for Virginia because not enough residents had been willing to pay him. "Many" in Flushing, wrote the dominie disapprovingly, "have become imbued with divers opinions." He expressed his scorn in a Latin tag: *quod homines tot sententiae* (as many men, so many opinions).[13]

The form of the rebuke from Flushing was legalistic. Remonstrances are statements of grievance. Although they are not laws or even proposed laws, they are formal protests or petitions for redress. Magna Carta allowed barons to remonstrate with the king of England. Jews in the Bible remonstrated with the kings of Israel. Now Stuyvesant was on the receiving end.

"Right Honorable," the remonstrance began, "You have been pleased to send unto us a certain prohibition or command that we should not receive or entertain any of those people called Quakers because they are supposed to be, by some, seducers of the people." Here already in the first sentence was a whiff of defiance: Peter Stuyvesant himself considered Quakers seducers of the people, and his word was law; he would not appreciate being lumped among "some." Defiance became forthright in the next sentence. "For our part we cannot condemn them in this case, neither can we stretch out our hands against them, for out of Christ God is a consuming fire, and it is a fearful thing to fall into the hands of the living God." In the course of their remonstrance, the men of Flushing would give several reasons for challenging Stuyvesant, but they began with their most important: God told them to do it, and they obeyed—and feared—the Almighty more than their director-general.

Then the remonstrance introduced a new argument. In defying Stuyvesant, were Flushing's signers in fact breaking the law? The remonstrance admitted that it looked as though that were the case. "For the present we seem to be unsensible for the law and the Law giver." Yet the men of Flushing argued that they were following the tolerant laws of Holland. "The Lord hath taught . . . the civil power to give an outward liberty in the state. . . . The law of love, peace, and liberty . . . extending to Jews, Turks, and Egyptians . . . is the glory of the outward state of Holland." Even Jews, Muslims (Turks), and gypsies (Egyptians) could worship as they liked in Holland, so long as they did so in the privacy of their homes; surely Quakers enjoyed the same liberty. In a community as small as New Amsterdam, everybody knew everything; the men of Flushing must have known, or surmised, that the company had corrected Stuyvesant's anti-Lutheran and anti-Jewish edicts in the past. If the law of Holland governed the possessions of the Dutch West India Company, Stuyvesant was breaking the law, not them.

They bolstered this argument by referring to their town charter, granted by Stuyvesant's predecessor as director-general in 1645. According to this document, the residents of Flushing were to "have and enjoy the free libertie of conscience according to the costome and manner of Holland, without molestation or disturbance from any Madgistrate . . . or any other Ecclesiasticall Minister."[14] Now, in 1657, the remonstrance cited "the patent and charter of our Towne . . . which we are not willing to infringe and violate."

Like a good legal brief, the remonstrance offered multiple justifications for the case it was making: the laws of the home country and the words of the village's founding document. But these were justifications drawn from the outward liberties of the outward state. The law that mattered most to the men of Flushing was the inner law, the law with which they had begun—the law of God.

They returned to the point again and again. "When death and the Law assault us . . . the powers of this world can neither attach us [*attach*—a legal term meaning *seize*], neither excuse us, for if God justifye who can condem and if God condem there is none can justifye. . . . Our desire is not to offend one of [our Saviour's] little ones, in whatsoever form, name or title hee appears in, whether Presbyterian, Independent, Baptist or Quaker, but shall be glad to see anything of God in any of them, desiring to doe unto all men as we desire all men should doe unto us, which is the true law both of Church and State; for our Saviour sayeth this is the law and the prophets."[15]

The remonstrance was loaded with allusions to the Bible: God the consuming fire was from Deuteronomy 4:24 and Hebrews 12:29; God alone justified or condemned in

Romans 8:33–34; the comparison of Protestant sectaries to Christ's "little ones" drew on Matthew 18:6, Mark 9:42, and Luke 17:2; Christ declared the golden rule to be "the law and the prophets" in Matthew 22:40.

Accounts of the origin of religious liberty in America typically ascribe it to enlightenment rationalism: to John Locke, whose *Letter Concerning Toleration* would resonate powerfully in English thought and politics at the end of the seventeenth century, or to René Descartes, whose free-thinking *Discourse on Method* was published in Holland ten years before Peter Stuyvesant arrived in New Amsterdam. These gave an educated gloss to the concept of religious liberty, impressing minds of philosophical bent who wished to shake free of the religious ferment and controversies of the Reformation and Counter-Reformation.

Our religious liberty in America is considered a simple side effect of the number of religions that are in fact here. All keep each other free by resisting the efforts of any one to dominate. As James Madison would put it 130 years after the Flushing Remonstrance, "security . . . for religious rights" depends on "the multiplicity of sects." When "society itself [is] broken into so many parts, interests, and classes of citizens . . . the rights of individuals or of the minority will be in little danger."[16]

But philosophy did not make the men of Flushing take action. Neither did practical sociology. It took God to do that. In America religious liberty without the force of God's injunction is a discussion topic or, at best, a habit.

The remonstrance was written by Edward Hart, the town clerk, on December 27, 1657, and signed by Tobias Feake, the *schout* (a Dutch legal office, equivalent to district attorney), and William Noble and Edward Farrington, two of the town's magistrates. They were joined by twenty-six other men: William Thorne Sr. and Jr., Edward Tarne, John Store, Nathaniel Hefferd, Benjamin Hubbard, William Pidgion, George Clere, Elias Doughtie, Antonie Field, Richard Stocton, Edward Griffine, John Townesend, Nathaniell Tue, Nicholas Blackford, Michah Tue, Philip Ud, Robert Field Sr. and Jr., Nicholas Parsell, Michael Milner, Henry Townsend, George Wright, John Foard, Henry Semtell, and John Mastine.

None of these men, except the first four, were officials. They were ordinary men speaking up for other ordinary men. Liberty in America sometimes comes from the top (as discussed in chapter 1, Governor Yeardley had a commission to call an assembly in Jamestown), sometimes from the middle (the assembly he called took up its new job with a will). Sometimes it comes from the masses. The status of the men who remonstrated is suggested by the fact that six of them did not sign their names but made marks instead: William Thorne Jr.'s mark, for example, is a scrawl. Philip Ud's is a stylized capital P. George Clere's looks like three letters of an alphabet unknown to ordinary men. They could not write their names, but they laid down a marker.

The Flushing Remonstrance was a greater challenge to Stuyvesant's statesmanship than the intrusions of Hodgson and the other Quakers because the remonstrators were not Quakers. Hodgson and his fellows preached their outré doctrines; the Flushing Remonstrance asserted a right for them and for believers in myriad doctrines to live and worship in

New Amsterdam. Contrary to what Madison would say, they were not speaking for themselves but for a principle.

Hart presented the remonstrance to Stuyvesant on December 29. According to the official records of New Amsterdam, Stuyvesant "immediately" ordered Hart to be arrested and held in the fort at Manhattan's southern tip, "which was done." Stuyvesant then proceeded with a general crackdown. His own meticulous records supply the details. On New Year's Day 1658, the two magistrates, Noble and Farrington, appeared before him, in response to a summons, and were "immediately arrested."[17]

On January 3, Hart appeared before Stuyvesant and was grilled. The purpose of the interrogation was to find out who was behind the remonstrance; Hart answered as evasively as he could. Who wrote the remonstrance? Hart said he did, "according to the intentions of the people." Did all the signers individually tell him what to write? Hart said "no one in particular" gave him directions, but he "gathered the utterances of the people" at a town meeting. Where was the meeting held? Michael Milner's house. Where was the document signed? Some signed at Milner's house, others at their own homes (signers and locations were reviewed in detail). Who called the town meeting? Hart did not know. Who suggested writing the remonstrance? Hart did not know. Had Hart shown it to Feake, Noble, and Farrington, the schout and the magistrates, before the meeting? Hart had read it to them but did not know whether they approved it. "Having heard the answers of the clerk," the record concluded, "it was resolved to send him to prison until further order."[18]

On January 8, Noble and Farrington began to crack; they asked for permission to leave their confinement in the fort and move about Manhattan, promising to appear whenever they might be summoned. Permission was granted. Two days later they submitted a "humble petition" in which they said that they had been misled by Feake; they thought the remonstrance was simply an inquiry to know Stuyvesant's mind, not an attempt to change it. They promised to "offend no more," adding that they would "ever pray" for Stuyvesant's "health and happiness."[19]

Stuyvesant received a letter from Flushing on January 22 asking whether the town court should proceed with business in view of Noble's and Farrington's "trubell." Stuyvesant directed it to suspend its operations until he could come to Long Island himself and "give there some necessary orders."[20]

Hart cracked on January 23. He now testified that it was Feake who had advised him to draw up the remonstrance. He begged forgiveness. "Forasmuch as I have written a writing whereat you take offense . . . my humble request is for your mercy."[21] In recognition of his past service, his large family, his timely obeisance, and—most important—his laying the blame on Feake, Hart was pardoned.

On January 28, Feake formally became the scapegoat. Stuyvesant condemned the schout in a statement that was a drumroll of accusation. "Tobias Feake . . . had the audacity . . . to be a leader and instigator in the conception of a seditious, mutinous, and detestable letter of defiance . . . signed by himself and his [ac]complices . . . wherein they justify and uphold the abominable sect of Quakers, who vilify both the authorities and the Ministers of the Gospel and undermine the State and God's service. . . . As an example to others he deserves severe punishment."

But Feake had cracked too, "confessing his wrongdoing and promising hereafter to avoid such errors."[22] Feake was dismissed from his job and fined two hundred guilders (twice the fine levied on the Quaker Robert Hodgson). If he did not pay, he would be banished from New Amsterdam.

By his own lights, Stuyvesant had been politic, even merciful. He had stifled dissent in his domain without corporal punishment or prison sentences longer than a few weeks. Quakers, shorn of their allies, would be easier to isolate and expel whenever they reappeared. More important, their sympathizers, propagators of a dangerous doctrine of religious liberty, had been intimidated into silence.

The collapse of Hart, Feake, Noble, and Harrington is disheartening. We want bold thoughts and inspiring words to be sustained by brave actions. Unlike the Quakers they defended, the men of Flushing were unwilling to wear the martyr's crown.

Actual martyrdom was a reality among the English to the northeast. By the late 1650s, New England had become home to half a dozen English colonies. One of them, Rhode Island—where Fowler had sailed and where Waugh, Wetherhead, and Hodgson had been sent—allowed Quakers in its midst. (The dominie of New Amsterdam called Rhode Island "the *latrina* of New England.")[23] But Massachusetts Bay, the largest of them, expelled Quakers and condemned to death those who returned. From 1659 to 1661, four recidivist Quakers, one of them a woman, were hanged on Boston Common.

Stuyvesant enjoyed his victory for four and a half years. Then in August 1662, trouble returned to Flushing. The magistrates of Rustdorp, a neighboring village, reported that "the abomnible sect, called of Quakers" were meeting every Sunday at the home of John Bowne. Bowne, an Englishman, had recently arrived in Flushing, building a farmhouse there in 1661. He had married Hannah Feake, a relative of Tobias (some accounts call her his daughter, others his niece). Hannah had gone beyond Tobias in sympathy for Quakers by becoming one herself. In time her husband joined her as a convert. The informers who reported the meetings at Bowne's house asked Stuyvesant to prevent them "one way or another."[24] The way Stuyvesant chose was to order the new schout of Flushing, Resolved Waldron, to arrest Bowne and bring him to New Amsterdam.

When Bowne appeared before the director-general, he would not remove his hat. Stuyvesant had it removed for him and fined him 150 guilders, plus court costs, with the threat of doubling the fine in case of a second offense and banishment in case of a third. Bowne refused to pay.

Bowne was a true believer, which made Stuyvesant hesitate. When Robert Hodgson had similarly refused to acknowledge the sentence meted out to him, Stuyvesant had applied the whip, but the only result of that savagery had been that one of his own subjects had complained in sympathy. Stuyvesant now held his hand, keeping the new Quaker in prison for five months, perhaps hoping that he would crack. In January 1663, when it became clear that Bowne would not, Stuyvesant shipped him off to Holland to be tried by the company at its Amsterdam headquarters.

At his trial, Bowne, like the signers of the remonstrance before him, relied on both inward and outward law. He argued that his treatment at Stuyvesant's hands was "contrary . . . to justice and righteousness." It also violated "that liberty promised us" in Flushing's founding charter.[25]

Ignoring inward law, the company decided on pragmatic grounds. In a double-minded letter to Stuyvesant, the company began by declaring that it shared his aversion to Quakers. "We heartily desire that these and other sectarians remained away" from its New World outpost. Yet the sectarians continued to settle there. "We doubt very much whether we can proceed against them rigorously without diminishing the population and stopping immigration, which must be favored at a so tender stage" of the colony's existence. Amsterdam, the company noted, "has always practiced this maxim of moderation and consequently has often had a considerable influx of people."[26] New Amsterdam would benefit from a similar policy.

The company accordingly directed Stuyvesant to "shut your eyes" and "allow everyone to have his own belief," so long as he gave no offense to his neighbors and obeyed the government.[27] Stuyvesant might have objected that disobeying him was precisely what the Quakers and their sympathizers had done, but, good company man that he was, he obeyed his bosses. Bowne returned to his house in Flushing. Quaker fervor and Flushing's principles had created facts on the ground to which the company and even its rigorous man on the spot finally bowed.

In 1664 Stuyvesant was ordered to bow again, this time by superior enemy force. England's post–civil war interval of republican government had ended; the restored royal dynasty revived her imperial ambitions. An English armada sailed into the harbor of New Amsterdam and demanded that Stuyvesant hand over his domain.

As on the island of St. Martin twenty-two years earlier, once again there was Stuyvesant, a Dutch flag, and a cannon (this one, his). He stood on the rampart of his fort with a gunner, resolved to fight the invader. But the dominie, speaking for Stuyvesant's frightened subjects, persuaded him to surrender peacefully.

The articles of capitulation guaranteed that the people of New Amsterdam, renamed New York after Charles II's brother, the Duke of York, "shall enjoy the liberty of their Consciences."[28] What Stuyvesant had resisted with such determination survived him. Two decades later an English governor of the new colony described its patchwork religious makeup thus: "New York has first a Chaplain, belonging to the Fort, of the Church of England; secondly a Dutch Calvinist [minister], thirdly a French Calvinist, fourthly a Dutch Lutheran; abundance of Quakers preachers men and women especially; Ranting Quakers; Singing Quakers . . . some Independents, some Jews; in short, of all sorts of opinions there are some, and the most part, of none at all."[29]

Stuyvesant died in 1672, at his bouwerie, or farm, north of town; the road that led to it is still called the Bowery. Bowne died in 1695 at his farm, which still stands in what is now Queens, in a neighborhood thick with Chinese restaurants.

England's colonies, especially Virginia and Massachusetts, conquered the American creation story, as England conquered New Amsterdam; as they became considered sole sources of the American experience, the Flushing Remonstrance faded from the map of the American mind. Its importance is the effect that its principles had on New York and that New York would have on the country. Rhode Island and Pennsylvania were religiously tolerant colonies— Rhode Island small and sui generis, Pennsylvania large and influential. But New York became and remains the nation's most populous city, as New York State was for over a century (1810–1960) its most populous state. For many years, New York had the largest megaphone, thanks to its cultural and media prominence. From Alexander Hamilton, writing Federalist essays in New York newspapers, to *Hamilton, An American Musical*, what New Yorkers thought, other Americans would think or react to.

Flushing's Quakers suffered for religious liberty; the Flushing Remonstrance proclaimed it; John Bowne practiced it. It became the norm, then the rule, for their town, and for its country.

chapter three

TRIAL OF JOHN PETER ZENGER

Liberty of Expression

AFTER DEFEATING THE DUTCH, BRITAIN SOWED the Atlantic seaboard with colonies from Spanish Florida to French Canada. New Amsterdam established religious liberty, but liberty of expression would be the work of British colonists.

Britain's colonial governments showed a family resemblance. All had popularly elected assemblies, like the Virginia House of Burgesses. The chief executive was a governor, answerable to the king or queen. (Most were appointed directly by the sovereign; some were appointed by proprietors—private persons, like William Penn, who had been given chunks of the continent as royal favors; a few were chosen by their colonial assemblies.) Governors were assisted by councils, whose members were generally chosen by London. Over time criminal trials and lawsuits were removed from the purview of governors' councils and assigned to courts, with judges, juries, and lawyers. But ambition, interest, and faction—that is to say, politics—tugged at these formal structures of government, as they do always and everywhere.

One destabilizing factor was inattention. Britain did not always send its best administrative talent overseas. One early eighteenth-century governor of New York, Henry Hyde, Lord Cornbury, was accused of lurking on the streets of New York City at night in order to accost male passersby and tug their ears. On his midnight rambles he dressed as a woman. A portrait of him, so garbed, hangs in the New-York Historical Society. The story and the painting are quite possibly hoaxes, produced by New Yorkers who disliked him. One of his successors, however, caused very real problems.

William Cosby belonged to that class of gentlemen who earned office by marrying well, in his case to the sister of an earl. As governor of Minorca in the Mediterranean, he acquired a reputation for lining his pockets, but in 1732, still married, he was transferred across the Atlantic to fill the vacant governorships of New York and New Jersey. (Neighboring colonies occasionally shared the same governor; New York's and New Jersey's previous one had died of an epileptic seizure.)

Between the death of the old governor and the arrival of the new one, six months passed. Transatlantic travel was slow, but Cosby also dawdled. In the interim his duties were filled by Rip Van Dam, the senior member of the governor's council. When Cosby arrived, he demanded that Van Dam give him half the salary he had earned while serving as his stand-in.

This was getting off on the wrong foot. Van Dam refused. Governor Cosby sued him in New York's supreme court. The chief justice, Lewis Morris, ruled for Van Dam, whereupon Cosby dismissed him from the bench, replacing him with one of his colleagues, James DeLancey.

Governor Cosby, fresh off the boat, had run afoul of two powerful forces. One, felt throughout the colonies, was an interest in studying the law and in upholding those who administered it fairly. This disposition was transplanted from Britain, which had a rich and respected legal culture. American colonials took it to heart. Justice Morris appealed to this legal-mindedness in a tart letter of reproof he sent Cosby. "The people of this province . . . are very much concerned both with respect to their lives and fortunes, in the freedom and independency of those who are to judge of them. . . . But if judges are to be intimidated so as not to dare to give any opinion but what is pleasing to a governor," New Yorkers "may possibly not think themselves so secure."[1]

The second force Cosby defied was the pride of local grandees. Lewis Morris was the scion of a family that had made its fortune in Barbados before moving to the North American mainland. He owned large properties in both New York and New Jersey and the largest library (three thousand volumes) in the colonies. He forbade his steward to loan his copy of Tacitus "to anyone whatever," lest it "come into a country fellow's hand, to daub and dirty."[2] Morris bolstered his social standing by office-holding and electioneering. He had been active in the politics of both New Jersey and New York for years: he was one of those who had made life miserable for Lord Cornbury. He was not intimidated by Cornbury's most recent successor.

Powerful New Yorkers and their families jostled each other, jockeying for influence. The cross-currents of family politics pitted landowners, like the Morrises, against merchants. Morris's replacement on the bench, James DeLancey, happened to be a leader of the merchant faction. He was also not yet thirty years old, half Morris's age—the final insult. Morris sought revenge via a third force, newly manifest in New York and America: the power of the press.

The first newspaper in colonial America had appeared in Boston in September 1690: *Publick Occurences Both Foreign and Domestic*—a monthly offering three pages of local and foreign news items (the latter lifted from months-old British journals), plus a blank fourth page for readers' notes. It lasted only one issue, the governor and council of Massachusetts suppressing it for propagating "doubtful and uncertain reports."[3] But early in the eighteenth century, other newspapers appeared, first in Boston, then in other towns.

Printing was a complicated process. Ink was made from the soot of oil lamps, paper from linen rags. The type for each page was set in a wooden frame by hand and inked using leather balls. A screw press, operated by pulling a long wooden handle, brought the type in contact with the paper. Each sheet that was printed was then hung up to dry before being sorted, folded, and finally delivered. Printing was laborious and smelly—at the end of the day the inky leather balls were cleaned with urine—but, once the type was set, a skilled printer could do a page in as little as fifteen seconds.

Newspapers maintained the formula of local news, often uncertain, and foreign news, always old. Sometimes they deliberately stirred up controversy. The *New England Courant*, a Boston newspaper printed by James Franklin and his apprentice and younger brother Benjamin, feuded with Cotton Mather, a prominent clergyman, over the efficacy of inoculation as a treatment for smallpox. Mather said it was helpful, the *Courant* scoffed (Mather was right, the newspaper wrong).

The Franklins were outsiders attacking Boston's clerical establishment; Morris was a disgruntled member of New York's establishment, seeking redress. But he willingly used the Franklins' methods.

The printer he turned to was John Peter Zenger. Zenger had landed in New York as a boy in 1710, one of a wave of German Protestant refugees fleeing the wars of Louis XIV. Zenger's father had died on the voyage across the Atlantic; once in New York, Zenger's mother apprenticed him to William Bradford, New York's printer.

Bradford printed almanacs, pamphlets, religious works (including the Book of Common Prayer), and, beginning in 1725, New York's lone newspaper, the weekly *Gazette*. He also acted as the official printer of all laws and public proclamations. For Bradford to help Morris would be biting the hand that fed him. Zenger, however, willingly set up a competing newspaper, New York's second, the *Weekly Journal*, which began publishing in November 1733.

The *Weekly Journal* rarely named Governor Cosby, but it was filled with attacks on "SCHEMES OF GENERAL

OPPRESSION AND PILLAGE . . . RESTRAINTS UPON LIBERTY AND PROJECTS FOR ARBITRARY WILL [caps in the original]."⁴ Zenger lacked the literary powers to produce these; they were written by James Alexander and William Smith, two lawyers allied with Morris. When they needed reinforcement, Zenger reprinted essays by English contrarians condemning official malfeasance there.

Zenger also published songs and bogus ads, all tacitly anti-Cosby (one ad asked after a missing spaniel, intended as a reference to a Cosby supporter; another ad mentioned a monkey—Cosby himself). The *Gazette* answered with defenses of the governor, but they were tepid.

The *Weekly Journal*'s polemics were not written for their own sake. They were intended to influence public opinion and win victories for Morris's allies at the polls. Only the king could name a replacement for Cosby, but the people could embarrass and annoy him. The city had an elected common (or city) council (the mayor was appointed by the governor); in September 1734, after ten months of journalistic back and forth, the Morrisites won control of the council.

Cosby decided it was time to silence his critic. His weapon was the doctrine of seditious libel, expounded in Britain early in the seventeenth century. Any statement that held the government or its personnel up to contempt might cause riot or rebellion and was therefore considered criminal.

If the law gave Cosby a weapon, it also gave him an obstacle. In October Chief Justice DeLancey, acting at Cosby's behest, addressed the grand jury—the body responsible for bringing cases to trial. He asked them to consider the problem of seditious libels: "They are arrived to that height, that they call loudly for your animadversion."[5] The grand jury, however, refused to act. Ordinary New Yorkers, it seemed, sympathized with Zenger.

In November Cosby did what Peter Stuyvesant would have done at first, ordering, via the governor's council, four issues of the *Weekly Journal* to be burned and Zenger imprisoned. He was confined in the town jail, which was located in the basement of city hall, a newish building on Wall Street. His bail was set at four hundred pounds, a punishing sum (his net worth at the time was forty pounds). At first, he was forbidden to see, or even write notes to, anyone, but after a week he was allowed pen and paper and visits (through a hole in his cell door) with his wife. By this means he kept the *Weekly Journal* going while he awaited trial.

Alexander and Smith now shifted from being Zenger's contributors to being his lawyers. In April 1735 they appeared in court to argue before Chief Justice DeLancey that he be removed from the case. They challenged the commission under which he acted as Morris's replacement, which stated that he was to serve at Governor Cosby's "pleasure." Yet the customary tenure for English judges was service during "good behavior"—meaning that they served for life, so long as they committed no crimes. The good behavior standard guaranteed their independence. A judge who only served at pleasure would do the bidding of whomever had been pleased to appoint him.

Questioning DeLancey's right to preside over his own courtroom was an aggressive gambit. The chief justice responded with an even more aggressive one—disbarring Alexander and Smith.

When Zenger petitioned the court for someone to represent him, DeLancey was fair-minded enough to assign him another lawyer, John Chambers. Chambers set about his task conscientiously, but no lawyer in New York was as good as Alexander or Smith, and so Zenger's supporters looked to Philadelphia for help.

The help they summoned was Andrew Hamilton, a Scotsman who had settled in America at the end of the previous century. He made his mark as an advocate when he was still in his twenties. "[He is] an ingenious man," an acquaintance wrote, "and, for a lawyer, I believe a very honest one."[6] He had honed his skills at the Inns of Court in London, handled cases for the Penn family, proprietors of Pennsylvania and Delaware, and was elected speaker of the Pennsylvania Assembly. By 1735 he was considered the best lawyer in British North America. James Alexander had known him professionally for years.

Chief Justice DeLancey scheduled Zenger's trial for August. It was held in city hall; Zenger was brought upstairs from his cell to attend it. Despite the summer heat, DeLancey and the lawyers labored under the shoulder-length horsehair wigs worn in English courtrooms (sixty years later Thomas Jefferson would compare the look to "rats peeping through bunches of oakum," or rope fiber).[7]

The jurors were sworn in: twelve male property owners picked from a list generated by the clerk of the court. Chambers had done his best work for Zenger in the jury selection process: the first list of potential jurors had been packed with Cosby supporters—tradesmen he dealt with, political allies who had lost their seats on the Common Council to

Morrisites. Chambers asked for, and got, a second list of random men.

The attorney general of the colony, Richard Bradley, a Cambridge-educated lawyer, opened the case against Zenger. He wrapped Cosby in royal robes. "His Excellency the Governor of this province . . . is the King's immediate representative here." "Defendant Zenger," on the other hand, was a dangerous disturber of the peace. The *Weekly Journal* had "greatly and unjustly scandalized" the governor; such attacks on officialdom, if unchecked, "create differences among men, ill blood among the people," and even "great bloodshed between the party libeling and the party libeled."[8]

Chambers, opening for the defense, began by poor-mouthing himself, admitting his "inabilities" as a lawyer but declaring that they would be counterbalanced by his client's innocence. This was good courtroom theatrics, and Chambers went on to outline a cautious but plausible legal strategy based on the *Weekly Journal's* reliance on indirection and innuendo: who, really, was the object of its attacks? "For general[itie]s are uncertain, and no one can tell who are meant."[9] Perhaps Zenger had printed harsh things, but was Cosby in fact his target?

Andrew Hamilton then took over from Chambers, and what he said startled the court. He announced that he would save the prosecution "trouble" by admitting that his client had published the material it considered so scandalous. Hamilton said nothing about mistaken identity. He seemed to have given up before he began.

In an account of the case written afterward by Zenger himself, he noted "there was silence in the court for some time."[10] DeLancey broke it by asking Bradley to elaborate on his opening statement. The attorney general explained the law of seditious libel and appealed for good measure to St. Paul (Acts 23:5): "For it is written, thou shalt not speak evil of the ruler of thy people."

Hamilton in reply said that he agreed that government was sacred. But he denied that "the just complaints of . . . men who suffer under a bad administration" could be considered libelous.[11]

Although Hamilton had offered to save the prosecution trouble, he was willing to take considerable trouble himself. He was sounding the first note of an argument that the law of libel, as it was then understood, was too broad: government could, and should, be criticized if what its critics said of it were true. He would ring the changes on this thought in an oration, interrupted by occasional dialogue with DeLancey or Bradley, of almost thirteen thousand words. (In comparison, recent presidential inaugural addresses average two thousand words.)

If DeLancey had been older or more experienced, he would have cut off the prolific defense attorney. But Hamilton had been in courtrooms longer than DeLancey had been alive, and he easily outmaneuvered the young chief justice. When DeLancey rebuked him for statements he considered legally inadmissible, Hamilton responded politely and made the same point later or in some other way. Hamilton meant to make a case and put on a show, and he would not be deterred.

He aimed his first shot at Cosby's pretensions, as expounded by Bradley. "Is it not surprising," Hamilton asked, "to see a subject, upon receiving a commission from the King to be a governor of a colony in America, immediately imagining himself to be vested with all the prerogatives belonging to the sacred person of his Prince?" Because kings were untouchable, were their colonial appointees? Hamilton used the king as a club to knock Cosby down, simultaneously playing the roles of a royalist and a mugger. But even as he mocked the governor, he goaded his audience: "it was yet more astonishing to see that a people can be so wild as to allow of and acknowledge these prerogatives and exemptions, even to their own destruction."[12] Upstarts do not arise in a vacuum; the passivity of the people enables them.

Hamilton challenged the reigning doctrine of seditious libel by attributing it to the Star Chamber, a royal court of appeals that became increasingly capricious and heavy-handed under the Tudors and Stuarts; it was abolished on the eve of the English Civil War and made a byword for oppression. "That terrible Court," Hamilton called it, was "where those dreadful judgments were given and that law established which Mr. Attorney [general] has produced for authorities to support his cause."[13] Later, Hamilton called a particular feature of current libel law—launching prosecutions, like Zenger's, without the approval of grand juries—"a child if not born, yet nursed up and brought to full maturity, in the Court of Star Chamber." DeLancey tried to embarrass Hamilton by citing a prosecution without grand jury in a medieval case long before the Star Chamber came into existence, whereupon Hamilton embarrassed him by giving a detailed sketch of that very case and explaining that it offered no precedent for what Cosby and DeLancey were doing to

Zenger now.[14] He all but said, Don't argue legal history with me, young man.

Hamilton praised the institution of the jury (and appealed to the self-esteem of the jurors sitting before him). "You are citizens of New York," he told them; "you are really what the law supposes you to be, honest and lawful men. . . . In your justice lies our safety." And again: "Jurymen are to see with their own eyes, to hear with their own ears, and to make use of their own consciences and understandings in judging of the lives, liberties or estates of their fellow subjects."[15] Jurors were not bit players in the drama of a trial but major actors.

What Hamilton wanted the jurors in Chief Justice DeLancey's courtroom to see and hear was a political truth: that a free press was a necessary defense of freedom. Governors, appointed by the sovereign, were formally immune to popular displeasure, but the elected members of every colonial assembly and council since Jamestown were not, and they had the power to advise or stymie overweening governors. But suppose a governor, using bribes or threats, had his colony's elected officeholders under his thumb? (Governor Cosby did not have the Common Council of New York under his thumb, but Hamilton ignored that.) When officeholders were unresponsive, what recourse against misgovernment did the people have? Hamilton answered: "It is natural, it is a privilege, I will go farther, it is a right which all freemen claim . . . to complain when they are hurt; they have a right publicly to remonstrate the abuses of power . . . to put their neighbors upon their guard against the craft or open violence of men in authority, and to assert with courage the sense they have of the blessings of liberty."[16] He went on,

"Were this liberty to be denied then the next step" would be to make the people slaves. For what was slavery but "suffering the greatest injuries and oppressions without the liberty of complaining; or if they do [complain], to be destroyed, body and estate, for so doing?"[17]

Complain and *complaining* are not neutral descriptive words; they can imply peevishness, ill temper, bad character. "'Tis the voice of the sluggard: I heard him complain, 'You have waked me too soon, I must slumber again,'" wrote Isaac Watts in a popular book of poems for children. But Hamilton, in a bold reversal, made complaint a cornerstone of liberty.

He scattered memorable observations in passing. "Power," he said at one point, "may justly be compared to a great river [which], while kept within its due bounds, is both beautiful and useful; but when it overflows its banks, it is then too impetuous to be stemmed, it bears down all before it and brings destruction and desolation wherever it comes."[18] In the northern reaches of the colony, the Hudson and Mohawk Rivers flooded regularly, and within living memory a hurricane had raked the colony, punching a channel through Fire Island; New Yorkers understood his imagery.

Hamilton took Bradley's invocation of religion and stood it on its head. "We well know that it is not two centuries ago that a man would have been burnt as a heretic for owning such opinions in matters of religion as are publicly wrote and printed at this day." But in New York the Flushing Remonstrance and John Bowen had intervened. "In taking these freedoms in thinking and speaking about matters of faith or religion, we are in the right." Then, Hamilton lodged the stinger. "From which I think it is pretty clear that in New York a man may make very free with his God, but he must take special care what he says of his governor."[19] Liberty was not just for the conscience or even for public worship; it was for secular man and his political situation.

Hamilton himself invoked historical heroes of liberty, one Roman, one English. Lucius Junius Brutus overthrew Rome's last king, then approved the execution of two of his own sons who had plotted a royal restoration. John Hampden, a member of Parliament during the reign of Charles I, was tried for refusing to pay a tax on the grounds that the king had levied it illegally; Hampden later died in battle during the English Civil War. These were formidable heroes: two rebels, one who gave his life, another who took the lives of his sons. There was an implied threat here: push free men too far and this is what they will do. The attorney general's opening statement had held up the specter of bloodshed; Hamilton's closing statement warned, don't bring it on.

Hamilton's peroration was masterly. "I am truly very unequal to such an undertaking," he began. "I labor under the weight of many years." Hamilton was fifty-nine years old, but ill health made him look older. "Yet old and weak as I am, I should think it my duty, if required, to go to the utmost part of the land where my service could be of any use in [defending] the right of remonstrating (and complaining too)"—that word again—"of the arbitrary attempts of men in power." He continued,

Men who injure and oppress the people under their administration provoke them to cry out and complain;

and then they make that very complaint the foundation for new oppressions and persecutions.

But to conclude; the question before the Court and you gentlemen of the jury is not of small nor private concern. It is not the cause of a poor printer, nor of New York alone, which you are now trying. No! It may in its consequence affect every freeman that lives under a British government on the main[land] of America.

It is the best cause. It is the cause of liberty. [By your] impartial and uncorrupt verdict, [you will] have laid a noble foundation for securing to ourselves, our posterity, and our neighbors that to which nature and the laws of our country have given us a right: the liberty, both of exposing and opposing arbitrary power . . . by speaking and writing the truth.[20]

Attorney general Bradley seems to have suspected the power of Hamilton's summation, for he tried deflating it with mockery. Hamilton, he replied, "had gone very much out of the way, and had made himself and the people very merry."[21] He directed the jury's attention instead to the law and to the interpretation of it that would be given by the chief justice; the chief justice then did the same.

The jury retired for what Zenger later called "a small time."[22] When they returned, they gave their verdict: *not guilty*. The courtroom audience burst into cheers; the next day Zenger walked free after nine months in jail.

A twentieth-century biographer of Andrew Hamilton wrote that the jury roll of the Zenger trial was "a list that should be honored permanently!"[23] Here are their names:

Hermanus Rutgers, Stanly Holmes, Edward Man, John Bell, Samuel Weaver, Andries Marschalk, Egbert van Borsom, Thomas Hunt (foreman), Benjamin Hildreth, Abraham Keteltas, John Goelet, and Hercules Wendover. These ordinary people had done an extraordinary thing.

The trial and the verdict were an intersection of the top and the bottom of colonial society: two grandees, Cosby and Morris, started the fight; a crack lawyer, Hamilton, was hired to wage it; and twelve random men settled it.

Hamilton had accepted no fee for his performance; the occasion was payment enough. But the Common Council awarded him the keys to the city, delivered in a solid gold box, inscribed with suitable mottoes: *NON NUMMIS— VIRTUTE PARATUR* (Won Not by Money, but Virtue) read one.

Governor Cosby died of tuberculosis in 1736, and Lewis Morris's faction made a big push in the elections for the colony's assembly in the following year. "The sick, the lame, and the blind were all carried to vote," wrote one contemporary.[24] Morris and his son, Lewis Jr., were elected to the assembly, which made Lewis Jr. Speaker; Zenger was named official printer.

The popular tide crested, then withdrew. The acting governor, George Clarke, who had been secretary of Cosby's governing council, instituted a few changes on which the Morrisites had campaigned: most important was holding assembly elections not when the governor called them but at scheduled intervals. The interval chosen was three years. The people would have their say not at the governor's whim but regularly and frequently.

The elder Morris and his allies were rewarded (others might say, bought off). Alexander and Smith were reinstated as lawyers. The wheels of empire, turning in London, made Morris himself royal governor of New Jersey in 1738. This plum job got him out of New York, and he held it until he died in 1746. Leaderless, the Morris party in New York withered away. Lewis Morris, it turned out, was a populist in the most limited sense: he cared about oppression when it was directed at one person, himself. John Peter Zenger also died in 1746; his family carried on the *Weekly Journal* a few years more.

Hamilton had died at home in Philadelphia in 1741. A Latin elegy celebrated his defense of *Eboracumque novum* (New York) and Zenger; it ran in the Philadelphia *Gazette*, a newspaper owned and operated by the transplanted Bostonian Benjamin Franklin.[25]

Hamilton's vision of freedom of the press was limited to true statements; falsehoods might still bring down the law's wrath. Even this partial defense of freedom of the press rested on shaky legal foundations. Hamilton had argued the law as he believed it should be, ignoring what it manifestly was. The jury's verdict was a fluke, a one-off. Seditious libel continued to be a crime in New York until 1804, when another Hamilton—Alexander, no relation to Andrew—gave his last major speech as a lawyer in defense of an accused journalist. "The office of a free press," Alexander Hamilton said, is "to give us early alarm and put us on our guard against the encroachments of power."[26] This Hamilton lost this case, but his argument persuaded the legislature to change the law the following year.

Yet Andrew Hamilton's great performance in 1735, and the brave response of the jurors to it, had consequences nevertheless. Hamilton had told the jury in his peroration that "your upright conduct this day" would "entitle you to the love and esteem of your fellow citizens" and the "honor" of "every man who prefers freedom to a life of slavery." So it happened. A year after Zenger was freed, he published *A Brief Narrative of the Case and Trial of John Peter Zenger,* including notes compiled by James Alexander and the text of Hamilton's argument, supplied by Hamilton himself. *A Brief Narrative* circulated throughout the English-speaking world—reprinted in Boston and London, attacked by a pamphleteer in Barbados (probably the royal attorney there). To all but the Caribbean critic, Zenger, his defenders, and the jurors who freed him became symbols of liberty.

There was a special consequence in America. The upright conduct of the New York jury laid down a marker, and a model, for what other colonial juries would do in similar cases. Since the law of seditious libel could not be enforced, colonial authorities, with few exceptions, gave up trying to enforce it. As a result the press in colonial America flourished.

There were additional reasons for a burgeoning newspaper culture here: a widespread population called for numerous newspapers; Benjamin Franklin, as a trainer of printers, worked to satisfy the demand far beyond Philadelphia (and, as a business partner, shared in their profits). But the light hand of the law made America's colonial press the freest in the world.

Its liberty nourished more than political liberty. Books of sermons and other religious works poured off American presses, vastly outnumbering political pamphlets throughout the eighteenth century. The Zenger trial did not start the flood but helped ensure that it would continue.

Half a century later, Gouverneur Morris, a grandson of the elder Lewis, would call the Zenger verdict "the morning star" of liberty in America. He spoke from family pride. But he was right.[27]

chapter four

DECLARATION OF INDEPENDENCE

"Certain Inalienable Rights"

I N 1735, AS ANDREW HAMILTON FLAYED THE ROYAL governor of New York, he declared that "we are governed by the best of kings."[1] Only forty years later, most of British North America was in revolt against Britain, its parliament, and its king, in the name of liberty.

Crisis was the child of victory. From 1689 on, Britain had fought a series of world wars against France. One of the theaters of conflict was North America. France's American empire, which stretched from the St. Lawrence River via the Great Lakes and the Mississippi River to the Gulf of Mexico, was vast, enveloping, and empty. Britain's, which hugged the Atlantic coast, was smaller, encircled, and populous. By 1763, thanks to superior generalship and colonists' numbers, Britain had wrested all of America east of the Mississippi from France.

The thirteen colonies stretching from Maine (then part of Massachusetts) to Georgia were liberated from the fear of French attack and, they soon realized, from dependence on British protection. At the same time, they found themselves entangled in Britain's efforts to pay off the debt left over from the great struggle. Her statesmen were determined to replace a patchwork empire, in which ear-tuggers and pocket-liners had been carelessly sent to misrule its far-flung parts, with a well-run business concern that would replenish the imperial coffers.

The effort backfired. The very prospects that had drawn settlers across the ocean—making a living, enjoying a measure of self-rule—made them resent new taxes and cherish their privileges. In 1765 a stamp tax on all sorts of paper, from legal documents to playing cards, prompted delegates from nine colonies to meet as a congress in New York's City Hall to discuss their grievances and petition the king and Parliament for relief. Parliament repealed this tax, but others followed; new protests begot reprisals. In the fall of 1774, a Continental Congress met in Carpenters' Hall, a craft guild's house of assembly in Philadelphia. The delegates to this meeting were picked in a variety of ways: Connecticut's were chosen by a patriotic colonial governor and legislature; Massachusetts's by its legislature, acting at loggerheads with its royalist governor. After Virginia's royal governor dissolved the House of Burgesses for expressing too-radical opinions, it simply moved to a tavern in the colonial capital, where it reconstituted itself as a convention—representing the people without royal approval—and chose representatives to go to Philadelphia.

The first Continental Congress called for a boycott of British goods and a second meeting to be held in the spring of 1775. By the time the Second Continental Congress opened in the Pennsylvania State House in May, the cycle of resistance and repression had given way to battle. A column of British troops sweeping the countryside around Boston for protest leaders and caches of arms exchanged fire twice with local militias; its march back to barracks had been a fighting retreat against swarming, enraged locals.

The Congress sent George Washington, a Virginian veteran of Britain's last colonial war, to take command of the New Englanders flocking to besiege Boston. It tried to raise funds and supplies and secretly explored the possibility of foreign help. It was not yet committed, however, to a separation. The king's ministers and Parliament, who had proposed and approved all oppressive measures, were the villains. The king himself, George III, was still young (turning thirty-seven) and popular. He looked enough like George Washington that coin collectors cannot say which man the big-nosed heads on crude colonial tokens inscribed *GEORGIUS TRIUMPHO* are meant to honor. Maybe he would turn out to be "the best of kings."

The dream of royal reconciliation did not last. In the fall of 1775, George III informed Parliament that he "would put a speedy end to these disorders" by military force.[2] The Royal Navy burned Falmouth, Maine, and Norfolk, Virginia. In early 1776 Thomas Paine, an immigrant British tax collector, published *Common Sense*, a pamphlet calling for independence and assuring its readers "we have it in our power to begin the world over again."[3] It sold 150,000 copies, in a population of three million (the equivalent of a sale of six-teen and a half million copies today). On June 7 Richard Henry Lee, a Virginian whose eloquence was enhanced by the black silk glove he wore over his left hand maimed in a hunting accident, moved in Congress "that these United Colonies are, and of right ought to be, free and independent states." After a month of debate, his motion was carried on July 2—a date, wrote Massachusetts delegate John Adams, that would be celebrated with worship, parades, games, guns, bells, and bonfires "from this time forward forever more."[4]

Why? Why independence? Why break up what bid fair to become the greatest empire on earth?

Congress, besides doing the deed, had thought to explain it, and, anticipating the result, had assigned the job to a five-man committee on June 11.

The oldest member, at seventy, was Benjamin Franklin, the most famous and probably the smartest American then living—printer, politician, wit, and scientist. For sixteen years he had lived in London, acting as a lobbyist for Pennsylvania and other American colonies to the British government. For most of that time he was a dedicated imperialist, approving the Stamp Act as a necessary measure and maneuvering to have his illegitimate son William named royal governor of New Jersey. In his vision, however, the colonies and the home country would be equal partners in empire. No one in Britain shared his vision. In 1774 the Privy Council, the king's advisors, gave him a public dressing-down for his Americanist sympathies; he returned home, dedicated to independence and to revenge. In June 1776 he had just returned from a two-month mission to Canada trying to spread the revolution there.

Roger Sherman, age fifty-five, was a shoemaker, surveyor, and self-taught lawyer who had been in Connecticut politics for twenty years. In appearance he was plain as a board and just as stiff. But, as a colleague later wrote, he was "cunning as the Devil . . . you may as well catch an eel by the tail."[5]

John Adams, forty, was a Harvard-educated lawyer who, under the guidance of his cousin Samuel, had been a figure in the politics of protest in Massachusetts for seven years. His pen, lively and discursive in private letters, labored when he turned it to polemics. But when he spoke he was both compelling and indefatigable—one fellow delegate to the Continental Congress called him "our Colossus on the floor"—though thanks to some self-critical mechanism, he could not recall and preserve his great efforts.[6]

Thomas Jefferson, thirty-three, was a planter and lawyer, and the youngest member of Virginia's seven-man delegation. The typical Virginia politician was an orator (the unimpressed would say a ranter). Jefferson was quiet and shy; under stress he suffered migraines. But when he sat down to write he was transformed, showing a style that was both sweet and urgent, singing and staccato. "The God who gave us life gave us liberty at the same time," he wrote in 1774; "the hand of force may destroy, but cannot disjoin them."[7] Note the alliterations (life, liberty), the internal rhymes (destroy, disjoin), the bold antitheses (God, force). No other writer in America had that combination of lightness and power.

Robert R. Livingston, twenty-nine, of New York, was a Hudson Valley grandee who was sent to Congress almost as a matter of inheritance. His father, Robert R. Livingston, had been a delegate to the Stamp Act Congress. The Livingston clan was so numerous and included so many Roberts that this father and son both bore the repetitive middle name Robert to distinguish themselves from other Robert Livingstons.

Of these five men, Jefferson was the obvious choice to do the committee's work. Though Sherman and Livingston would go on to long and honorable careers, they contributed nothing to the declaration. Franklin was an ironist, unbeatable for a joke or a hoax, less suited to the task at hand. Adams later claimed that he demurred on the grounds that he had "a great Opinion of the Elegance of [Jefferson's] pen and none at all of my own."[8] Jefferson lodged in a bricklayer's house two blocks from the State House. Working in the second-floor parlor on a portable writing desk, he produced a seventeen-hundred-word document in a few days. Adams and Franklin, to whom he showed it, suggested several small changes: Jefferson described human rights as "sacred and undeniable," which scientist Franklin made "self-evident." Congress was given the draft at the end of June. After Richard Henry Lee's motion passed on July 2, Congress turned to the declaration to edit it, approving the final version and sending it to the printer on July 4.

The Declaration of Independence has three sections: an introduction, a conclusion, and, in between, a bill of indictment against George III, and secondarily, against the British people. Most of the items in the bill of indictment accuse the king of suspending or ignoring America's colonial assemblies and of ordering actions that those assemblies would never have approved: appointing judges and administrators ("swarms of new officers") responsible to him, not them; maintaining troops in America in time of peace under his command, not theirs (British Redcoats had been occupying Boston, ostensibly to keep order, since 1768). The hopeful experiment in self-rule begun at Jamestown a century and a half earlier was unraveling.

One of Jefferson's most passionate items arraigned George III for forcing the slave trade on America ("he has prostituted his negative for suppressing every legislative attempt to prohibit or to restrain this execrable commerce"). It is the fashion to scoff at Jefferson for including this bit of arrant hypocrisy. Every colony represented in Philadelphia in 1776 had slaves, and many, including Virginia, depended on their labor. Virginia had indeed asked that the slave trade be restricted, but it could afford to: the colony had all the slaves it needed; new imports would only decrease the value of those already there. Yet, as historians of slavery have come to understand the immense profits that Britain derived from the slave trade, Jefferson's complaint recovers some credibility. Yes, we were hooked, and willingly, but the mother country was an eager pusher.

Congress did not want to raise the question of slavery; our enemies were already raising it for us ("How is it," Samuel Johnson, the great English Tory and abolitionist, had asked in 1775, "that we hear the loudest *yelps* for liberty among the drivers of Negroes?").[9] The "drivers of Negroes," and their non-slave-driving colleagues, cut this accusation out of the declaration.

Jefferson, with all the pride of an author and all the sensitivity of a still-young one, squirmed over this and every other editorial change. Franklin, sitting beside him and observing his unhappiness, offered the balm of an anecdote, supposedly about one John Thompson, a friend of his youth, who after serving an apprenticeship to a hatter planned to open a shop of his own. Thompson designed a "handsome signboard" with a picture of a hat and the inscription, "John Thompson, *Hatter, makes* and *sells hats* for ready money." But every friend he showed it to suggested a shortening of his slogan—"*'Sells hats!'* says his next friend. Why, nobody will expect you to give them away; what is the use of that word?"—until all that was left was his name and the picture of the hat.[10]

Congress was not so drastic; it trimmed less than a third of Jefferson's handiwork, leaving a little over thirteen hundred words. And it left his introduction virtually untouched.

The declaration's opening paragraph is a polite salutation to its audience and a description of what is to follow. The declaration will explain "the causes" of the American Revolution—"the separation"—to "mankind." Who is included in "mankind"? The British, obviously, against whom we were fighting. Also Americans, who were doing the fighting—or not (John Adams later guessed that only a third of Americans supported independence; the remainder were opposed or neutral). Also, crucially, potential allies: France, Britain's longtime enemy; Spain, another British rival. But such was Jefferson's power of suggestion that "mankind" potentially opens out to mean everyone, present or future. The declaration is Congress's recital of its reasons to the world and to posterity.

But before the declaration gets to the reasons—the indictment of Britain and its king—it pauses to give a lesson in political philosophy. It is brief, only half a paragraph, yet without feeling pinched; Adams's praise of Jefferson's elegance was never more justified. The lesson covers revolution, government, and human nature, and glances at God. Jefferson, with a touch of the professor, begins with the most fundamental topic, human nature, adding implications and reservations as he goes. But, as ordinary humans immersed in our lives and the news, we might examine his argument in reverse order.

Revolutions, the declaration admits, are rare, and rightly so. "Prudence . . . will dictate that governments long established should not be changed for light and transient causes . . . all experience hath shown that mankind are more disposed to suffer while evils are sufferable, than to right themselves by abolishing the forms to which they are accustomed." Government had been compared to a ship or a boat since Plato and Horace. Jefferson is saying, don't rock it. *Prudence, established, experience,* and *accustomed* stand like four grave helmsman against the turbulence represented by *light* and *transient*. In these two sentences the American revolutionary seems to echo the pragmatic rhetoric of his English contemporary Edmund Burke (a pro-American member of Parliament, it is true, but later to become the philosopher of modern conservatism).

But suppose the evils of misgovernment are not "light and transient"? Suppose evils are the result, not of accident, ignorance, or even the bad policies of a particular set of lawmakers (who might, in time, be replaced by other, wiser ones)? Suppose evils arise from the "form of government" itself? Evils so fundamental require radical remedies. It then becomes "the right of the people to alter or to abolish" the current form "and to institute new government." When Andrew Hamilton invoked Brutus and Hampden in the trial of John Peter Zenger, he warned what men might be driven to. Now, says Jefferson, Americans have been driven to it.

A new government should not be just any government, however. Revolution is not for the purpose of disruption; change for its own sake is like a sick man turning over in bed. The new government, wrote Jefferson, should rest on a "foundation" of right "principles" ("laying its foundation on such principles [as] shall seem most likely to effect [the people's] safety and happiness").

What principles are they? The declaration has explained when revolutions should happen (rarely, and only to right evil forms of government) and why (to establish proper forms). It must also explain what the right forms of government are.

The declaration is not a constitution, an enduring structure or semipermanent list of hows and don'ts. Congress would get to work on writing a constitution later in July (the document, known as the Articles of Confederation, would take more than a year to complete). But the declaration outlines two features that a good form of government must have.

The first feature is that good government rests on consent ("deriving [its] just powers from the consent of the governed"). This was the principle tentatively enacted at Jamestown in 1619.

The second feature of a good government is that it acknowledges and upholds rights ("to secure . . . rights, governments are instituted among men"). Rights, plural. The declaration has gone beyond the Flushing Remonstrance and Andrew Hamilton's address to the Zenger jury. Good government looks to more than the right to worship or the right to complain; there are multiple rights in its purview.

The two features, consent and the range of rights, are related. Could there be an ideal sovereign, a "best of kings," who would guarantee every legitimate right without being answerable to his subjects? No. The ideal sovereign is, in the first place, incredible, because even good sovereigns die or change. George III had looked very good—until he stopped looking good at all. The all-powerful ideal sovereign is, in the second place, logically impossible because the power of the governed to give or withhold consent is one of the very rights that good government must uphold.

It is important to know that good governments secure rights and possess the consent of the governed. But this is all still rather abstract. What rights, besides consent, does the declaration have in mind?

Jefferson listed three. "Among these [rights] are life, liberty and the pursuit of happiness." *Life* and *liberty* seem obvious: you cannot be killed or imprisoned without good reason—in the English legal tradition, only as punishment for a crime and only after a trial. Gallows, jails, and stocks were features of ordinary eighteenth-century life, but no one was sent to them at whim. Even Governor Cosby gave John Peter Zenger his day in court.

To our ears *pursuit of happiness* sounds startlingly open-ended, even zany—like ad copy for a cruise ship or a reality show. But the phrase had a long, serious existence before it appeared in the declaration. It was used, more or less, by William Blackstone, the eighteenth-century English academic and jurist, whose *Commentaries on the Laws of England* was canonical for lawyers on both sides of the Atlantic. Blackstone wrote that, since living justly makes us happy, "the foundation of what we call ethics, or natural law," could be summarized thus: "that man should pursue his own true and substantial happiness."[11] Jefferson knew Blackstone's work, though he disliked it, for Blackstone was a man of the English establishment and a protégé of George III. But Blackstone's words, or words almost like them, had appeared in the work of other legal commentators and political philosophers, including John Locke. Their most recent incarnation had been on June 12, 1776, in a Declaration of Rights promulgated by Virginia (it would become the opening of Virginia's first state constitution). This document listed, among the rights enjoyed by "all men," "pursuing and obtaining happiness and safety." Jefferson had Virginia's Declaration of Rights in his Philadelphia parlor as he wrote his own declaration; assuming he needed any reminder about happiness, it was no further than his desktop.

But maybe the most expansive word in the declaration's list of rights is *among*. Life, liberty, and the pursuit of happiness do not exhaust the list. They are only the three rights Jefferson chose to specify, among uncounted, unnamed others.

Good government may be founded anew when it forgets its purposes, which are to heed consent and uphold rights. But government is a human institution. Men make it, staff it, live with it. So we must also ask, what are men?

Many areas of study—history and art, philosophy and science—give their various answers. For political purposes, the declaration says this: "they"—men—"are endowed by their Creator with certain inalienable rights." (This is the only change Congress made to Jefferson's draft, a matter of style not substance; he had written "inherent and inalienable rights," which must have struck his colleagues as one alliteration too many.)

Here the declaration joins hands, from however great a distance, with the Quakers and other sectarians of the seventeenth century. *Alienate* is a legal term referring to the transfer of ownership. A man can alienate whatever he owns, from a landed estate to a writing desk. But rights are not like that. They are bolted to us; they are part of us; they are aspects of our nature.

They have that character because the Creator made us that way. Our rights are not granted by kings, invented by a scribe in a parlor, or voted by continental congresses. They are outside human fashioning, created by God.

That does not guarantee that they will be honored in the world. They can be ignored, mocked, trampled. So they were, Jefferson and his fellow delegates believed, by George III. But any such curtailment was against nature. More, it was a profanation, because the Creator willed otherwise.

How religious was Thomas Jefferson? Years after 1776 he spent some time editing the Gospels, separating what he considered the authentic sayings of Jesus from the spurious ones. He also wrote that the ethics Jesus taught were superior to those taught by the Greeks and the Jews. No doubt these efforts and opinions retained some afterglow of belief, but Jefferson meant them as exercises in philosophy. His Jesus was like Socrates or Jefferson himself: a wise, good man, the best of his kind, but the same kind as all other men. All Christian theology, which made Jesus the Son of God, Jefferson dismissed as perversions of its founder's career and teachings. Jefferson's God, similarly, was a philosopher's God, a cause and a sustaining hum. God almost vanished into His greatest creation, nature itself (the first paragraph of the declaration spoke of "the laws of Nature and of Nature's God"). Now and then Jefferson could break out in pious anxieties, but for the most part he had no more religion than a cat. John Bowne and Tobias Feake, Robert Hodgson and Robert Fowler, would not have known what to make of him. On one thing, however, they all agreed, and it was important: rights were inextricably human because their origins were extrahuman, fashioned by the Creator of everything.

Jefferson was not the only American to put this thought into contemporary language. He never claimed that the declaration was original; a year before he died, he said he had only formulated "the common sense of the subject . . . whether expressed in conversation, in letters [or] in printed essays."[12] He said so, in part, as backhanded self-promotion: if he had only written what everybody thought, then the declaration was all the more to be honored. By forfeiting the status of lonely genius, he acquired that of universal bard.

But Jefferson's denial of originality, especially concerning this key point, was also simple truth. In 1766, during the Stamp Act crisis, John Dickinson, a wealthy Pennsylvania lawyer, had written that our rights "are created in us by the decrees of Providence, which establish the laws of our nature. They are born with us; exist with us; and cannot be taken from us by any human power."[13] In 1775, during the present crisis, Alexander Hamilton, an immigrant college student in New York, said that our rights "are written, as with a sunbeam, in the whole volume of human nature, by the hand of the divinity itself, and can never be erased or obscured by mortal power."[14] Jefferson probably never read Hamilton's youthful effusion, but he had certainly read Dickinson's; Dickinson was a far more prominent patriot than he was— author of America's first political best seller, *Letters from a Pennsylvania Farmer*, and, in 1776, a fellow delegate to the Continental Congress.

The declaration made one more point about men. All of them "are created equal." Elections determined by majority vote, as in Jamestown's first General Assembly, presumed equality, of the voters at least; the declaration's phrase was more sweeping. It would have many aftershocks.

Jefferson's document calls itself the Declaration of Independence, but it starts with an essay on liberty—why we are entitled to it, what it is, and its relevance to the matter at hand. Liberty is America's reason for being.

Congress ordered two hundred copies of the declaration to be printed and distributed across the new country. On July 9, Commander in Chief George Washington had one read to his troops, who were then in New York City awaiting a British attack (the Royal Navy had begun landing troops on Staten Island a week earlier). After the reading was finished, a patriot mob went to Bowling Green, a park at the southern tip of Manhattan, and toppled an equestrian statue of George III, which was melted into bullets.

When he was an old man, Jefferson stated that the declaration was signed the day of its date, but his memory played him false. Signatures were affixed to a handwritten parchment copy on August 2. Some of the signers were late arrivals to Congress who had not participated in the vote for independence; other voters had not been there to sign (for example, Robert Livingston had been called back to New York to serve in the legislature there). John Dickinson refused to sign, believing that a constitution and formal alliances should precede independence, though he served as a private in the Delaware militia the following year when that state and Pennsylvania were under attack.

The act of signing, which technically made all the signatories traitors, was accompanied with some gallows humor. Charles Carroll of Carrollton signed from Maryland (the suffix to his name distinguished him, like Livingston's extra Robert, from other family members—his father was Charles Carroll of Annapolis, his grandfather Charles Carroll the Settler). Carroll, a planter and merchant, was reputedly the wealthiest member of Congress; as he signed, someone quipped, "There go a few millions."[15] Carroll lost no millions, but Richard Stockton, a signer from New Jersey, was captured by the British in November 1776 and held—shackled, freezing, and starving—in prison for five weeks before being released on parole. About the same time, John Hart, another New Jersey signer, evaded capture by fleeing his farm and hiding out in nearby caves. Later in the war, George Walton of Georgia and three South Carolinians—Thomas Heyward, Arthur Middleton, and Edward Rutledge—were made prisoners of war and held for months. They were treated with only ordinary roughness and released in prisoner exchanges.

These are the signers of the Declaration of Independence (two of the colonies used what strike us as antiquated names):

New Hampshire: Josiah Bartlett, William Whipple, Matthew Thornton

Massachusetts Bay: John Hancock signed as president of Congress; Samuel Adams, John Adams, Robert Treat Paine, Elbridge Gerry joined him from their state

Rhode Island and Providence Plantations: Stephen Hopkins, William Ellery

Connecticut: Roger Sherman, Samuel Huntington, William Williams, Oliver Wolcott

New York: William Lloyd, Philip Livingston, Francis Lewis, Lewis Morris (grandson of John Peter Zenger's patron)

New Jersey: Richard Stockton, John Witherspoon, Francis Hopkinson, John Hart, Abraham Clark

Pennsylvania: Robert Morris (no relation to the New York Morrises), Benjamin Rush, Benjamin Franklin, John Morton, George Clymer, James Smith, George Taylor, James Wilson, George Ross

Delaware: Caesar Rodney, George Reed, Thomas McKean

Maryland: Samuel Chase, William Paca, Thomas Stone, Charles Carroll of Carrollton

Virginia: George Wythe, Richard Henry Lee, Thomas Jefferson, Benjamin Harrison, Thomas Nelson Jr., Francis Lightfoot Lee (brother of Richard Henry), Carter Braxton

North Carolina: William Hooper, Joseph Hewes, John Penn

South Carolina: Edward Rutledge, Thomas Heyward Jr., Thomas Lynch Jr., Arthur Middleton

Georgia: Button Gwinnett, Lyman Hall, George Walton

If these men escaped prosecution for treason, they would belong to the elite of a new nation. Most were already leading figures in their colonies, now to become states. They were overwhelmingly lawyers, merchants, or plantation owners, with a handful of doctors and a few wild cards thrown in: Franklin was sui generis, John Witherspoon was a clergyman and college president, lawyer Francis Hopkinson doubled as a composer and organist.

The declaration they signed increased in stature over the years, from an American announcement to a sacred text. We celebrate our independence not, as John Adams predicted, on the day that Richard Henry Lee's motion calling for it passed but on the day that Jefferson's words immortalizing it were endorsed. Conversely (and perversely), scholars point out that the declaration was not that important to begin with. America's revolutionary leadership had many things on its mind in the summer of 1776, from setting up postindependence state governments, which would be the seats of all real political power for years to come, to running the war (soon to take a sharp turn for the worse: Stockton was seized and Hart fled because the British chased Washington and his army out of New York and across New Jersey).

Scholarly downgrading privileges inside baseball over insight, logistics over psychology. Americans were a verbal people; they wrote, read, spoke, listened, and argued among themselves. They could not consider a thing really done unless they said what it was; sometimes they considered it done simply because they said it. The declaration pinned a lawyerly list of offenses on a faithless king and his people, prefaced with sweeping claims. The congressmen who signed it wrangled over the offenses but endorsed the claims with hardly a quibble. That is what they believed, and they put their names to it as a pledge of their lives, fortunes, and sacred honor.

Independence is what every breakaway colony achieves. But the Declaration of Independence is about more than throwing the rascals out. Our nationhood begins with an essay on liberty.

chapter five

CONSTITUTION OF THE NEW-YORK MANUMISSION SOCIETY

"These Our Brethren"

THE EMBARRASSMENT FELT BY THE CONTINEN-tal Congress in editing Thomas Jefferson's denunciation of George III for fostering the slave trade had a long backstory—far longer than the lifetime of anyone then living.

African slaves were first brought to the New World by Portugal and Spain early in the sixteenth century. England, the colonial latecomer, followed their practice. At the end of August 1619, only a few weeks after Jamestown's first General Assembly adjourned, Governor George Yeardley and Abraham Piersey, keeper of the Virginia Company's warehouse, went to Point Comfort, the colony's port at the mouth of the James River, to meet the *White Lion*, an English privateer carrying a Dutch letter of marque, or license to attack enemy vessels. The *White Lion* had raided a Portuguese ship, the *St. John the Baptist*, off the coast of Yucatan. The Portuguese were carrying several hundred Africans from Luanda, in what is now Angola, to Veracruz—a typical cargo in a traffic that had been going on for decades. The *White Lion* took some Africans off its defeated foe and landed in Jamestown with "20 and odd Negroes," which Yeardley and Piersey bought "at the best and easiest rates they could."[1] (This description of the transaction comes from a letter to the Virginia Company by John Rolfe, the widower of Pocahontas.)

The number of enslaved Africans in Virginia increased slowly at first (four years later there were twenty-three). But once tobacco became an established crop, the need for field hands grew exponentially. By 1670 the number of black slaves outstripped the number of white indentured servants (the labor of the latter was cheaper to buy, but it was time limited because indentures, or labor contracts, ran only for a specified number of years). A few African slaves lucky enough to be given their own plots of land to work in their spare time were able to earn enough money to purchase their freedom; one, Anthony Johnson, himself became a planter and a slave owner. But the vast majority remained tied to their work and their status. From the first, slavery was loaded with racial meaning. All slaves were black; most blacks were slaves. Between blacks and whites, the laws fixed a gulf. In 1630 a white settler, Hugh David, was "soundly whipped" in public on a Sunday for "lying with a Negro."[2]

The proportion of Virginia's population that was enslaved hovered around two-fifths throughout the eighteenth century (the proportion of South Carolina's was higher, sometimes rising over half). But slavery existed throughout the thirteen colonies. The colonies where the slave population was lowest—1–3 percent in New Hampshire, Massachusetts, and Connecticut—still accounted for thousands of slaves. These colonies profited from serving their slave-rich siblings, either by participating in the slave trade or by supplying them with goods that they did not produce locally.

Antislavery sentiment began to stir after the institution was well rooted. Initially it was confined to religious outliers appealing to the golden rule. The first attack on slavery published in America was a petition to a February 1688 meeting of Quakers in Germantown, Pennsylvania, by four recent converts. The petitioners asked their slave-owning brethren to "consider well . . . you who doe it, if you would be done at this manner?"[3] Over time, additional antislavery arguments besides the golden rule were put forward. In 1767 the *Virginia Gazette*, published in Williamsburg, the colonial capital, printed an antislavery essay signed Philanthropos, which drew on philosophy, practicality, and aspiration. Slavery, the essayist wrote, was a "violation of Justice," and "dangerous to the safety of the Community," and "destructive of the growth of arts & Sciences."[4] Slaves were held without their consent; they might rebel; and the availability of enslaved labor bred indolence among masters.

Philanthropos was Arthur Lee, himself a slave owner (and youngest brother of the two Lees who would sign the Declaration of Independence). As the American Revolution approached, a number of patriot slave owners perceived the contradiction between their principles and their way of life, unaided by Samuel Johnson's taunts. In 1774 George Washington wrote a loyalist in-law that it was time for Americans to assert their rights or "custom and use will make us as tame & abject Slaves as the Blacks we Rule over with such arbitrary Sway."[5] Washington expressed an inverted golden rule: stand firm or we will be done by as we do unto others.

How to resolve the contradiction? Slave owners could give their own slaves liberty, and some did so, often for religious reasons. In 1771 John Pleasants, a Quaker tobacco merchant in Virginia, died, leaving a will that asked his heirs to free his slaves once they reached the age of thirty. His son Robert agreed with his father's desires; other heirs didn't. Rival Pleasantses disputed the terms of John's will in court, but by 1799 about seventy-eight slaves had been freed. Robert Carter III of Nomini Hall, a plantation in Virginia's Northern Neck, became a Baptist in 1778, then a follower of the mystic Emmanuel Swedenborg a decade later. In the 1790s he began the gradual emancipation of his five hundred slaves. George Washington drafted a will in July 1799, five months before he died, directing that his 123 slaves be freed at the death of his wife. Washington was neither a Quaker nor a Swedenborgian. Yet he enjoined his executors "to see that *this* clause respecting Slaves, and every part thereof be religiously fulfilled ... without evasion, neglect or delay."[6] He wanted the blot of arbitrary sway scrubbed from his record, even at the last minute, for the good of his reputation, and possibly also of his soul.

During the American Revolution, Britain offered freedom to the runaway slaves of Americans, and thousands seized the chance. Free blacks fought on the American side too. Emmanuel Leutze's heroic painting, "Washington Crossing the Delaware," shows the Continental Army, after the string of disasters that landed Richard Stockton in prison and forced John Hart into hiding, striking to turn the tide of battle. One of the oarsman in George Washington's boat, on the starboard bow, is black. This is historically accurate. The Fourteenth Massachusetts, a regiment of former sailors who handled the crossing, had white, Indian, and black soldiers, as did some other northern units. Washington would be the last American officer to command integrated troops until the Korean War.

Yet the small numbers of freedmen and private manumissions were not enough to compensate for the work of reproduction and the ongoing slave trade, which kept the nation's slave population ever increasing. Americans who wanted the institution curtailed or ended would have to work together for legal change.

New York was a middling state where slavery was concerned. It did not support the plantations of Virginia and the Deep South, but it was bound to slavery as both a business partner and as a practitioner. Colonial New Yorkers made rum out of Caribbean sugar. Small farmers and artisans before and after the American Revolution employed slave laborers. The wealthy were attended by enslaved servants. An English visitor to Robert Livingston's Hudson River estate, eager to meet a transatlantic man of enlightened views, was surprised to find himself being served at meals by barefoot black boys wearing fine embroidered coats. The first post-independence census would count 21,193 slaves in New York, out of a total population of 314,366 (there were 4,682 free blacks). Local newspapers statewide were dotted with ads offering to buy or sell slaves and with inquiries after runaway property. For example, from the *Albany Centinel*: "Twenty Dollars Reward [for] a Negro Woman, named BETT, with her two children: She stole away and carried away a large Cheese, a number of silver Tea spoons, and several other articles. . . . Also, RAN AWAY, About two months since, a Negro Man, named BILL, or WILL [who] induced the abovementioned Negro Woman, (whom he calls his wife), to go off with him, so that it is probable they will be found together."[7] More slaves lived in New York City than in any other American city except Charleston.

On January 25, 1785, nineteen New Yorkers met in the house of John Simmons, innkeeper. The American Revolution had been particularly harsh on New York, which the British had conquered in the grim fall of 1776. Washington's prudent generalship, and the help of Britain's longtime enemy France, had won victory by 1781. Yet the enemy had not evacuated the city until the end of 1783. A third of it had burned; all its trees had been cut for firewood. Commerce had only just revived.

The men gathering at Simmons' house looked to a civic and moral revival. Most of those present were Quakers, many of them interrelated. Robert and Thomas Bowne bore the name of Peter Stuyvesant's Quaker antagonist. John Murray Sr. and Jr. gave their name to a hill north of the city. Elijah Cock, Effingham and Lawrence Embree, Samuel Franklin, John and William Keese, Edward and Joseph Lawrence, Willet Seaman, and William Shotwell were additional Friends, as Quakers were known. Others in attendance were veterans—James Cogswell, William Goforth, Melancton Smith, and Robert Troup. The meeting was called to order by Troup, a twenty-eight-year-old lawyer who had been both a British prisoner of war and a general's aide at one of America's great victories, Saratoga. Troup was an amiable young man whom everybody liked; one friend would call him "a better antidote to the spleen than a ton of drugs."[8] This January meeting had the serious purpose of forming "A Society for Promoting the Manumission of Slaves, and Protecting such of them as have been or may be Liberated."

In the chaos of the American Revolution, many slaves in and around New York had freed themselves simply by disappearing. Slave catchers, known as man-stealers or blackbirders, hunted for runaways and scooped up free blacks if authentic runaways were not to be found. In November 1784, city authorities had foiled an attempt to spirit away a group of free blacks on a ship bound either for Charleston or the Bay of Honduras.[9]

This was the immediate stimulus for the New Yorkers to meet, but they had larger ends in view. A committee of five—Embree, Franklin, Murray Sr., Smith, and Troup—was appointed to draw up the society's regulations and bylaws for approval at the next meeting, February 4. This time the society met at the Merchant's Coffee House, the city's largest. This was a larger meeting, attended by George Clinton, James Duane, John Jay, and Alexander Hamilton.

These were ornaments of the New York elite. George Clinton, an upstate landowner and speculator, was the state's first postindependence governor, now serving his third term (he would serve four more, earning the nickname "Old

Incumbent"). James Duane, who had married into the Livingston clan, was New York City's first postoccupation mayor. John Jay, another Livingston in-law, had been a Revolutionary spymaster, diplomat, and politician who had helped write the state's constitution. Alexander Hamilton was the newcomer to this group: he was the same age as Robert Troup and had roomed with him at King's College, later Columbia, before the American Revolution. Like Troup, he had served in the war, though in a loftier position: George Washington had tapped him to be a colonel on his staff.

The list of attendees reflected a unique political moment. New York's political vanguard (loyalists having been driven into exile or hiding) had led a successful revolution. In the years to come, they would split into hostile parties: Jay and Hamilton on one side, contending with Clinton and Melancton Smith (Jay and Clinton would run against each other for governor twice, each of them winning once). But now a united elite joined with Quakers—always outsiders, pursuing their own goals—in a common cause.

The society's bylaws began with a preamble, probably written by Troup, stating its goals and its inspiration. It included two sentences on the immediate crisis, the depredation of slave catchers: "The violent attempts lately made to seize and export for sale, several free Negroes, who were peaceably following their respective occupations, in this city must excite the indignation of every friend to humanity, and ought to receive exemplary punishment. . . . Destitute of friends and of knowledge, struggling with poverty, and accustomed to submission, [free blacks] are under great disadvantages in asserting their rights."

The first efforts of the society, then, would be directed to preventing black New Yorkers from being enslaved elsewhere. Man-stealing, a southbound underground railroad, was a monstrous practice, well worth stopping. Campaigning to stop it also conveniently focused attention on evil masters somewhere else (the luckless free negroes were seized for *export*). This smacked of an always popular form of charity: charity at a distance. The owners of Bett and Bill, advertising in the *Albany Centinel*, need not be concerned.

The opening of the preamble, however, was both more comprehensive and more specific: it addressed an all-American problem, focusing particularly on New Yorkers. The language echoed and amplified that of the Declaration of Independence: "The benevolent Creator and Father of men, having given to them all an equal right to life, liberty, and property, no Sovereign power on earth can justly deprive them of either; but in conformity to impartial government and laws to which they have expressly or tacitly consented."

Like Jefferson, the society invoked the Creator. But its Creator was more personal—not nature's God but a benevolent Father. Its villain was not George III but any unjust sovereign power. That would include unjust power that had been elected; that might include America.

The society shared Jefferson's emphasis on consent. Punishment could be justly administered only by governments to which men had "expressly or tacitly" given theirs. ("Tacitly" was added to include persons—women and children—who did not vote.)

The preamble went on: "It is our duty, therefore, both as free Citizens and Christians, not only to regard with compassion, the injustice done to those among us who are held as slaves; but to endeavour, by lawful ways and means, to enable them to share equally with us, in that civil and religious Liberty, with which an indulgent providence has blessed these States, and to which these our brethren are, by nature, as much entitled to as ourselves."

This sentence is not as elegant or as dense as Jefferson at his best, but there is a lot packed in it. It is a political and religious duty ("as free citizens and Christians") not just "to regard" but "to endeavor." To act, not just to sympathize. "By lawful ways and means" could be a counsel of conservatism: working within the laws as they now exist. But it could also be a counsel of activism: changing the laws to better suit our goal, which is enabling slaves "to share equally with us" in liberty. Why do we have such a goal? Because "our brethren" are "as much entitled to [it] as ourselves." All men are created equal.

Christianity suffuses the entire preamble. As God is a father, so men are brethren. America is free because "an indulgent providence" has "blessed" it. To be sure, Americans had won their liberty by fighting for it; the veterans at the Merchant's Coffee House had fought, personally. But their efforts had been secured by providence. The preamble, mean-while, does not neglect enlightened philosophy: slaves are entitled to liberty "by nature."

The preamble's echoing of words in the Declaration of Independence—*equal, consented, life, liberty*—are not bor-rowings from it but terms taken from the same source used by Jefferson: the common stock of American political ideas. Troup was not writing out of his head; he and Jefferson both were writing out of America's head.

Still, there are important differences between the society's preamble and the declaration. Slavery, an embarrassment so glaring that it had to be brushed aside in 1776, takes center stage in 1785 alongside the benevolent Father—no longer an adjunct of nature but a person and a personality—Who wishes that it be done away.

After the preamble, the bylaws set the dues—eight shillings, or a dollar, to join, four shillings every quarter to stay a member—and called for elected officers. At the next meeting John Jay was elected president.

Jay, a descendant of wealthy merchants, was a hardheaded man. One of his wartime assignments had been to run the state's Committee for Detecting Conspiracies; revolutionary-era New York was a dark ground of conflicting loyalties. "Punishments," Jay wrote, "must of course become certain, and Mercy dormant, a harsh System repugnant to my Feelings, but nevertheless necessary." As a diplomat, he had remarked that treaties were valid only so far as they reflected the interests of the parties; otherwise, they "had never signified anything since the world began."[10]

Jay's best portraits, however, show a face marked by acquaintance with grief. He was the grandson of a Huguenot refugee; two of his siblings had been blinded by smallpox, and two others suffered from mental problems.

He was sincerely committed to the gradual abolition of slavery. He wanted language approving such a goal included in the constitution he had helped write for New York State in 1777: "The rights of human nature and the principles of our holy religion loudly call upon us to dispense the blessings of freedom to all mankind."[11] The proposed language was voted down. In a letter written three years later, he stated that until America adopted such a measure, "her prayers to Heaven for liberty will be impious. This is a strong expression," he added, "but it is just."[12]

Yet Jay himself owned five slaves. He bought them, he said, in order to free them, once they had worked off their purchase price, thrift tracking charity; he calculated that Benoit, a slave he bought in 1779, would earn his freedom by 1787.[13] Jay was not the only slave-owning member of the society: Troup owned two.

Troup tried to resolve the anomaly via that favorite recourse of small-group politicians, a committee. At the society's February 1785 meeting, he was assigned to a committee of three members, along with Hamilton and White Matlack, a silversmith who had been expelled from the Quakers for his too-zealous support of the American Revolution. The committee's mandate was "to Report a Line of conduct to be recommended to the Members of the Society in relation to any Slaves possessed by them."[14]

At the society's November 1785 meeting, the Troup committee presented four resolutions. "All slaves" age twenty-eight or younger "who shall be owned by any of the members of this Society" should be freed when they turned thirty-five; all slaves older than twenty-eight and younger than thirty-eight should be freed "within seven years of the present time"; all other slaves should be freed when they turned forty-five, those who were now that age or older to be freed "immediately"; and finally, members should not sell any slaves except on the condition that their purchasers agree to adopt this schedule of manumission.[15]

These recommendations struck the rest of the society as too bold, and they were killed by that other favorite recourse of small-group politicians, another committee. Troup's report was assigned to a second committee for reconsideration; that committee dragged its heels until November 1787, when it was dissolved at its own request. The manumission of the Manumission Society's slaves would be left, at least in the short run, to the initiative of members.

One thing the society did do, as early as May 1786, was begin planning for a school in the city to educate the children of "poor Africans."[16] In its very first meeting, the society had noted that free blacks fell easier prey to man-stealers because they were "destitute . . . of knowledge." Education would make them better able to defend their rights.

The African Free School was opened for boys in 1787; girls were admitted five years later. All were taught reading, writing, and arithmetic; girls were taught needlework, boys astronomy needed for navigation. Both sexes were enjoined to avoid "immorality," "idleness," and "fiddling, dancing or any noisy entertainments in their houses."[17] In 1797 an evening school was added for adults. By the time it was folded into the public school system in the 1830s, the African Free School had seven branches scattered across the city.

Protecting free blacks was important (the society also compiled a list of them, against which the victims of man-stealing could be checked). But liberating slaves required political action. The society successfully petitioned the state legislature to achieve small but crucial reforms: forbidding new slaves from being brought into the state or current slaves from being taken out of it; freeing the slaves of exiled loyalists that the state government had confiscated as punishment. Finally, in 1799, Gov. John Jay, serving his second term, signed an act for the gradual abolition of slavery. Slave children born after July 4 that year were to be freed after twenty-eight years (for males) or twenty-five years (for females). Eighteen years later a new law mandated that all slavery in the state would end by July 4, 1827.

New York's slowness in ridding itself of slavery has cast the New-York Manumission Society into retrospective disrepute. Scholars sniff at its gradualism. Every other northern state except New Jersey had begun the process of abolition, or completed it, before the Manumission Society was even founded. Massachusetts ended slavery at a stroke by a decision of its state supreme court in 1783; Pennsylvania passed a gradual emancipation law in 1780, New Hampshire in 1783, Connecticut and Rhode Island in 1784; Vermont never had any slaves to begin with. The society's willingness to dispense lifestyle advice to its charges in the African Free School—no fiddling or dancing at home—seems paternalistic and, given the later direction of American popular culture, just plain dumb (without fiddling and dancing, by blacks and whites, what popular culture would we have?). The quasi-aristocratic status of leaders like Jay, and the aristocratic aspirations of *arrivistes* like Hamilton, give the society a veneer of elitism (the many Quaker outsiders in its ranks are, for the purposes of this indictment, forgotten).

No such reservations occurred to William Hamilton, a black carpenter, orator, and journalist, when slavery finally ended in New York in 1827. He marked the occasion with a speech at the African Zion Church, which he had helped found, on the fourth of July: "This day has the state of New-York regenerated herself—this day has she been cleansed of a most foul, poisonous and damnable stain."

How, in Hamilton's opinion, had this happened? "The cause of emancipation," he said, "has ever had its votaries, but they stood single and alone." Philanthropos might write an essay, but then it was thrown out with the newspaper it was printed in. "After the revolution, they drew nearer together." Common hopes bred fellowship, and fellowship bred action. Hamilton mentioned New York's Quakers as an organized body of slavery opponents. "That venerable body of religionists, called Friends, ought ever to be held in grateful remembrance by us."

But there was a still greater body. "The most powerful lever, or propelling cause was the Manumission Society."

Hamilton paused to savor an almost ecstatic thought. "How sweet it is to speak of good men! [It] yields a pleasure such as the young feel when talking of their lovers, or the parent feels, when telling of the prattle of their infants." So much for paternalism, if the patriarchs are compared to young lovers and beloved infants.

Hamilton then proceeded to speak of men "who ought to be deeply inscribed on your memories, and in your hearts: The names of Washington and Jefferson should not be pronounced in the hearing of your children until they could clearly and distinctly pronounce the names I am about to give." Hamilton was proposing a parallel hierarchy of founding fathers—the founding fathers of manumission.

The first name he gave was "that great and good statesman, the right honorable John Jay. . . . Blessed God! How good it is, he has lived to see, as a reward, the finishing of a work he helped to begin." Jay, then eighty-one years old and long retired from politics, still had two more years to live. Hamilton next named five more men: John Murray—"a man that calumny never did approach, but that she bit her tongue"; Samuel Franklin—"good"; John Keese—"the zealous, the virtuous, the industrious"; Alexander Hamilton—"that excellent soldier"; and Robert Bowne—"that man of more than sterling worth." (Rumor had it that William Hamilton was Alexander's illegitimate son, which was almost certainly untrue, though the white Hamilton's antislavery convictions make him a legitimate precursor.)

Hamilton then called a roll of nineteen other members of the society, including Robert Troup. "These are the men that formed the Manumission Society, and stamped it with those best of principles, found in the preamble to the constitution, framed by them. It is too excellent to pass over."[18] And so he read it.

There is a historians' fashion that identifies all propelling causes with large forces or, if with individuals, then only with little known ones. Many causes, great and small, undermined slavery in postrevolutionary New York. The state filled with antislavery immigrants as New England sent its surplus population westward. New York's Dutch, so long set in their ways, began at the end of the eighteenth century to abandon many customs, from Dutch-language church services to slave owning. More important than demography or cultural assimilation, slaves freed themselves. The 1799 law seemed like permission to run away: if the institution was doomed, why not escape it now? In its wake, manumissions spiked as slaves and masters negotiated short-term deals: I will still work for you, if you promise to free me after five years, or two.

All these factors played their part. But the best of principles, and a common commitment to them, was, as William Hamilton said, a powerful lever.

The Manumission Society was a fortuitous alliance of outsiders and insiders—oddball Quakers and Manhattan elitists. But whatever side they came from, they were determined to lead. Change requires action, which requires some person, or group of people, to be the first to take it. Change always requires what William Hamilton called a "propelling cause."

New York's moment of regeneration in 1827 found no imitators; the other remaining northern slave state, New Jersey, had passed its own gradual abolition law in 1804. New York only moved itself out of the column of slave states. A vital move. New York would be a political swing state throughout the nineteenth century, pivoting from party to party, its gyrations often deciding close elections. Its partisan preferences were never more consequential than during the Civil War, which many New Yorkers resisted, even to violence. How much stronger would they have fought if a culture of slave owning had persisted there?

The Manumission Society was not thinking of future wars when it first met in 1785. They were moved by an all-American idea: that slavery deprived "our brethren" of liberty.

chapter six

CONSTITUTION

"Blessings of Liberty"

T HE NEW-YORK MANUMISSION SOCIETY WAS A private organization in one state. In the 1780s the constitution of the entire country cried out for revision.

The problem was war debt. The American Revolution was the longest war the United States would fight until Vietnam; paying for it was the responsibility of Congress, which, under America's first constitution, the Articles of Confederation, was the totality of the national government (there was no executive and no national judiciary). Each state sent two to seven delegates to Congress; each delegation, whatever its size, cast one vote. The articles assigned Congress various powers—declaring peace and war, adjudicating boundary disputes between the states. They did not, however, give Congress reliable access to funds. It could ask the states for money, but the states, which held all real power under the system, gave only as much as they could or would. Robert Morris, the Philadelphia merchant tapped by Congress to manage the nation's finances, said that begging the states for funds was like "preaching to the dead."[1] In 1783 the enemy finally went home, but America's debts remained.

Some states, which had incurred their own war debts, were no better off than the country. Massachusetts, where the shooting started, tried to restore its finances in peacetime via a regressive tax on land, which provoked hard-pressed farmers to rebel—a disturbance named after Capt. Daniel Shays, one of the Revolutionary War veterans who led it.

The political elite of the country recognized that some change in the structure of the national government was needed. Congress called on the states to send delegates to a constitutional convention in Philadelphia in May 1787. Over the previous four years, Congress had moved from Philadelphia to Princeton, Annapolis, Trenton, and finally New York. But the new convention assembled in Congress's wartime home, the Pennsylvania State House, the same hall in which it had declared independence and approved Jefferson's declaration.

The meeting got off to a slow start. The first out-of-state delegates arrived when they were supposed to, on the second Tuesday of the month, but thanks to late starts and slow travel, a majority of states was not represented until May 25.

About half the delegates would attend every session, but the rest came and went, for reasons personal or public. William Blount of North Carolina and Abraham Few and William Pierce of Georgia left the convention to serve as delegates to Congress, which was meeting in a tavern in

New York. James McHenry of Maryland left to tend a sick brother; William C. Houston of New Jersey left to suffer his own mortal bout of tuberculosis. Two of the three delegates sent by New York, John Lansing Jr. and Robert Yates, went home in the second week of July, unhappy with the nationalistic tenor of the proceedings. Their colleague, Alexander Hamilton, also became a truant, feeling that he could not cast his state's vote by himself. New Hampshire appropriated no funds to cover the expenses of its delegates, John Langdon and Nicholas Gilman; they arrived in the last week of July only because Langdon decided to pay for both out of his own pocket. John Francis Mercer of Maryland arrived in August, gave a couple dozen disputatious speeches, and left after two weeks. Rhode Island, which was happy with the Articles of Confederation as they were, refused to send any delegates at all. Seventy men were chosen by the other twelve states to attend; fifty-five made it, at one time or other.

The delegates were mostly planters, lawyers, or state office holders. Eight had signed the Declaration of Independence; twenty-one had fought in the American Revolution. Among these patriots were the two most famous Americans in the world at that time. The first item of business the convention performed was to elect George Washington its president. Washington had earned his fame by commanding a revolutionary army for eight and a half years, then going home—a feat that recalled the semimythical Roman hero Cincinnatus and few nonmythical persons in all of history. The motion to elect him was to have been made by the other world-famous American, Benjamin Franklin, scientist, diplomat, wit, and jack-of-all-trades, but rain and indisposition kept the eighty-one-year-old Philadelphian home that day; Robert Morris, serving as another one of Pennsylvania's delegates, made the motion instead. The vote to elevate Washington was unanimous.

A few of the delegates left little trace on the meeting or on history. William Blount and Jared Ingersoll (Pennsylvania) each spoke only once, on the last day the convention met, evidently to put themselves on the record. Nicholas Gilman (New Hampshire), Thomas Fitzsimmons (Pennsylvania), Richard Bassett (Delaware), and Alexander Martin (North Carolina) never said a word. Delaware's Jacob Broom, a farmer, surveyor, and toolmaker, is the only delegate of whom no image or description survives. When the National Constitution Center in Philadelphia commissioned life-size statues of all the delegates who stayed to the convention's end, for display in a "Signers' Hall," the sculptor showed Broom with a hand over his face, as if rubbing it, so as not to have to imagine what he looked like.

The convention met six days a week, Monday through Saturday. A quorum was seven delegations, representing a majority of states. As in Congress, each state cast one vote. Any motion, once voted on, could be reconsidered, which encouraged open-ended discussion and second thoughts. Exchanges between speakers were sometimes short, even sharp; at other times, a speaker might hold the floor for an entire day or even one day running over to the next. Most of the delegates were intelligent and well informed, a few had moments of eloquence, a very few were funny: when Elbridge Gerry (Massachusetts) worried that the vice president would be a mere tool of the president, Gouverneur Morris

(Pennsylvania) observed he would be the only heir that ever loved his father. Other delegates struck their colleagues as tedious, inaudible, pedantic, or vain. Yet the general tone was serious and respectful. There were no altercations; everyone had his say. George Washington, the president, spoke only three times, briefly.

At the end of July, the convention named a committee of detail to prepare a draft based on all the provisions agreed to so far, then took a ten-day break. The delegates had decided on a bicameral Congress, joined by an executive and federal courts—a structure similar to the governments of most states, which had in turn imitated their colonial predecessors (with elected governors in place of royally appointed ones). The new Congress would have the power to levy taxes and tariffs, the necessary prelude to solving America's debt crisis. Edmund Randolph, Virginia's young governor, wrote a first draft; James Wilson of Pennsylvania, a transplanted Scot who was one of the most learned and voluble delegates, rewrote it. Their handiwork was presented to all the delegates when they reconvened in the first week of August. Then began a clause-by-clause review, assisted by a committee on postponed matters, to remind them of issues they had left unresolved in their wake.

At last, on September 8, the draft of the new Constitution was given to a committee of style for a final rewrite. This five-man committee was chaired by William Samuel Johnson (Connecticut), the only delegate who had maintained an uneasy neutrality during the Revolution. An Anglican with an honorary degree from Oxford, he had defended colonial rights but thought independence was a bridge too far. Once it was secured, however, he served the new nation in Congress and had just been chosen president of the former King's College, patriotically renamed Columbia. His fellow committee members belonged to a younger generation. Rufus King (Massachusetts) had sympathized with his state's hard-pressed farmers until their violent protests made him keen for national reform. James Madison (Virginia) had made a name in state and national politics both as a theorist and a wire-puller; his friend and ally, Alexander Hamilton (New York), was the convention's exotic—a West Indian immigrant, rumored to be illegitimate, perhaps even a bit black, a veteran both of George Washington's staff and of the last American charge at Yorktown.

The fifth committee member was Gouverneur Morris, tall, handsome, witty, and arrogant (he was a grandson of Lewis Morris, the New York powerhouse who had backed John Peter Zenger, and half brother of Lewis Morris, a signer of the Declaration of Independence). He had recently lost a leg in a carriage accident, which he replaced with an elegant peg. Although he had skipped the entire month of June to tend to family business, once he returned he spoke more often than any other delegate, including those who had been present for every session. This burst of eloquence induced his colleagues to give the work of polishing the amended draft to him.

Unlike Jefferson in Philadelphia eleven years earlier, Morris was editing rather than creating. By eliminating legalisms and redundancies, he massaged the twenty-three articles of the draft down to seven. One example of his compression: the committee of detail devoted an entire article to declaring that "the Government shall consist of supreme legislative, executive, and judicial powers." Morris simply began his first three articles by announcing that "all legislative powers," "the executive power," and "the judicial power" should be vested in their respective branches. It was a small cleanup, but many of them made for a large cleanup.

Morris's original contribution was his rewrite of the document's preamble, which he transmuted from a roll call—"We the People of the States of New Hampshire, Massachusetts" and so on "do ordain, establish and declare this Constitution"—into an elegant miniature essay on the purposes of government, complete with alliteration and internal rhymes. Morris's final purpose, given the place of honor at the end of his statement, was to "secure the Blessings of Liberty to ourselves and our Posterity." The preamble was a contract and a will, and liberty was the most important item concerned: Morris and his fellow delegates, speaking (they hoped) for the American people, wanted it for themselves and meant to pass it on.

The committee of style's rewrite was done on September 12. With a few small changes, it was signed on September 17 by thirty-eight delegates from eleven states. Hamilton had returned to sign as the lone New Yorker. A thirty-ninth signature, of John Dickinson, who had gone home sick, was added by fellow Delawarean George Read.

Here are their names:

President and deputy (or delegate) from Virginia: George Washington
New Hampshire: John Langdon, Nicholas Gilman

Massachusetts: Nathaniel Gorham, Rufus King

Connecticut: William Samuel Johnson, Roger Sherman

New York: Alexander Hamilton

New Jersey: William Livingston, David Brearley, William Paterson, Jonathan Dayton

Pennsylvania (since the convention was meeting around the corner, the state sent many men, who lasted until the end): Benjamin Franklin, Thomas Mifflin, Robert Morris, George Clymer, Thomas Fitzsimons, Jared Ingersoll, James Wilson, Gouverneur Morris

Delaware (which, being just down the river from Philadelphia, also sent a full, and patient, quotient): George Read, Gunning Bedford Jr., John Dickinson, Richard Bassett, Jacob Broom

Maryland: James McHenry, Daniel of St. Thomas Jenifer, Daniel Carroll (The odd first name "Daniel of St. Thomas" was a favorite in the Jenifer family, which used it to distinguish Daniel of St. Thomases from plain Daniels.)

Virginia: John Blair, James Madison Jr.

North Carolina: William Blount, Richard Dobbs Spaight, Hugh Williamson

South Carolina: John Rutledge, Charles Cotesworth Pinckney, Charles Pinckney (the Pinckneys were second cousins), Pierce Butler

Georgia: William Few, Abraham Baldwin

The convention had debated and written the Constitution in secret to allow for maximum freedom of discussion. One of George Washington's three utterances had been to chide whichever delegate had left a copy of proposed resolutions behind him in the State House, where it might have been seen by prying eyes. "Let him who owns it, take it," Washington scolded at the end of one session, tossing it down and leaving the room.[2] No one claimed the wayward paper.

Once the Constitution was done, however, there followed a months-long, nationwide public debate in which it was praised, attacked, explained, and confuted. America's print culture, nourished by the Zenger verdict, did not guarantee outcomes for or against the Constitution or for any important decision; it left the burden of persuasion to advocates pro and con. The legacy of voting established at Jamestown left the burden of decision to the people.

Congress had asked the states to send delegates to Philadelphia, and the convention notified Congress of its handiwork. The new Constitution, however, declared that it would go into effect once it was approved, neither by Congress nor by the state legislatures, but by conventions elected in each state for the purpose. Nine of thirteen would be sufficient to bring the new form of government into being.

America had gone outside its existing structures to write the Constitution; it would go outside them once more to make it real. Devising and writing had been done by a few dozen men in conclave; approving would be done by the people at large and their representatives, specially chosen for the task.

The anti-Constitution campaign had begun at the convention itself. Three delegates refused to sign on the last day: Edmund Randolph and George Mason of Virginia and Elbridge Gerry of Massachusetts. Randolph soon came around to back the new document, but Gerry got into a shouting match with a supporter of the Constitution at his state's ratifying convention, and Mason was a doughty opponent at his. Gerry thought the new Congress had too much power; Mason thought the new system would end in a monarchy or a tyrannical aristocracy—which he did not know, "but one or the other, he was sure."[3] The antis had the most organized media operation, a clearinghouse for tracts run by George Clinton, governor of New York (the two New York delegates who had left the convention in July were his political allies and ideological soul mates). Some of the antis' criticisms were subtle: most republics in history—Greek city states, Rome before it grew—had been small; could the stronger, more unified government the Constitution proposed retain its republican character over a country as large as the United States? Some criticisms were outlandish: the Constitution had created an executive, the president, and forbidden religious tests for office; could an American-born Pope get the job?

The Constitution's supporters wielded all the influence and art they could muster in their home states and kept in touch with each other via many anxious letters. They won an early victory at Pennsylvania's ratifying convention, which met, like the constitutional convention itself, at the State House in Philadelphia, but they won it in a bum's rush by muscling unhappy delegates to the hall for a quorum. The losers indignantly told all of America how they had been bullied, whereupon the winners realized they would have to proceed more cordially, arguing rather than straight-arming. James Madison was a model of argument and industry; he helped Alexander Hamilton and John Jay write a series of pro-Constitution essays for the newspapers in New York City, where he was serving in the old Congress, then returned to his home state to lead the pro-Constitution forces at its ratifying convention in Richmond. George Washington seemed to do nothing; but the prestige of his signature (and of his counsel, delivered in private letters) counted as much as his colleagues' efforts.

There was an outpouring of commentary, including one anti-Constitution pamphlet by female historian Mercy Otis Warren. There were riots over ratification in several cities—in Albany, New York, rival parades of pros and antis fought each other with clubs, stones, and bricks—but happily no deaths. All in all the process was a tribute to what Massachusetts politician Nathan Dane called "the attention of this intelligent people."[4]

Delaware, Pennsylvania, and New Jersey ratified in December 1787; Georgia and Connecticut in January 1788, Massachusetts in February, Maryland in April, South Carolina in May. New Hampshire became the decisive ninth state to ratify on June 21, 1788; Virginia, not yet knowing what New Hampshire had done, ratified four days later. New York followed in July, North Carolina in 1789, Rhode Island in 1790. The new federal government assembled for the first time in New York City in the spring of 1789.

The Constitution is a web of interlocking parts. James Madison argued that its very complexity guaranteed liberty, since officeholders in every branch of government—executive, legislative, or judicial; federal or state—would resist the power grabs of rivals in the interest of defending their own turf.

One vital layer of complexity had been added at the constitutional convention itself. After long, sometimes angry bargaining between large and small states, the new Congress was divided into two bodies: a House of Representatives in which seats would be assigned to states on the basis of population, and a Senate, in which each state would fill two seats. Representatives would be elected by popular vote, senators by their state legislatures. Thus, large and small states, local voters and local politicians, would all have their say.

Another layer of complexity was suggested by the long struggle for ratification. The Constitution guaranteed certain rights—there could be no ex post facto laws (criminalizing deeds after they were done) and no bills of attainder (criminal verdicts rendered by legislatures instead of courts). Yet there was no freestanding bill of rights specifying the liberties that the men of Flushing and the Zenger jurors had claimed and to which the declaration and the constitution of the New-York Manumission Society had alluded. In fact many state constitutions had bills of rights; Virginia's said, among other things, that "all men are equally entitled to the free exercise of religion" and that "freedom of the press is one of the great bulwarks of liberty, and can never be restrained but by despotic governments."

Roger Sherman of Connecticut had cited the states' bills of rights as reasons for not adding a new one to the federal Constitution; "being in force," they "are sufficient."[5] But their very existence made the lack of one in the Constitution glaring. As the ratification debate unfolded, it became clear that most antis would be reconciled to the new system if there were an implicit promise that a bill of rights be added via the amending process laid out in Article V. The new Congress, which met in the spring of 1789, accordingly sent what are now the first ten amendments to the states that summer; they were ratified by December 1791. The "free exercise of religion" and "freedom . . . of the press" found themselves protected from congressional interference in the same amendment.

Three interlocking features of the Constitution were especially important guarantees of liberty, despite being relatively little noticed, certainly not in their relation to each other. All concerned status, class, or caste. There was no king, no nobility, and no mention of slaves. No American, on paper at least, was to be different at birth from any other.

The executive power was vested, according to Article II, in a president, who should hold office for a four-year term and "be elected."

The rebels who had torn down the gilded statue of George III and melted it into bullets were obviously no friends of kings. But kingship was woven into their world and sometimes into their very thoughts.

One political philosopher known to every well-read patriot was the last-generation English politician and journalist Henry St. John, Viscount Bolingbroke (d. 1751). Bolingbroke, after a brilliant start, spent the bulk of his life as a disappointed gadfly, explaining in lively magazine articles that England's ills were the work of corrupt insiders (that is, the politicians who had displaced him). This diagnosis, shorn of its local particulars, struck Americans as a perfect description of their unhappiness in an unresponsive empire. Bolingbroke's solution was a patriot king, a royal outsider above the swamp of politics, who alone could drain it. It was a fantasy, and a singularly unrepublican one, but seductive even so. George Washington, John Adams, and Thomas Jefferson all had Bolingbroke on their shelves.

In the nineteenth century, the Scottish author and antiquary Sir Walter Scott would claim that he had found in the papers of Charles Edward Stuart, cousin of George III and forlorn sprig of a rival dynasty, a memorial from American supporters, written during the American Revolution, asking him to be their sovereign.[6] Nothing came of it: Charles was a Catholic drunkard living in exile in Italy—not a promising candidate for a king of America. It is certain that, as the war wound down, Washington received a letter from one of his officers, Col. Lewis Nicola, urging him to aspire to a throne himself. "I believe strong arguments might be produced for admitting the title of king," Nicola wrote.[7] Washington replied, immediately and angrily, "You could not have found a person to whom your schemes are more disagreeable."[8] During the constitutional convention, Alexander Hamilton, taking his leave of absence, reported to Washington that the people he encountered on his way home, weary of misgovernment, were willing to "substitute something not very remote from that which they have lately quitted."[9]

All this was gossip or speculation. But gossip and speculation, like dreams, often express unconscious fears—or desires. Royalty was like a gravitational field; resisting it required firmness.

Article I, sections 9 and 10, forbade a second form of stratification: neither the United States nor any state could grant titles of nobility. As there would be no royal family under the Constitution, so there would be no noble ones.

Nobility had been thin on the ground in colonial times. Only one American had ever been ennobled—Sir William Pepperell, a Maine merchant who was made a baronet in recognition of capturing a French fortress in Nova Scotia during one of England's colonial wars. The only English nobleman to take up residence in America was Thomas, Lord Fairfax, who owned a tract of Virginia as large as New Jersey and settled in the Shenandoah Valley. George Washington's half brother Lawrence married into the Fairfax family, which gave young George his first job as a surveyor.

Many a nobleman fought on America's side in the American Revolution, however. Baron von Steuben, whose title came from his native Prussia, wrote the drill book for the American army, served as its inspector general, and would die at the estate he had been given in northern New York. The Marquis de Lafayette became a brigadier general, a surrogate son to the childless George Washington, and America's favorite Frenchman. His grave in Paris would be covered with soil he brought from Bunker Hill. One native-born general, William Alexander, claimed to be a nobleman, as the senior male relative of a defunct line of Scottish earls. The House of Lords, to whom he had applied for confirmation, had not recognized his title, though his American comrades did, punctiliously calling him "Lord Stirling" throughout the war. "The troops commanded by Lord Sterling [*sic*]," wrote Washington after one battle, "behaved with great bravery."[10]

Could there be a homegrown nobility? In 1783, Washington's artillery commander, Henry Knox, founded a fraternal organization of Revolutionary War officers, the Society of the Cincinnati. Cincinnatus had gone home to his plow after saving Rome, but what would the American Cincinnati go home to do? They had chapters in each state (plus one in France)—a fact that, at a time when even churches were regional and there were no other large organizations of any kind, struck some Americans as politically dangerous. "One set of men dispersed through the union and acting in concert," warned Elbridge Gerry at the constitutional convention, might "delude" voters into supporting their candidate for president.[11] The additional fact that membership in the Cincinnati was (and still is) hereditary seemed doubly dangerous. The first president of the Cincinnati, George Washington, would indeed become the first president of the United States (though he would certainly have gotten the job whether he had belonged to many organizations or to none).

Offices in the colonial administration of America had been awarded by the king based on a combination of merit and family connection. Now that Americans were independent, they could elevate their fellows based on merit—as long as they did not erect another web of family connection.

There would be no kings or nobles under the Constitution. But almost one in five Americans—just under seven hundred thousand—were slaves. The most brutal form of stratification was far and away the most common.

Slaves are discussed several times in the Constitution: in determining the population of states for the purpose of representation (Article I, Section 1), in guaranteeing the slave trade until 1808 (Article I, Section 9, and Article V), and in providing for the return of fugitive slaves from the states they had escaped to, to the states they had fled (Article IV,

Section 2). Nowhere, however, are the words "slaves" or "slave" used; instead they are called "other Persons," "such Persons as any of the States . . . shall think proper to admit," or "Person[s] held to Service or Labour."

Gouverneur Morris, who did not suffer fools, at one point rebelled against these evasions, moving that the clause guaranteeing the "importation of such Persons" be changed to the "importation of slaves into North Carolina, South Carolina and Georgia." He "wished it to be known that this part of the Constitution was a compliance with those states."[12] Morris's fellow delegates shushed him.

Why? James Madison gave the most interesting answer: it would be "wrong to admit in the Constitution the idea that there could be property in men."[13]

Madison's answer was simple, avoiding both Morris's sarcasm and the circumlocutions that provoked it.

His answer was hypocritical. The idea was forbidden, but the property remained (Madison was a slave owner).

His answer was aspirational. The property remained, but the name was to be kept out of the Constitution like a stain. Slavery, to Madison and to most of his colleagues in Philadelphia, was an embarrassment. Perhaps one day it would wither away.

The delegates to the constitutional convention, and their contemporaries, took two steps to hasten the process. Guaranteeing the slave trade until 1808 implied that it would be banned thereafter (the bill to do so would be signed in 1807, a year ahead of time, by Thomas Jefferson, the president Madison served as secretary of state). Another step to weaken slavery was taken immediately. Even as the constitutional convention sat in Philadelphia, Congress, meeting in its tavern in New York, passed a law organizing the Northwest Territory, the barely settled frontier bounded by Pennsylvania, the Ohio and Mississippi Rivers, and the Great Lakes. The Northwest Ordinance declared "there shall be neither slavery nor involuntary servitude in the said territory." Five future states—Ohio, Indiana, Illinois, Michigan, and Wisconsin—would be free of it.

Slavery was a hardy plant. It would take more—much more—than cutting its roots and preventing its growth into the old Northwest to kill it. But these were starts.

Taken together, these three provisions—no king, no nobility, no mention of slaves—established in fundamental law one of the principles of the declaration: there were no orders of mankind; all men are created equal. It was necessary to put it in black and white because the human tropism toward royalty, rank, and bondage is so strong. The Bible contains denunciations of royalty—Thomas Paine, the English immigrant pamphleteer, cited Samuel's (and God's) unwillingness to give Israel a king in his best seller, *Common Sense*—but it also contains many passages that accept it. A spasm of equality passed through the western world with the Enlightenment, but other intellectual currents, romantic and radical, would follow, generating their own inegalitarian consequences. Whatever scripture or the spirit of the age says, humanity inclines to hierarchy. We are raised by parents, and we raise children; some forms of hierarchy are as natural as birth and death.

George Washington was so mindful of the pull of kingship that he planned to remind America, in his first inaugural address, that there could be no Washington dynasty because he was childless: "I have . . . no family to build in greatness upon my country's ruins." (Madison ghosted a shorter, less confessional address, which Washington ended up giving instead.) Many of Washington's successors were similarly placed, having no children or no sons (office-holding then being restricted to men). The third president, Thomas Jefferson, had only daughters; the fourth, James Madison, only a stepson; the fifth, James Monroe, only daughters; the seventh, Andrew Jackson, only adopted children. But the second president, John Adams, had three sons, the eldest of whom, John Quincy Adams, became the sixth president. Who knows what a political landscape crowded with founding presidential sons might have looked like?

We know that political dynasties proliferated at the lower levels of American politics. The Pinckney cousins who signed the Constitution were one of many examples (Charles Cotesworth would run for vice president once and president twice, all three times unsuccessfully; Charles was more successful, serving as congressman, US senator, and governor). In January 2019, Rodney Frelinghuysen retired after twelve terms as a congressman from New Jersey. He was the fifth member of his family to serve in Congress, the first being Frederick Frelinghuysen, who was sent to the Continental Congress in 1778.

America's appetite for foreign nobility is insatiable. We mock titles and pomp, boast of our simple superiority to them—and lap them up. During the Madison administration, Betsy Patterson, daughter of a wealthy Baltimore merchant, married Jerome Bonaparte, Napoleon's youngest brother. *Le tout* Washington gaped at the couple, especially at the beautiful, and beautifully (under)dressed, Betsy. "Mobs of boys," wrote one spectator, "have crowded around her splendid equipage to see what I hope will not often be seen in this country, an almost naked woman."[14] Napoleon, furious that a family member had married a commoner, annulled the match. But Betsy wore her surname as a badge of honor for the rest of her life.

Slavery was the most tenacious form of hierarchy, rooted in habit and economics. For decades, only a few words, and a few silences, stood against it.

Men want liberty. But they want other things as much, sometimes more. They will surrender liberty for the sake of security and take other people's liberty in order to bolster their own self-esteem.

Securing the blessings of liberty takes vigilance and effort.

chapter seven

MONROE DOCTRINE

"Movements in This Hemisphere"

GEORGE WASHINGTON WAS INAUGURATED THE first president of the United States under the new Constitution in April 1789. Three months later the Bastille fell. The American Revolution was the first of what would become an age of revolutions, which would test and ultimately expand our commitment to liberty.

The French Revolution destroyed Europe's most sophisticated absolute monarchy in Europe's most populous country. The shock to France's neighbors and the stimulus to France's energies generated a world war that would last for twenty-five years. Beginning in 1791, a slave revolution and war of independence turned France's richest Caribbean colony, Saint-Domingue, into the black republic of Haiti.

How to respond to the French Revolution perplexed American politics for years. Was the new France, as our ambassador in Paris during its earliest days, Thomas Jefferson, thought, a sister republic deserving our best wishes? Or was it, as his successor Gouverneur Morris believed, a belligerent despotism that meant us no good? America went to war with France's great rival, Britain, in 1812, an objectively pro-French act, though we took it for our own reasons. The question of the French Revolution's nature was never truly answered, only mooted with the final defeat of Napoleon, its last avatar, at Waterloo in 1815.

The United States had given Haiti's rebels some tactical help in the late 1790s in order to frustrate French attempts to retake it. At the request of the American consul there, Alexander Hamilton even sketched a constitution for the new country—a military dictatorship with wishful checks and balances built in. (His suggestions were not followed, the Haitians opting for dictatorships pure and simple.) But black Haiti was a phenomenon that the American slave republic preferred to shun and ignore for decades.

As the 1820s began, the world saw a new wave of revolution. In 1820 Spanish liberals forced their king to accept a constitutional government; in 1821 Greeks rose up against their Ottoman overlords. In this hemisphere, the Spanish empire, which stretched from California to Buenos Aires, had been contending with native-born rebels for a decade.

Americans felt a natural sympathy for these struggles. Spain's liberals wanted a constitution; America had one. Greeks were Christians; so were almost all Americans. Between the United States' and Spain's colonies lay no unbridgeable racial barrier: their societies were mestizo, but their would-be leaders belonged to the local white upper classes. The colonial revolutions also tempted American appetites: the Spanish empire represented a world of potential trade that Spain had kept to itself for three centuries.

The most eloquent American supporter of the new revolutionary moment was the most eloquent man in America, Speaker of the House Henry Clay. A Virginian transplanted to Kentucky, he looked like an ordinary farmer. But when he opened his mouth, he could sigh like a lute or ring like a trumpet. He was a drinker, a gambler, a flirt, and a politician to the marrow of his bones. He had been chosen Speaker in 1811, at age thirty-three, on his very first day in the House—a meteoric rise appropriate to his ambition and his glittering personality.

He expressed his sentiments on the new era in an oration on the House floor in March 1818. Formally, he was making a motion to appropriate funds to send an ambassador to what is now Argentina, but he used the occasion to survey all the revolutions in Spain's New World domain. "Within this vast region, we behold the most sublime and interesting objects of creation; the loftiest mountains, the most majestic rivers in the world; the richest mines of the precious metals.... We behold there a spectacle still more interesting and sublime—the glorious spectacle of eighteen millions of people, struggling to burst their chains and to be free." Clay's feelings toward the struggling eighteen millions were fraternal. They were like "an elder brother," long "abused and maltreated ... rising, by the power and energy of his fine native genius, to the manly rank which nature, and nature's God, intended for him."[1] Their rights, and ours, were the same. As we had asserted ours, so they were claiming theirs. All men of the Western Hemisphere were created equal.

A cooler view was taken by Secretary of State John Quincy Adams. Former president Adams's eldest son was destined— some might say condemned—to public service. During an episode of adolescent funk such as even the hardest-working young men experience, John Quincy's father had warned him that if he did not rise "to the head . . . of your country," it would be due entirely to his own "laziness" and "sloven- liness."[2] The lesson stuck. Unlazy, unslovenly John Quincy became a diplomat at age twenty-seven, a US senator at age thirty-six, a diplomat again, and then secretary of state, in 1817, at age fifty.

In March 1821 he had a private talk with Clay, which he recorded in his copious and exacting diary. The two men had known each other since 1815, when they served on the American commission that negotiated the treaty ending the War of 1812. They had worked reasonably well together then, though their temperaments could not have been more different—nor could their views about Spain's escaping colo- nies now. "So far as they were contending for independence," Adams told the Speaker, "I wished well to their cause; but I had seen . . . no prospect that they would establish free or liberal institutions." Clay looked to nature, Adams to history: "They have not the first elements of good or free government. Arbitrary power, military and ecclesiastical, was stamped upon their education, upon their habits and upon all their institutions. Civil dissension was infused into all their sem- inal principles." Spain's children had no Jamestown in their upbringing. As far as Adams was concerned, they were fated to be despotic or turbulent, likely both. He went on: "Nor was there any appearance of a disposition in them to take any political lesson from us." Jefferson had written about the laws of nature and nature's God, but Spanish Americans did not read him. If we and they belonged to the same hemispheric family, they were the prodigal sons.

Adams and Clay did agree on one thing: the revolutionaries were bound to win. "That the final issue of their present struggle would be their entire independence from Spain," said Adams, "I had never doubted."[3]

The reaction of European governments to the revolutionary wave was almost entirely hostile. After Napoleon's defeat, his victorious enemies were determined that there should be no repetition of continental carnage. Peace required order, which seemed to require political stability. A Quadruple Alliance of Britain, Austria, Prussia, and Russia was formed to ensure that result. The powers agreed to hold congresses every two years to coordinate their policies. A second alliance, inspired by Czar Alexander of Russia, embraced all these powers except Britain. Adams had known Alexander when he was minister to Russia a decade earlier; the czar struck him as polite and pro-American (American merchants did a thriving Baltic trade). When they met on the streets of St. Petersburg—both men were regular walkers— they would chat about the cold or Adams's young son. Intellectually, however, Alexander was a reactionary mystic who saw himself as doing the Lord's work; his tripartite group called itself the Holy Alliance.

France wished to become a peer and partner of its vanquishers. Since its monarchical government, restored after

Bonaparte's fall, was as hostile to revolution as they were, perhaps it could use repression as a way of getting back into their good graces.

In April 1823 France invaded Spain in order to rescue its king from the constitutionalists. The invasion was the special project of the French foreign minister, the Vicomte de Chateaubriand. Chateaubriand was a poet even more than a politician, a minor nobleman whose life had been upended by the French Revolution. His memoirs are ornamented by vignettes, always appalled, of the revolution's leaders, even as they occasionally acknowledge their impressive qualities (nature molded the head of one, he wrote, "either for imperium or for the gallows"[4]). Chateaubriand also left a purely admiring portrait of George Washington, whom he met during a period of exile. Washington seemed to him to be everything that the zealots of his own country were not: "Silence envelopes Washington's deeds. He moved cautiously; one could say that he felt charged with the liberty of future generations, and feared compromising it."[5] Chateaubriand wished above all to spare Spain his own and France's sufferings at the hands of noisy wreckers.

He wished something more: to turn the new nations of Spanish America into monarchies, ruled by princes of the House of Bourbon, Spain's royal dynasty.[6] He had already sent an army across the Pyrenees; now he wanted to send rulers across the Atlantic. Spain's former colonies could pass directly from an arbitrary dependence to an arbitrary independence. The Holy Alliance would be pleased to see revolution defeated the world over and think the better of France for doing it.

This scheme was disfavored by the European power that did not belong to the Holy Alliance, Britain. Britain's motives were economic—it was as entranced as America by the prospect of trading with the former Spanish empire and did not want the sequestered status quo restored under a new royalist guise. As the greatest naval power on earth, it had the means to stop any armada of Bourbon princes. But before things came to such a pass, perhaps Britain could warn France and the Holy Alliance off.

In September 1823, Britain's foreign minister, George Canning, made an offer to the American ambassador to London. (Canning, who had been a part-time journalist earlier in life, had a notoriously tart tongue. Adams, who had met him when he himself had been ambassador to London, noted it in his diary: "He had a little too much wit for a minister of state."[7]) Canning now asked if the United States would be willing to go "hand-in-hand" with Britain in a joint statement concerning Spanish America. The two countries would declare that its independence seemed assured and that neither Britain nor America coveted any part of it but that they could not see any of it "transferred to any other Power with indifference" (this was the veiled warning against the scheme of the Bourbon princes).[8]

The American ambassador wrote home for instructions in the middle of September. Steamboats already existed, but not reliable oceanic ones; communication was slow. President James Monroe received his account of Britain's offer a month later.

Monroe had long memories of Anglo-American relations, all of them grim. As a young lieutenant, he had been shot in the shoulder at the Battle of Trenton in 1776, and as a middle-aged member of James Madison's cabinet, he had tried to repel a British raid on Washington during the War of 1812. But new times might require new measures. Monroe sought the advice of the two men he most respected in the world, Thomas Jefferson and James Madison.

At the tail end of Monroe's term, these three would be called the Virginia Dynasty. The term was apt. They had followed each other in the White House for two terms apiece. Jefferson, conveniently, was eight years older than Madison, who was seven years older than Monroe. The Constitution forbade hereditary succession; they were a succession of soul mates, friends, and almost-neighbors: virtual siblings.

"Shall we entangle ourselves," Monroe began, "in European politics?"[9] Fraught words: Jefferson had warned, in his first inaugural address, against "entangling alliances."[10] But Monroe thought the time for entanglement had come. "Has not the epoch arrived when Great Britain must take her stand, either on the side of the monarchs of Europe, or of the United States? . . . My own impression is that we ought to meet the proposal of the British government."

His former president friends each gave him the answer he wanted, Jefferson most ringingly. "By acceding to [Britain's] proposition, we . . . bring her mighty weight into the scale of free government, and emancipate a continent at one stroke. . . . With her on our side, we need not fear the world."[11]

Encouraged with these approvals, Monroe put the question to his cabinet in November 1823. The cabinet then was a small body, initially composed of only three secretaries—state, treasury, and war—boosted to four in the late 1790s with the addition of the secretary of the navy. The attorney general, the administration's lawyer, was a sort of junior member (there was as yet no such thing as a Department of Justice).

William Crawford, Monroe's treasury secretary, was a Georgia politician, handsome and imposing, who had made an almost-successful bid to succeed James Madison as president; when it fell short, he contented himself with waiting until the end of the Virginia Dynasty. In the fall of 1823, he was out sick. Attorney General William Wirt would also miss some discussions. Secretary of the Navy Samuel Southard was new on the job, having been appointed that September, and would say little.

The burden of deciding America's reaction to Britain's offer thus fell on the president, Secretary of State Adams, and Secretary of War John Calhoun. Calhoun, a South Carolinian educated in Connecticut (Yale, Litchfield Law School), was as precocious as Adams or Clay—elected to Congress at age twenty-eight, tapped for Monroe's cabinet at age thirty-five. Adams and Calhoun became friendly— they were both smart, ambitious, and inclined to gloom. Adams recorded in his diary a conversation they had about Washington's meager burial ground for congressmen. "There are plain, modest and tasteless marble monuments," Adams wrote, "which the lapse of a few short years will demolish. We were remarking how exclusively by the nature and genius of our institutions we confine all our thoughts and care to the present time. We have neither forefathers nor posterity."[12] Calhoun meant to leave a lasting mark.

The cabinet's first discussion of Spanish America was in a meeting at the White House on November 7. (The marauding British had burned the White House to the ground during the War of 1812, but Monroe had rebuilt it.) Monroe did not tell his cabinet what Jefferson and Madison had advised him, though he made his own preference for an Anglo-American statement clear.

Calhoun agreed with the president. Our ambassador in London, he said, should be given "discretionary power . . . to join in a declaration against the interference of the Holy Allies."[13]

Adams objected. He did not want to see Europeans interfering in our hemisphere, but he did not want to join Britain in saying so. "It would be more candid," he said, "as well as more dignified" to state our own objections directly to France and Russia instead of "com[ing] in as a cock-boat in the wake of the British man-of-war."[14] Adams had his own memories of Anglo-American hostility—he had seen the smoke and heard the cannon of the Battle of Bunker Hill from his father's house in Braintree in 1775—and he stayed truer to them. Despite, or perhaps because of, his many years abroad, he was the prickliest nationalist in the room.

The president made no decision at that meeting, though he continued to worry about the possibility of French and Holy Alliance interference; in his diary, Adams accused Monroe of "panic" and Calhoun of feeding it.[15] When the cabinet met again on November 15, the secretary of war suggested that the Holy Alliance could restore all of Spanish America to Spain with only ten thousand men. Adams countered that this would no more happen than that Chimborazo (the tallest mountain in Ecuador) would sink into the sea. In his diary he called Calhoun "moon-struck."[16]

There was a major change in the diplomatic scene the following day, when a letter from our ambassador in London arrived in Washington, reporting that Britain was no longer interested in cooperating with us. Canning had conveyed a warning directly to the French: they and the Holy Alliance must leave Spanish America alone. Chateaubriand had a vision, but Canning had a navy. Britain's foreign minister had checked the ambitions of France's and no longer needed a joint Anglo-American declaration.

Our ambassador did not then know what Canning had said to the French, only that he was no longer interested in speaking to us. But the questions he had raised remained, even after his offer had vanished. What did America think about the world's new revolutions? What did it think about what Europe thought about them?

At the next cabinet meeting, on November 21, Monroe made a surprising announcement: he would address these questions in his annual message to Congress, to be delivered at the beginning of December. (We now call the annual message the State of the Union address, and it is given as a speech to a joint session, but in the nineteenth century, it was released in written form.) Diplomats communicate privately, often in strictest secrecy; diplomats abroad spend much of their time trying to discover what other diplomats have said. By including foreign policy in his annual message, Monroe would make his diplomacy public.

He would make it public to tell the world, but more importantly, to tell the American people. Foreign affairs, no less than taxes, budgets, morals, and all the other domestic issues that had been the stuff of day-to-day politics since the

Jamestown General Assembly, were ultimately the responsibility of voters—of ordinary Americans. Diplomats discussed and spied; policy makers deliberated and schemed in private. But the electorate had the final say and so had to be told and persuaded.

He read to the cabinet a sketch of his ideas. His passages on Spanish America followed their thinking, minus Calhoun's alarm: independence seemed certain; we would not meddle in whatever mutual arrangements Spain and its former colonies chose to make, but we would not look kindly on other European powers making new arrangements of their own. It was obvious, and therefore unnecessary to state, that we were saying this independently, not in concert with Britain.

Then Monroe added this coda: he condemned France's invasion of Spain "in terms of most pointed reprobation," recognized Greek independence, and asked Congress to appropriate funds to send an ambassador there.

Here was a new wrinkle: the cabinet had been arguing about European interference in Spanish America; now the president would be offering critical opinions of European affairs.

Adams protested. "For more than thirty years, Europe had been in convulsions [while] we had looked on safe in our distance beyond an intervening ocean." But "this message . . . would have the air of open defiance to all Europe."[17] He became as alarmed as Calhoun: Spain, France, and even Russia might break off diplomatic relations in response. He asked the president to reconsider.

The cabinet broke up without coming to any conclusion, but Adams went back to Monroe the next day to lobby him, suggesting that he make "an earnest remonstrance against the interference by force of the European powers with South America, but to disclaim all interference on our part with Europe; to make an American cause, and adhere inflexibly to that."[18]

To make an American cause: here was the point. What was an American cause? The United States had declared its independence, and its principles, to a candid world and the opinion of humanity in 1776. But what did our independence and our principles require us to say during world wars? During world wars in which we were not (yet) involved? In a world marked by far-distant, but not entirely unconnected, small wars and revolutions?

In recent decades, the phrase *the Atlantic World* has infected the scholarly mind. It is one of those grand, lighter-than-air concepts, like the Frontier Thesis, which explain a lot, though less than those who use them imagine. The Atlantic World posits four continents—Europe, Africa, North and South America—in continuous interconnection. It is simpler to say that men had ships and that ships were the internet of the age.[19] Ships carried men; men carried newspapers. Shots fired in Greece, Madrid, or Buenos Aires were eventually "heard" in St. Petersburg, Paris, and London—and Washington. They might not, of course, concern us, but even distant shots sometimes did.

In his appeal to Monroe, Adams raised a second important point: How would Congress react, particularly the House, Clay's domain? "What would be Mr. Clay's course in this case I could not foresee," Adams said, but Monroe "well knew" that when Clay had first hailed Spanish American independence on the House floor in 1818, "his main object was popularity for himself."[20]

Making an American cause was everyone's ideal, but making political points was everyone's business. Monroe was in the homestretch of his last presidential term. Clay was running to succeed him. So was Adams. So was Calhoun. So was the absent Crawford (he was thought to be the frontrunner, but his indisposition, all the world soon learned, was the result of a stroke, a revelation that would shatter his prospects).

The foreign policy positions advanced by these men were designed to give them advantages as presidential candidates. Calhoun expected Holy Alliance invasions of the Western Hemisphere because combating, or preparing against them, would highlight him and the War Department. Adams insisted we not be a cockboat in the wake of the British man-of-war to refute any suspicions that his many years of service abroad, and even his wife, Louisa Catherine—who was half English, born, raised, and married in London—had de-Americanized him. Clay hailed the glorious spectacle of revolution in Spanish America so that he could bathe in its reflected glory here.

The diplomatic historian Ernest May wrote a book analyzing the domestic politics behind the foreign policies of the Monroe administration's main actors. Yet, for all its merits, it has the air of a book explaining that the sun rises in the east. In democratic republics almost all officeholders will be politicians; that is the alternative to hereditary succession, and politics will inform their every move. Politics—with a small *p*, jockeying for advantage, jabbing one's rivals—never needs to be discovered; it is omnipresent and unkillable.

At the same time, politics can be, and sometimes is, about more than itself. The most effective politicians take positions that express their natures and their beliefs. Calhoun had gravitated to the War Department because he was both combative and efficient: a belligerent administrator. Adams's father had been on the committee to write the Declaration of Independence, and his son had followed his father in everything; John Quincy was all-American by inheritance, upbringing, and conviction. Clay found the spectacle of Spanish American revolution glorious because he believed in liberty. "He loved his country partly because it was his own country," Abraham Lincoln would say of him years later, "but mostly because it was a free country."[21] All politicians calculate the odds; the best ones put themselves wholeheartedly behind their bets.

Monroe's annual message was issued on December 2. It began with a warning that foreign policy—"the condition of the civilized world"—would occupy more of the annual message than it usually did. "The people being with us exclusively the sovereign, it is indispensable that full information be laid before them on all important subjects, to enable them to exercise that high power with complete effect. If kept in the dark, they must be incompetent to it." This was pure Monroe: whenever responsibility rests with the people, they must understand so that they can decide wisely.

Most of the message in fact surveyed domestic affairs—post roads, forts, budgets ("on the first of January there was a balance in the Treasury of $4,237,427.55")—or the most routine matters of foreign relations (tying up loose ends of the treaty that ended the War of 1812).

The revolutions that had roiled the world and the cabinet first appeared, as in a bank shot, in a paragraph discussing not Europe or Spanish America but the Pacific Northwest. Russia, Britain, and the United States had been harvesting furs along the North American coast—what is now Alaska, British Columbia, Washington, and Oregon—and the three countries were considering an amicable division of their spheres of activity. In these discussions, the message added, the United States had asserted, "as a principle in which [its] rights and interests [were] involved, that the American continents . . . are henceforth not to be considered as subjects for future colonization by any European powers." This was pure Adams: stay out of our half of the world.

Further along, the message touched the world's revolutions directly, citing "the heroic struggle of the Greeks" and the "great effort" Spain's constitutionalists had made to improve Spain's condition. What did we think of these struggles and efforts?

"The citizens of the United States cherish sentiments the most friendly in favor of the liberty and happiness of their fellow men on that side of the Atlantic." But there was no "pointed reprobation" of France's invasion of Spain, no proposal to immediately recognize the Greeks. "In the wars of the European powers in matters relating to themselves we have never taken any part, nor does it comport with our policy so to do." European revolutionaries could expect our sympathies, not our help.

The message then pivoted to American revolutionaries, who could expect something more.

"With the movements in this hemisphere we are of necessity more immediately connected. . . . The political system of the allied powers"—the Holy Alliance—"is essentially different . . . from that of America. . . . We owe it, therefore, to candor and to the amicable relations existing between the United States and those powers to declare that we should consider any attempt on their part to extend their system to any portion of this hemisphere as dangerous to our peace and safety." No new colonies, no Bourbon princes.

The message repeated the point. "With . . . existing colonies . . . we have not interfered and shall not interfere." Northern North America was British and Russian; the Caribbean was a salad of British, French, Spanish, and Dutch islands. None of these were any of our business, "but with the governments who have declared their independence and maintained it . . . we could not view any [European] interposition for the purpose of oppressing them, or controlling in any other manner their destiny" as anything but "an unfriendly disposition toward the United States."

The message repeated the point one more time for good measure: "It is impossible that the allied powers should extend their political system to any portion of [North or South America] without endangering our peace and happiness."

This was Monroe's message, delivered in public, to Europe's monarchs: We sympathize with those you oppress, though we will not interfere with your oppression. But we will treat any new efforts you make to oppress in this half of the world as interference with us.

This was a declaration of geopolitical division.

Equally important, it was also a declaration of philosophical separation. Since all the nations of Europe then were monarchies, and all the nations of the Americas were republics, Monroe had said: no more kings. He was passing judgment on Europe's political systems as well as its imperial pretensions. His message extended Article II of the Constitution to the hemisphere.

Russia, the holiest of the allies, instructed its minister in Washington that Monroe's message deserved "the most profound contempt."[22] Britain was somewhat happier with it, and Canning even tried to take credit for it, telling Parliament in 1826 that he had "called the New World into existence to redress the balance of the Old."[23]

It was an expression of the president's opinion only, speaking, he hoped, for his countrymen but calling for no legislation or appropriations. Five years later, when John Quincy Adams had become president himself and Henry Clay his secretary of state, Clay wrote one of his diplomats, a bit shamefacedly, that if ever there were European aggression in this hemisphere, "the declaration of the late president" would be upheld or not by "Congress alone." It would not be mentioned again until James Polk's first annual message in December 1845, in which he iterated "the principle avowed by Mr. Monroe . . . that no future European colony or dominion shall, with our consent, be planted or established on any part of the North American continent."[24] (A whole continent had fallen out of Polk's summary.) Adams, who was then a feisty seventy-eight-year-old, said that he "approved entirely" of Polk's remarks.[25]

The Monroe Doctrine did describe the future development of the Western Hemisphere, more or less. Three home-grown monarchs had already assumed thrones—Emperor Jacques and King Henri in Haiti and Emperor Augustin in Mexico. In the 1860s Haiti would belatedly produce one more emperor, Faustin. But Jacques was murdered, Henri committed suicide, and Augustin was deposed and exiled, then shot after attempting to return. Only Faustin, exiled, would die in bed. There would be dictators and perpetually reelected presidents aplenty—arbitrary power, as John Quincy Adams had said, was indeed stamped upon the habits of too many in the New World. But an old form of bondage, like colonialism itself, had passed away. President Monroe's message announced, and ratified, its exit.

The Monroe Doctrine can seem like a patchwork of rhetoric and action. We say fine things about liberty everywhere (we "cherish sentiments the most friendly" to it). But we will only support it when Europeans meddle in our hemisphere. In fact it fuses aspiration and prudence. Our friendly sentiments in favor of liberty are real, and we will resist those who would undermine it where we can and where their schemes would most menace us.

Henry Clay might have been bolder, John Quincy Adams more reticent. President Monroe made America, as far as we were able, the advocate of liberty in the world.

chapter eight

SENECA FALLS DECLARATION

Women's Suffrage

WARS SOMETIMES OPEN SOCIAL SPACE FOR women. When men go off to fight and die, women take their places, running households and family businesses. Lucy Knox, wife of George Washington's commander of artillery, wrote her husband, Henry, in 1777, hoping that "you will not consider yourself as commander in chief of your own house" after the war, "but be convinced . . . that there is such a thing as equal command."[1]

In New Jersey some Revolutionary War–era women enjoyed equal rights to vote, thanks to the state's first post-colonial constitution, ratified on July 2, 1776, which spoke of voters as "inhabitants," not "freemen," the word often used in other states. The phraseology may have been inadvertent— the constitution was rushed together in the face of an impending British invasion—but New Jersey's women took note. A property qualification limited the number who might vote, since in marriage all property belonged to the husband. But single women and widows worth more than fifty pounds ($2,500 today) were eligible, and there were enough of these to constitute a voting bloc, which acquired a nickname—the "petticoat vote."

Soon the space for women shrank again. Besides tradition and traditional interpretations of the Bible, the weight of Anglo-American law impinged on them. William Blackstone's *Commentaries on the Laws of England*, a transatlantic legal digest that had served as a textbook since its publication in the 1760s, explained the doctrine of coverture. "The very being or legal existence of the woman is suspended during the marriage, or at least is incorporated and consolidated into that of the husband: under whose wing, protection, and cover, she performs everything; and is therefore called in our law-french a *feme-covert*." Blackstone added, gallantly, "that even the disabilities, which the wife lies under, are for the most part intended for her protection and benefit. So great a favorite is the female sex of the laws of England"—and of America.[2]

New Jersey's women eventually lost their vote—not by law but by ordinary political skullduggery. In 1807 the state suffered an election that was corrupt even by New Jersey standards (the issue was, should the capital be in Newark or Elizabeth: real property values were at stake). In the enthusiasm of the contest, some towns reported more votes cast than they had residents. Ashamed of what its political culture had produced, the state reformed itself by purging its voting rolls of women and free blacks.[3]

If change were to come, it would very likely begin in western New York, which by the 1820s had become a proving ground for reforms, religions, and enthusiasms.

The American Revolution had destroyed the region's former occupants, the Iroquois Confederacy, too many of whom had sided with the British. The land opened for settlement; the Erie Canal (finished in 1825) brought commerce, canal towns, and factories. New York, which had been the fifth largest state in 1790, had become the largest by 1810.

The rolling countryside was also a "psychic highway," a transmission belt for visionaries, moralists, and organizers.[4] America's first homemade religion (Mormonism), its first political third party (the Antimasons), and its longest lasting utopia (the Oneida Community, whose members shared property and spouses) flourished there. Innovators and improvers of all sorts arose, argued, and as often as not vanished—so many that the region was called, at first derisively, then simply descriptively, the burned-over district.

Elizabeth Cady was born in 1815 near this hotbed, in Johnstown, a colonial-era village north of the Mohawk River. She was well-off and well educated. Her father was a judge who had served a term in Congress; her mother was an offshoot of the Livingston clan. At age sixteen Elizabeth was given a piano; she attended a top-notch academy for young women in Troy, New York; she acted as her father's de facto law clerk.

But all her young life she balked at the limitations placed on her sex. Her parents lost five of their ten children, including all their sons. Her grieving father often told her how sad it was that she had not been born a boy. Elizabeth vowed to do as well as any boy and resented that she would not be recognized for it.

When she was twenty-four, she married Henry Stanton, an abolitionist orator immersed in the whirl of New York and national politics. Slavery had been extinguished in the state in 1827, but the Missouri Compromise seven years earlier had given it new life beyond the Mississippi River, admitting Missouri as a slave state and allowing slavery in any territory below its southern border. Slave owners and their representatives began speaking of bondage not as an embarrassing necessity but as a positive good. John Calhoun told John Quincy Adams, in one of their conversations as cabinet secretaries, that slavery had "many excellent consequences. . . . It was the best guarantee to equality among the whites."[5] Slavery, it became clear, would not wither away. Its critics resolved to fight it by propaganda and by massive petitions to Congress, asking that it be outlawed in the District of Columbia (where Congress had the authority to act).

Henry Stanton, born in 1805, served the antislavery cause as a paid speechmaker, what one clergyman called a "he-goat" man, "butting everything in the line of . . . march," made of "vinegar, aqua fortis and oil of vitriol, with brimstone, saltpeter and charcoal, to explode and scatter the corrosive matter."[6] Frederick Douglass, a runaway slave-turned-journalist who probably deserved the distinction himself, called Stanton "unquestionably the best orator" of the movement.[7] Elizabeth embraced the cause as her own.

A month after their marriage, in June 1840, the Stantons attended a World's Anti-Slavery Convention in London. Elizabeth made as much of an impression as her husband, one British abolitionist praising her "eloquence ... naivete ... clearsightedness, candor, openness" and "such love for all that is great and good."[8]

But there arose a difficulty, for her and for every other woman in attendance. Women had been active in the American abolition movement for years, organizing and signing petitions and forming women's antislavery societies. They were becoming more active in mainstream American politics too. In the presidential campaign of 1840, women supporters of Whig candidate William Henry Harrison wore sashes bearing his nickname—TIPPECANOE—and the name of his running mate—TYLER—across their chests. Prudish supporters of Democrat Martin Van Buren chided them for flaunting their bosoms; they replied that Harrison, the old Indian fighter, had protected their homes and families; they were supporting him in return, as was their right and obligation.

American women were not welcome at the World's Anti-Slavery Convention, however. The reasons were complex. British abolitionists were more staid than their American cousins. Many abolitionists, both in America and Britain, were Quakers, but there was a sectarian split in Quakerism (broadly speaking, between those who looked more to the Bible or more to the Inner Light for guidance), which made American women, who tended to follow the unfiltered Inner Light, doubly unwelcome.

There was a growing divide within American abolitionism itself, between purists and politicals. The purists, whose most prominent figure was the crusading journalist William Lloyd Garrison, viewed any institution tainted by slavery, including most churches and the entire American government, as hopelessly corrupt. Change could only come through exhortation and moral reform. The purists welcomed (moral) women as equal allies in the struggle. The politicals thought change could also come by campaigning and (with luck) officeholding and lawmaking. But this strategic choice made them reluctant to dilute the antislavery message with other causes, however worthy.

The first session of the London convention was consumed by debate on the status of the American women, with "cries of 'order, order,' 'divide, divide,' 'No, no, no, no, no' . . . just like a House of Commons uproar," one observer wrote.[9] At the end of the day, a motion to seat them as delegates was beaten by a large margin.

The fight radicalized the young American woman who witnessed it. There in London, or perhaps a year later back home, Elizabeth asked another female American abolitionist "if we could not have a convention for Women's Rights."[10]

The Stantons moved to Boston, then to Johnstown (Judge Cady, for all he wished his daughter had been a son, was always willing to support her), then finally to Seneca Falls, a factory town in the Finger Lakes region of central New York, whose long narrow lakes stretch out like a spectral hand.

The mid-1840s saw two turbulences at opposite poles of western New York's energy field. The politically minded founded an abolitionist third party, the Liberty Party (its main funder, Gerrit Smith, was a cousin of Elizabeth's). Its showing in the 1844 election, though tiny—sixty-two thousand votes nationwide for Smith, versus over a million each

SENECA FALLS DECLARATION

for the major party candidates—was catastrophic for abolitionists. The issue of that campaign was whether or not
the United States should annex Texas, then an independent slaveholding republic. Henry Clay, the Whig candidate,
was moderately opposed, abolitionists ardently so; Democrat
James Polk was as ardently in favor. The Liberty Party candidate took enough votes in New York, which would otherwise
have gone to Clay, to tip the state, and the Electoral College, to Polk. Abraham Lincoln, a Whig politician in Illinois,
wrote a chagrined letter to a local Liberty Party man about
the debacle. "As I always understood, the Liberty-men dep-
recated the annexation of Texas extremely; and this being so,
why they should refuse to so cast their votes as to prevent
it . . . seemed wonderful."[11] The Liberty Party determined
to keep trying; Henry Stanton threw himself into its efforts.

The purists experienced a debacle of their own when William Miller, a Baptist minister and a close reader of the Bible,
concluded that the second coming of Christ would occur in
1843 or 1844. So worldly a man as John Quincy Adams gave
Miller's prediction serious consideration.[12] The Great Comet
of 1843, visible at peak brightness in broad daylight, seemed
to highlight the prophecy. Here was the ultimate reason to
eschew sinful half measures: the unregenerate world would
end soon anyway. Its continuance as normal became known
as the Great Disappointment.

But toward the decade's end, thanks to Elizabeth Cady
Stanton, purism and politics would experience a novel, and
momentous, fusion.

By the summer of 1848, Stanton had been living in Seneca
Falls for a year. Life had not been easy. While her husband

153

was busy politicking, she had charge of their three children, boys ages six, four, and three. She may have miscarried shortly after moving into her new home; in June 1848, her sister-in-law lost two children fifteen days apart, the second to whooping cough while visiting the Stanton household. A picture of Stanton taken at this time—a daguerreotype, not a painting—shows her with two of her sons; she seems attractive, determined, and harassed.

On July 9, a Sunday, Stanton attended a tea party in nearby Waterloo at the home of Richard Hunt, a factory owner, and his wife, Jane. Also present were Lucretia Mott, whom Stanton had met at the London convention, Mott's sister Martha Wright, and Mary Ann M'Clintock, wife of a Seneca Falls stationer. All these women, except Stanton, were Inner Light Quakers and relatives by blood or marriage. Like her, they were all abolitionists and supporters of women's rights.

Years later Stanton recalled that on that afternoon "the general discontent I felt with woman's position ... the chaotic conditions into which everything fell without her constant supervision ... my experience at the World's Anti-Slavery Convention ... and the oppression I saw everywhere, together swept across my soul." The assembled women shared her distress. According to Hart family tradition, Richard, who took tea with them, asked, "Why don't you do something about it?" The women decided to hold a convention "to discuss the social, civil and religious conditions and rights of women" ten days later in Seneca Falls.[13] The venue would be the Wesleyan Chapel, the newest and largest church in town, built by antislavery Methodists. Local papers, including Frederick

Douglass's *North Star* in Rochester, an hour away to the northwest, ran the notice.

Conventions were expected to provide stimulation in the form of oratory. That would come from Lucretia Mott, already well known as a speaker (one newspaper called her "a regular ultra Barn-Burning kind of woman"[14]). Mott, who lived in Philadelphia, was in New York only briefly to visit relatives, hence the haste of Stanton and her friends in calling their meeting. More important, conventions made motions and passed resolutions. They sought to leave some mark on the world.

On July 16 Stanton went to Waterloo again, to the M'Clintock house. Sitting around the parlor tea table, she, Mary M'Clintock, and her two daughters, Elizabeth and Mary Ann, drafted a set of resolutions and a Declaration of Sentiments. (The tea table is now in the Smithsonian Institution.) The resolutions began by quoting Blackstone, who, before he examined the details of marriage law, declared that the fundamental precept of natural law was that "man shall pursue his own true and substantial happiness." Therefore, wrote Stanton and her colleagues, any laws "that conflict, in any way, with the true and substantial happiness of woman" were invalid.[15]

This was a bold and clever gambit, citing the exponent of the doctrine of coverture to justify women's rights. The Declaration of Sentiments began with a bolder one. As Stanton later wrote, the authors spent a long time casting about for the right rhetorical tone. Then, "one of the circle took up the Declaration of 1776 and read it aloud with much spirit and emphasis, and it was at once decided to adopt the historic document, with some slight changes."[16] This was brilliant. Blackstone was English; the Declaration of Independence was as American as it was possible to be. Quoting Blackstone against himself was combative—polemical judo. Adopting the Declaration of Independence was embracing: we all believe this; here is what it also means.

Such an embrace was necessary, given the incendiary implications of the women's critique. If they were comprehensively oppressed, then men were their oppressors. King and Parliament had been an ocean away; once America was free of them, they would trouble it no more. Men, however, were here to stay. Calling on them as fellow Americans took the sting out of the critique.

The preamble of the Declaration of Sentiments tracked that of the Declaration of Independence almost word for word—"We hold these truths to be self-evident: that all men and women are created equal"—"Such has been the patient sufferance of the women under this government, and such is now the necessity which constrains them to demand the equal station to which they are entitled."

The bill of indictment against George III, however, had to be scrapped and replaced. The "injuries and usurpations" suffered by women fell into several clusters. One concerned property rights. A crack in the doctrine of coverture had opened in the New York legislature, which had been debating the property rights of married women since the 1830s. In April 1848 the (male) lawmakers passed a Married Women's Property Act, guaranteeing to wives the property they owned at the time of marriage and any profits it might later throw off. Judge Cady, for all his conservatism, supported it: he wanted his daughter to be secure against the possible impecuniousness of her politico/orator husband.[17]

But more needed to be done. The Declaration of Sentiments surveyed society as a whole.

Man "has monopolized nearly all the profitable employments, and from those [that woman] is permitted to follow"—governess, schoolteacher—"she receives but a scanty remuneration."

"He closes against her all the avenues to wealth and distinction, which he considers most honorable to himself. As a teacher of theology, medicine or law she is not known."

"He has denied her the facilities for obtaining a thorough education—all colleges being closed against her." (The single exception as of 1848, Oberlin, proved the rule.)

"He allows her in Church [only] a subordinate position, claiming Apostolic authority for her exclusion from the ministry." The call for women to be ministers, and teachers of ministers, reflects the importance of religion in the burned-over district and in America. People seldom demand the right to do trivial things. It also reflects the Quakerism of Stanton's coauthors: that sect had had women preachers since the seventeenth century, when Peter Stuyvesant expelled Dorothy Waugh and Mary Wetherhead from New Amsterdam.

"He has [given] to the world a different code of morals for men and women, by which moral delinquencies which exclude women from society, are not only tolerated but deemed of little account in man." Alexander Hamilton was a founding adulterer caught in a notorious sex scandal, but, as one contemporary of his observed, "if he fornicates with every female in New York and Philadelphia, he will rise again, for purity of character . . . is not necessary for public patronage."[18] Women who behaved so, however, were branded adventuresses or criminals.

Stanton's contribution to the Declaration of Sentiments' bill of indictment was to call for the right to vote.

> He [man] has never permitted her [woman] to exercise her inalienable right to the elective franchise.

> He has compelled her to submit to laws, in the formation of which she had no voice.

> He has withheld from her rights which are given to the most ignorant and degraded men—both natives and foreigners.

> Having deprived her of this first right of a citizen, the elective franchise, thereby leaving her without representation in the halls of legislation, he has oppressed her on all sides.

Stanton's life to this moment—daughter of a former congressman, cousin and wife of Liberty Party stalwarts—prepared her to insist on this point. Many of her allies, men and women, balked at her boldness. Her husband told her that the demand would turn the convention "into a farce."[19] "Lizzie," said Lucretia Mott, raised among Quakers who seldom voted, "thou wilt make the convention ridiculous."[20] Stanton's answer was contained in the points she made in the Declaration of Sentiments: deprived of a role in making decisions, women were left at the mercy of the decisions of others.

Politicals like Henry Stanton feared that the call for women's suffrage would bring derision on causes like abolition, which were already hated enough. Purists like Mott disdained the act of voting itself as at best a distraction, at worst collusion in sin.

Defenders of the status quo had a traditional counterargument to any call for expanding the franchise. This was the concept of virtual representation. You may not be able to vote, but never mind; someone who has your interests, as well as his own, at heart can, and therefore virtually represents you. In nineteenth-century America, husbands and fathers virtually represented their wives and daughters. In 1776, Parliament in London virtually represented the empire as a whole.

Stanton fused the purity of principle with the grit of politics. And she rejected the notion of virtual representation, just as the Continental Congress, and the Jamestown General Assembly before it, had.

Her mention of male "foreigners," in the third article relating to the franchise, was a slap at immigrants—a burst of old-stock resentment directed chiefly at the Irish, who had been coming to America, and voting, in increasingly large numbers. It would reappear to taint her rhetoric in later years.

The convention began on the morning of July 19, 1848, a Wednesday. No one had thought to bring a key to the Wesleyan Chapel, so one of Stanton's nephews climbed through a window and opened the door from inside. The convention lasted two days. Women only were allowed on the first day, to hear and debate the resolves and the Declaration of Sentiments; men were invited on the second day and encouraged to sign the documents adopted in their final form. The temperature outside rose to the nineties; one woman years later recalled the chapel's "dusty windows."[21] Three hundred people packed into the building, filling the ground floor pews and the galleries along the sides and at the back.

The only item that provoked debate was Stanton's call for women to have the vote. On the second day, she spoke in favor. So did Frederick Douglass, the only black person who attended the meeting. His remarks no doubt anticipated the editorial he wrote in the *North Star* after the convention. He was not above teasing some of his fellow abolitionists. "Many who have at last made the discovery that negroes have some rights as well as other members of the human family, have yet to be convinced that woman is entitled to any." His conclusion was dignified: "if that government is only just which governs by the free consent of the governed, there can be no reason in the world for denying to women the exercise of the elective franchise."[22] The call to allow women to vote was submitted to a vote and passed.

One hundred persons signed the Declaration of Sentiments—sixty-eight women and thirty-two men. One quarter of them were Quakers; ten were members, or related to members, of the Wesleyan Chapel. More than two-thirds of the signers came to Seneca Falls with family members: parents, children, spouses, siblings (not all of them signed, though they were obviously all supportive).[23] Virtually all of the attendees, signers and non, were local and otherwise obscure (of twelve, all women, we know nothing). Listing so many names makes for an ungainly layout. Read them all anyway; on this day, they did something important.

Listed first are the women signers:

Lucretia Mott

Harriet Cady Eaton
(Elizabeth Cady
Stanton's older sister)

Margaret Pryor (mother of
George W. Pryor)

Elizabeth Cady Stanton

Eunice Newton Foote (wife
of Elisha Foote)

Mary Ann M'Clintock
(mother of Elizabeth W.
and Mary M'Clintock,
wife of Thomas)

Margaret Schooley (wife of
Azaliah Schooley)

Martha C. Wright (sister of
Lucretia Mott)

Jane C. Hunt (wife of
Richard Hunt)

Amy Post

Catherine F. Stebbins

Mary Ann Frink

Lydia Mount (mother of
Mary E. Vail, sister of
Richard Hunt)

Delia Matthews

Catharine C. Paine

Elizabeth W. M'Clintock

Malvina Seymour (wife of
Henry W. Seymour)

Phebe Mosher

Catherine Shaw (age
eighty-one, probably
the oldest signer)

Deborah Scott

Sarah Hallowell

Mary M'Clintock

Mary Gilbert

Sophrone Taylor

Cynthia Davis

Hannah Plant
(sister of Richard
Hunt)

Lucy Jones

Sarah Whitney

Mary H. Hallowell

Elizabeth Conklin

Sally Pitcher

Mary Conklin

Susan Quinn (age fourteen,
the youngest signer—
and the only woman of
Irish descent)

Mary S. Mirror

Phebe King
Julia Ann Drake
Charlotte Woodward
Martha Underhill (aunt of
    Edward Underhill)
Dorothy Matthews
Eunice Barker
Sarah R. Woods
Lydia Gild
Sarah Hoffman
Elizabeth Leslie
Martha Ridley
Rachel D. Bonnel (niece of
    William S. Dell, cousin
    of Thomas Dell)
Betsey Tewksbury
Rhoda Palmer
Margaret Jenkins
Cynthia Fuller
Mary Martin

P. A. Culvert
Susan R. Doty
Rebecca Race
Sarah A. Mosher
Mary E. Vail
Lucy Spalding (wife of
    David Spalding)
Lavinia Latham
    (mother of Hannah
    J. Latham)
Sarah Smith
Eliza Martin
Maria E. Wilbur
Elizabeth D. Smith
Caroline Barker
Ann Porter
Experience Gibbs
Antoinette E. Segur
Hannah J. Latham
Sarah Sisson

These are the men signers:

Richard P. Hunt (husband of
    Jane C. Hunt, brother of
    Lydia Mount and Hannah
    Plant, and the man who
    asked, "Why don't you do
    something about it?")

Samuel D. Tillman
Justin Williams
Elisha Foote (husband
    of Eunice Newton
    Foote)
Frederick Douglass

Henry W. Seymour
(husband of Malvina
Seymour)
Henry Seymour
David Spalding
(husband of Lucy
Spalding)
William G. Barker
Elias J. Doty
John Jones
William S. Dell (uncle of
Rachel D. Bonel)
James Mott
William Burroughs
Robert Smalldridge
Jacob Matthews
Charles L. Hoskins
Thomas M'Clintock
(husband of Mary Ann
M'Clintock, father of

Elizabeth W. and Mary
M'Clintock)
Saron Phillips
Jacob Chamberlain
Jonathan Metcalf
Nathan J. Milliken
S. E. Woodworth
Edward F. Underhill
(nephew of Martha
Underhill)
George W. Pryor (son of
Margaret Pryor)
Isaac Van Tassel
Thomas Dell (cousin of
Rachel D. Bonel)
E. W. Capron
Stephen Shear
Henry Hatley
Azaliah Schooley (husband
of Margaret Schooley)

At the end of the convention's second session, a committee of five—consisting of Stanton, two of the M'Clintocks, and two other women—was appointed to publish the proceedings.

Fifty-eight newspapers, from Massachusetts to Missouri, reported on the convention, including the *New-York Tribune*, then one of the largest dailies in the country. Twenty-four were hostile (the *Philadelphia Public Ledger and*

Daily Telegraph wrote that "the ladies of Philadelphia . . . are resolved to maintain their rights as Wives, Belles, Virgins, and Mothers, and not as Women"), sixteen were neutral, seventeen were positive ("Success to the cause in which they have enlisted!" wrote the *Herkimer Freeman*, adding a modernist touch: "A railroad speed to the end they would accomplish!").[24]

The speed with which their end was accomplished was much slower than that. The issue of slavery monopolized the nation's attention. The vote totals of antislavery political parties tell the story. In the 1848 election, most of the Liberty Party merged with antislavery Democrats and Whigs to form a new third party (zealously championed by Henry Stanton), the Free-Soil Party, which chose as its presidential candidate no abolitionist but former president Martin Van Buren, a wily opportunist who, after years of serving the interest of slave states, performed an about-face in order to get back in the game. This party won no electoral votes but took 10 percent of the popular vote (a quarter of the vote in New York State). Eight years later yet another new antislavery party, the Republicans, won almost 40 percent of the popular vote and carried eleven of thirty-one states. Four years after that, Republican Abraham Lincoln won the White House, and the country fell apart.

After the Civil War, Stanton and some of her women allies were impatient with the national focus on blacks at the expense of women. Imagine, she wrote bitterly, "Patrick and Sambo and Hans and Yung Tung . . . who never read the Declaration of Independence" making laws for women like herself. This prompted her old ally Frederick Douglass to explain the parlous condition of black freedmen: "When women, because they are women ... are dragged from their houses and are hung from lamp-posts ... then they will have an urgency to obtain the ballot equal to our own."[25]

In 1867 a referendum in Kansas to give the vote to women failed. But the west was poised to go the other way. Wyoming (1869), Utah (1870), and Washington (1883) approved women's suffrage as territories, followed by Colorado (1893) and Idaho (1896) as states. In the new century, more states joined in, including New York in 1917.

Elizabeth Cady Stanton had died in 1902. But a signer of the Declaration of Sentiments still lived in Geneva, New York, ten miles west of Seneca Falls. Rhoda Palmer had attended the convention with her father, Asa. Years later she remembered that they had had "an enjoyable time, excepting one little incident. Our carriage broke down on the way home, and we were obliged to stay overnight on the road."[26] In 1918, age 102, she was driven to the polls, without mishap, to cast her first ballot.

The Nineteenth Amendment to the Constitution—"The right of citizens of the United States to vote shall not be denied or abridged by the United States or by any State on account of sex"—was ratified in August 1920. A number of countries, from the United Kingdom to Latvia, had granted the right earlier nationwide, but Utah, Wyoming, and the Seneca Falls Convention led the way.

chapter nine

GETTYSBURG ADDRESS

"Conceived in Liberty"

THE MAN WHO OUGHT TO HAVE HEADED THE Republican ticket in 1860 was William Seward of Auburn, New York, fifteen miles west of Seneca Falls. Seward was a successful mainstream politician (governor, US senator), but with a record and connections about as radical as it was possible for a mainstream politician to have. He had declared that there was an "irrepressible conflict" between slavery and free labor.[1] He and his wife, Frances, knew Martha Wright, signer of the Declaration of Sentiments, who also lived in Auburn. He had made a neighbor of Harriet Tubman, the black liberator of slaves, selling her a lot for a house.

But there was a vein of what can only be called optimistic fatalism in Seward, related to his sunny temperament, which sometimes led him astray. Convinced he had the Republican nomination in the bag, he took a long European vacation before the 1860 convention. Later he would identify the decisive moment in the Civil War as the federal government's decision to reprovision Fort Sumter in Charleston harbor; once that was made, he was convinced, victory was assured (in other words, the Civil War was won even before the first shots were fired).

Seward was wrong in the first case; he would not be his party's nominee. He was right perhaps in the second case— the Union did win the Civil War—though victory would take great efforts, defining American nationalism.

Abraham Lincoln, the younger man (fifty-one to Seward's fifty-nine) who got the nomination instead, did not seem marked for greatness. Seward was no Adonis—a sloppy dresser with a big nose, described by one admirer as looking like a macaw. Lincoln looked odder—a body like a pine tree, surmounted by a rough-hewn, melancholy face, which he decided, midcampaign, to ornament with an unfortunate beard. He had run a spirited though losing race for the Senate in Illinois in 1858; before that he had served a few terms in the state legislature and one in the House of Representatives. He prevailed over Seward because the very meagerness of his record meant that he carried less baggage; because the nominating convention was held in Chicago, giving him a home state advantage (Lincoln men printed fake tickets to pack the galleries of the hall with supporters); and because Illinois was a populous battleground state, necessary for victory. Republicans had not carried it in 1856 and lost the election; they did carry it in 1860 and won.

Lincoln had said, in his most radical preelection speech, that the United States could not remain half slave and half free but must become "all one thing, or all the other."[2] If slavery could be kept from expanding into America's territories, then, he believed, it would wither and die. But he also said, in 1858, that slavery might not disappear for one hundred years (that is, the second term of the Eisenhower administration).[3] In the meantime, he assured southerners, their human property was as secure as "in the days of Washington."[4] In his first inaugural address, he stressed that he would uphold the fugitive slave law, which returned escaped slaves to their masters. This pledge caused Frederick Douglass to brand him, in an acrid editorial, a "slave hound."[5]

Lincoln was cautious because the American political system, from Jamestown through the Constitution, empowered slavery's supporters as well as its opponents. European countries had abolished slavery in their colonial empires decades before his election, and Russia's serfs would be emancipated the day before his inauguration. But these were the acts of imperial powers or of an autocrat. Free institutions, paradoxically, complicated the problem of slavery.

But how would secession and rebellion change the political equation? In the first years of Lincoln's administration, he and Congress showed both antislavery conviction and caution.

In the spring of 1861, Gen. Benjamin Butler, in charge of Fort Monroe at the mouth of the James River in Virginia (not far from Jamestown), suggested that slaves escaping to his lines should not be returned to their owners, who had applied for them under a flag of truce, but allowed to remain free, on the grounds that they were "contraband"—enemy goods that could be seized in wartime. Lincoln jokingly called the proposed policy "Butler's fugitive slave law"—it was, in fact, the negation of the fugitive slave law—but he approved it at Fort Monroe.[6]

In December 1862 he called for diplomatic recognition of the world's only black-run countries, Haiti and Liberia, the latter a settlement of freed American slaves on the coast of West Africa. One opposition newspaper worried about "strapping negro" ambassadors arriving in Washington; Lincoln evidently did not.[7]

Congress had declared the slave trade would be illegal beginning in 1808, the earliest date allowed under the Constitution; twelve years later, participating in it was made piracy, a capital crime. Yet only one American had ever been convicted of it, and his sentence had been commuted by President James Buchanan, Lincoln's predecessor. In 1860 a second American slaver, Nathaniel Gordon of Portland, Maine, was caught off the mouth of the Congo River with a cargo of nine hundred men, women, and children, bound for Cuba. Gordon was taken to the United States, tried, and sentenced to death; Lincoln, despite appeals for clemency, let him swing, granting him only a two-week stay of execution so that he might seek the mercy of "the common God and Father of all men" (including black men).[8]

Congress, meanwhile, dominated in both houses by Republicans, ended slavery in the territories and in the District of Columbia. It also passed a law freeing all slaves belonging to rebel officials or soldiers.

Republicans were, by definition, not Quaker or Garrisonian purists; they had chosen the path of politics. Lincoln was ever mindful of its pitfalls and the need to navigate around them. Before his inauguration in March 1861, seven slave states seceded from the Union—South Carolina, Mississippi, Florida, Alabama, Georgia, Louisiana, and Texas—on the grounds that the election of a Republican president was an intolerable affront to the institution by which they lived. After he tried (in vain) to hold Fort Sumter in a slave state's harbor, four more slave states—Virginia, Arkansas, North Carolina, and Tennessee—joined them. But four other slave states—Missouri, Kentucky, Maryland, and Delaware—remained in the Union. Holding them, especially Kentucky, which fronted hundreds of miles of the Ohio River, was paramount; needlessly offending them, unthinkable.

In August 1861 John Fremont, the army's commander in Missouri, declared martial law and freed all slaves belonging to rebel sympathizers there. Lincoln countermanded him, fearing his order would tip Kentucky out of the Union. Butler had asked permission to free slaves fleeing from a rebel state; Fremont, on his own initiative, had reached into homes and farms to free slaves in a state that was still loyal.

Lincoln tried to pave the road to liberty with gold, appealing to governors of loyal slave states to accept a program of gradual, compensated emancipation. He offered Delaware, the smallest, $719,200 to free its eighteen hundred slaves by 1893. Slavery would end, but even on its (slow) way out, it would pay. No slave-state governor accepted his offer.

What would become of blacks after slavery ended? Lincoln considered sending them to Africa or the Caribbean. "Colonization," as such schemes were called, was an old idea. James Madison, in his retirement, had endorsed it. So had George Washington's nephew, Bushrod Washington, a justice of the Supreme Court. (Washington himself seems never to have thought of it; many of the slaves he freed in his will continued to live near Mount Vernon, some of their descendants still working for the estate as paid employees in the twenty-first century.)

Most abolitionists hated colonization, which seemed to them simply a form of racial cleansing. But Lincoln thought it was simply realistic. He tried pitching it to a delegation of black men from the District of Columbia, invited to the White House for the purpose. Freedom for black Americans, he told them, would not mean equality. "On this broad continent not a single man of your race is made the equal of a single man of ours. Go where you are treated the best, and the ban is still on you."[9] Lincoln's grim analysis misjudged the racial feelings of the Seneca Falls Convention, where Frederick Douglass spoke, or possibly of Auburn, New York, where Harriet Tubman moved. But about most of America, North as well as South, he was surely correct.

All Lincoln's considerations, idealistic or hard-headed, were shaped by the progress of the Civil War.

It quickly became clear that the war would be neither short nor light. The bloodiest battle of the American Revolution, Camden, left twelve hundred casualties, American and British. The first great engagement of the Civil War, the First Battle of Bull Run, killed or injured four times as many. The butcher's bills lengthened prodigiously after that, with no end in sight.

In the West, the Union made steady but slow progress, retaking the Mississippi River. In northern Virginia, where rival armies maneuvered to destroy each other and seize the enemy's capital (Richmond the target for the Union, Washington for the rebels), the Union experienced a series of defeats.

In July 1862 Lincoln read his cabinet a draft of a proposed executive order, which would change both the strategic and the moral equations of the war. As of January 1, 1863, all slaves still in rebel territory would be freed. The Emancipation Proclamation would be issued under the president's authority as commander in chief during a war of rebellion. It would not touch slaves in loyal states or in parts of seceded states that the Union had occupied (such as portions of Louisiana and Virginia). But it would give slaves in the South who learned of it an incentive to malinger; it would inspire free blacks in the North to enlist as soldiers; it would recast the war as a moral struggle. It was no longer possible to wait until 1958; it was time to strike the heart of slavery now.

Seward, whom Lincoln had named secretary of state, suggested waiting until a battlefield victory to announce the idea, lest it look desperate. It was desperate, but one must never seem so. At last, in September, Union armies stopped a rebel invasion of Maryland at Antietam. There were twenty-three thousand casualties altogether, and the battle was a draw. But, though the enemy retreated in good order, he retreated; Antietam was victory enough. The Emancipation Proclamation, announced that month, went into effect on New Year's Day 1863.

But the rebellion had only been checked, not beaten. In the summer of 1863, the rebels made a second push north, into Pennsylvania. The combatants met, unexpectedly, at Gettysburg, a town and a nexus of roads twenty miles southwest of Harrisburg. A three-day struggle followed, ending on the Fourth of July, with sixty thousand casualties. Though the invaders managed to escape to Virginia, they had been decisively mauled.

Europe had seen deadlier battles; Leipzig, in the Napoleonic Wars, saw over a hundred thousand casualties. But that battle engaged the armies of eleven countries. All the dead at Gettysburg were Americans, certainly from Lincoln's point of view, since he never admitted the legal reality of secession.

It was hard to dispose of so many corpses. Five thousand dead horses and mules were burned; eight thousand men were shoveled over. Grieving relatives dug them up, searching for loved ones; so did hogs, scavenging.[10] At the initiative of the governor of Pennsylvania, an interstate commission was formed to bring order to this charnel field. Seventeen acres were set aside for a proper cemetery; the War Department donated caskets.

A ceremony of dedication was planned for the fall, and Edward Everett was engaged to deliver an oration. Everett, sixty-nine years old, was at the peak of an eminent career, having served as congressman, governor, president of Harvard, secretary of state, and US senator. He was also America's premier speechmaker. (He gave his most famous talk, on the character of George Washington, 129 times to raise money for the preservation of Mount Vernon.) He had also run against Lincoln, tangentially: in the 1860 election, he was the vice-presidential candidate of the Constitutional Union Party, a remnant of old Whigs who depicted themselves as the just middle between Democrats and Republicans—their single issue was preserving the Union, with no reference to slavery. Everett's ticket carried only three states. When the war came, he became a firm supporter of the Union cause. He and the organizers picked November 19 as the date of his performance.

President Lincoln was also invited to give brief "dedicatory remarks" after the main speech. He composed them in Washington ahead of time and took a train to Gettysburg the night before.

Everett did the job that was expected of him. As he did whenever he spoke, he brought his text to the lectern, then never looked at it, so keen was his memory. He described the three-day struggle in detail, from the first contact to the "expiring agonies." He poured scorn on the politicians who had taken their states into secession—"bold, bad men" who would "inherit the execration of the ages."[11] After the ceremony Lincoln would write Everett telling him that he had particularly liked his description of the nurses who had come to tend the injured and the dying, "to moisten the parched tongue, to bind the ghastly wounds, to soothe the parting agonies alike of friend and foe."[12]

Everett's speech lasted two hours—typical for a major effort in those more oral days. Lincoln himself was used to speaking at length. His first great speech, in Peoria, Illinois, in October 1854, lasted three hours.[13] His speech kicking off his presidential campaign, at Cooper Union in New York City in February 1860, lasted ninety minutes. At Gettysburg he spoke for two or three minutes.

The Gettysburg Address is not his greatest speech; that would be his second inaugural address in March 1865, the closest any president has ever come to prophetic utterance.

The Peoria speech and the Cooper Union address are more impressive, in their way, from sheer scope—as a symphony is more impressive than a song. But the Gettysburg Address is an epitome, a gathering of threads into one tight knot.

The first thread was military. We almost laugh now at the line "The world will little note nor long remember what we say here." Lincoln absolutely meant the follow-on: "but it can never forget what they"—the officers and men of the Union army—"did here." Lincoln did not go into the details of the battle—Everett had already done that, but he did not need to. Everyone was aware of the stakes. A rebel victory at Gettysburg would have put the invading army in striking distance of Washington, Philadelphia, or Baltimore. The nation's capital, its second and fourth largest cities, and the underbelly of its second largest state, would have all been at risk.

America does not have a parliamentary system, in which governments serve at the pleasure of sometimes fickle legislative majorities. But how could even a president and a Congress, serving for set terms, have withstood such a shock? The very Americanness of the victors would have encouraged defeatism; they were not armies from overseas, like the enemy in the American Revolution or the War of 1812, but citizen soldiers from a few states away. Why not let them whip their slaves in peace, as they had done for over eighty years under a united American government?

After such a debacle Lincoln would have been bound, not for Mount Rushmore or the currency, but for an afterlife as an idealist perhaps, but an impetuous and incompetent one. The buffs who compulsively reenact Pickett's Charge or the defense of Little Round Top have a point after all. Ideas show men how to live; words can inspire them to die. But battles, in turn, determine how ideas and words fare in the world.

The second thread of the Gettysburg Address concerns the world. This thread is scarcely visible, Lincoln touches on it so swiftly. Yet he, and the world, were mindful of the world's attention. The fate of the American experiment was being watched by more than Americans. Lincoln alludes to our exposure twice, toward the beginning of the address and at the very end. Could a nation governed as we are "long endure"? Could our form of government "perish from the earth"? Not "perish," but "perish from the earth"—that is, from human experience.

The other great free country on earth, for all its monar- chical and aristocratic trappings, was Great Britain. Its House of Commons had been reformed in 1832 to elim- inate inequities such as towns with few or no inhabitants sending two members to Parliament because they had done so once upon a time, while cities with a hundred thousand or more sent none, for the same reason. Yet inequities remained; workingmen could not vote. Was further reform desirable? The breakup of the American republic would suggest not.

English workingmen saw the connection between the Union's fate and their own. They saw it even though a Union naval blockade kept southern cotton from English textile mills, imperiling their livelihood. In December 1862 the workingmen of Manchester sent Lincoln an address, cheering him on. "The vast progress you have made in the short space of twenty months" in curtailing slavery "fills us with hope that every stain on your freedom will shortly be removed. . . . If you have any ill-wishers here, be assured they are chiefly those who oppose liberty at home."[14] Lincoln thanked them for their faith in him and America, in which he saw a portent of "the ultimate and universal triumph of justice, humanity and freedom."[15] Ultimate and universal—if justice, humanity, and freedom could pass the test here.

France's days as a restored monarchy had ended with a revolution and a Second Republic in 1848, filling liberals and radicals around the world with hope. "Thanks to steam navigation and electric wires," wrote an excited Frederick Douglass, the news of revolutions "flashes with lightning speed from heart to heart, from land to land, till it has traversed the globe."[16] In 1852 very different news traversed the globe when a nephew of Napoleon Bonaparte restored the empire as Napoleon III. France's second empire still flew the revolutionary tricolor, but the emperor's personal flag better depicted the new reality: the tricolor, overlaid with his coat of arms and a swarm of golden bees, his uncle's favorite insect.

Napoleon III's ambitions extended to our doorstep. In 1846 we had gone to war with Mexico, tearing off Texas, California, and everything in between. Even so we had not dictated to Mexico its form of government. Fifteen years later, while we were consumed with our Civil War, France landed an army in Mexico, captured the capital, and offered the crown of a newly decreed Mexican empire to a European prince. Here was a reactionary power replicating itself in the New World, making the dream of Chateaubriand come true. Rebellion in America had suspended the Monroe

Doctrine; America's dissolution would encourage despotism worldwide.

The third thread of the Gettysburg address examined history and looked to the future.

The fact of a victory on the Fourth of July offered an unmissable opportunity to clothe it in patriotism. Electric wires compounded the opportunity by bringing news of a second victory on the Fourth—the fall of Vicksburg, one of the last rebel strongholds on the Mississippi. Lincoln did not let the opportunity pass.

On July 7 he told a joyous crowd assembled on the White House lawn that the Fourth was the birthday of both the United States and the Declaration of Independence. "How long ago is it" since 1776, he asked. He offered a quick approximation: "Eighty odd years." He then noted two other momentous Fourths—in 1826, when Thomas Jefferson and John Adams died, "precisely fifty years after they put their hands" to the declaration; and 1831, when James Monroe followed them. Now, on the Fourth just past, the "gigantic Rebellion" had suffered two signal defeats. The coincidence of all these Fourths was "a glorious theme, and the occasion for a speech, but I am not prepared to make one worthy of the occasion."[17]

When he rose to speak at Gettysburg, he was prepared. His arithmetic now was accurate and rendered in the phrasings of the Bible. "Four score and seven years ago our forefathers brought forth on this continent a new nation."

Lincoln, his party, and the army were laboring to defend that nation; they were better entitled to the name of nationalist than anyone since the revolution. But what kind of nation was it?

It was, Lincoln went on, "conceived in Liberty and dedicated to the proposition that all men are created equal." His immediate target in saying so was, of course, slavery, the wholesale denial of the equality of millions. But he had larger goals in view.

Like Jefferson, he was fusing liberty and equality. The one presupposed the other. If men were not equal, then some men might justly assign (and deny) the rights of other men.

He was fusing this self-evident truth with America. The declaration was more than an announcement of a fact: here is a new country. It defined the fact it announced: here is what the country is about.

But the declaration was not the only founding document Lincoln referenced at Gettysburg. At the end of his remarks, he echoed another: the form of government that "shall not perish from the earth" was "government of the people, by the people, for the people."

This formulation had numerous antecedents. John Wycliffe, a fourteenth-century theologian, wrote a translation of the Bible into English that he declared to be "for the Government of the People, by the People, and for the People." The Bible nineteenth-century Americans read, however, was King James's; Wycliffe's was by then a historical curiosity. Lincoln's sources for his definition of America's government were closer to home.

In 1819, Chief Justice John Marshall delivered the Supreme Court's opinion in a case involving the constitutionality of the Second Bank of the United States (Daniel Webster was one of the lawyers representing the bank). The nature of the federal government had come up then too. "The government of the Union," Marshall wrote, "is, emphatically and truly, a government of the people. In form and in substance it emanates from them. Its powers are granted by them, and are to be exercised directly on them, and for their benefit."[18]

In 1830 Daniel Webster delivered a two-day speech in the Senate capping a debate, initially over western land policy, which had broadened into a discussion of the nature of the federal government itself. "It is, Sir," said Webster, ". . . the people's government, made for the people, made by the people, and answerable to the people."[19]

Lincoln had studied Webster's speeches, and as a former lawyer he was familiar with Marshall's decision. Before both of them was their original inspiration, the preamble to the Constitution, written by Gouverneur Morris.

The draft from which Morris worked had begun, "We the People of the States," listing all thirteen. Morris changed this to "We the People of the United States."

Morris had a very particular reason for his rewrite. Rhode Island had refused to send anyone to the Constitutional Convention, and New York had not been represented since midsummer, when two members of its three-man delegation went home in disgust, and their remaining colleague, Alexander Hamilton, virtually absented himself too, not feeling entitled to cast his state's vote alone (he came back in the home stretch to sign). It would have been indecent to have listed all thirteen states at the head of a document that two of them disapproved. Better to fudge the issue by not naming the states at all.

But Morris was also consciously making the point later elaborated by Marshall, Webster, and Lincoln.[20] The

Constitution was an act of the people. Neither Congress nor the state governments had written it, nor had they approved it (the ratifying conventions were one-time, stand-alone bodies, directly elected).

As the Constitution came from the people, so the government it created answered to them. All men were not merely created equal; they had an equal share in the government as citizens and voters.

Morris and Lincoln were also making a statement of responsibility. The people must maintain their government in its proper form, whether in daily politics or in the face of rebellion. No one else can do it for them.

Oral tradition holds that when Lincoln uttered his last sentence, he emphasized not the prepositions but the noun that was their object: not "*of* the people, *by* the people, *for* the people" but "of the *people*, by the *people*, for the *people*."[21]

Lincoln had fit two founding documents into a speech of 272 words. He was like a Chinese or Gothic carver, making a fruit pit into a sailing ship or a boxwood bead into the Heavenly Host. His remarks at Gettysburg were not the result of sudden inspiration; he had been turning such thoughts over in his mind, and his rhetoric, for years. But long familiarity, and the weight of circumstance—the threat of defeat, the world's attention, the silent dead—had sharpened them to a point.

When Lincoln finished, his remarks were greeted, according to the Associated Press report, with "long-continued applause."[22] The next day Everett sent him a note expressing the professional's judgment: "I should be glad, if I could flatter myself that I came as near to the central idea of the occasion, in two hours, as you did in two minutes."[23]

Was Lincoln's effort of historical compression honest? Would the founders and framers have been pleased to find themselves brought together in his epitome, for his purposes in 1863?

There are many who think not. Garry Wills's Pulitzer Prize–winning study of the Gettysburg Address is subtitled "The Words That Remade America." America was broken (that, looking at the five thousand caskets, seems indisputable); Lincoln had to make a new America. He also remade American history. "Through no foresight of the founders was slavery eventually abolished," declares political philosopher George Kateb. Lincoln transformed the founders and framers into something they were not. "They were, if you will, retrospectively speaking, lucky."[24]

Skepticism concerning Lincoln's argument seems to draw strength from some of Lincoln's own words at Gettysburg. "[Let us] here highly resolve," he said, as he swung into his conclusion, ". . . that this nation, under God, shall have a new birth of freedom." That makes the men responsible for the old birth ("conceived in Liberty") hair-powdered relics, does it not?

It does not, for the reason that Lincoln was a careful writer. His reading for pleasure ran to Burns and Byron, Artemus Ward and Petroleum V. Naseby, but he was also a lawyer who had worked his own way through Euclid. If he had wanted to say "a birth of new freedom," he would have. Instead he said "a new birth of freedom." The freedom of Jefferson, Morris, and the rest. Restored, not remade.

Lincoln's look backward was the same look that the Seneca Falls Convention had taken when it modeled its

Declaration of Sentiments on the Declaration of Independence or that Martin Luther King Jr. would take in his 1963 speech at the Lincoln Memorial when he invoked "the magnificent words of the Constitution and the Declaration of Independence" as "a promissory note to which every American was to fall heir."[25] Backward looks yield the pleasures of nostalgia: we have been here before. Because they are pleasing they are politic. But they can also look back to things that are real.

Lincoln well knew that many of America's revolutionaries had been satisfied with slavery and that their reading of the founding documents was different from his.[26] But he also knew that many others had found the continued existence of slavery embarrassing; that some of them had taken concrete steps to curtail or abolish it—Alexander Hamilton, via the Manumission Society—while others hoped it would wither away; and that even more of the founders, while showing no real discomfort with slavery, were devoted to the Union. That, for him, was enough.

Gettysburg and Vicksburg were turning points, though the turn was slow and bloody. By November 1864, however, enough progress had been made that voters reelected Lincoln and Republican majorities in Congress. The Thirteenth Amendment, abolishing slavery nationwide, passed Congress at the end of January 1865. The last rebel armies surrendered in April. In December Seward, still serving as secretary of state, certified that the Thirteenth Amendment had been ratified by three-quarters of the states and thus was part of the Constitution.

Words make ideas memorable; battles can exalt or destroy them. Politics cleans up afterward—or not. Slavery ended, but what would become of freedmen? In the last speech of his life, Lincoln said in passing that he would "prefer" that black men who were "very intelligent" or who had served "our cause as soldiers" be given the vote (he had come a long way from colonization).[27] It took two constitutional amendments, the Fourteenth (1868) and Fifteenth (1870), to give blacks citizenship and black men the franchise. Terrorism and indifference would make the last two amendments dead letters for over ninety years: hence King speaking in 1963 of the Declaration of Independence and Constitution as promissory notes that had yet to be paid.

But the Gettysburg Address had registered them in the American mind.

chapter ten

THE NEW COLOSSUS
Liberty Enlightening the World

ABRAHAM LINCOLN'S REPUBLICAN PARTY WAS
not the only new political force in the decade before
the Civil War. For a brief time in the mid-1850s, it
shared the stage with the American or Know-Nothing Party,
whose signature issue was hostility to immigrants.

Many American Party members were refugees from
Lincoln's former party, the Whigs, which had fractured and
collapsed after 1852 because of its inability to take a stand
on the question of slavery. The last Whig president, Millard
Fillmore, was the American Party's presidential candidate in
1856. But the passion that drove the new party was unease
and anger over swelling tides of immigrants, driven here by
famine, political unrest, or the search for a better life. The
Antimasonic Party of the burned-over district in the 1830s
had feared a fraternal organization, bound by secret oaths
and practicing hidden rituals; the American Party feared

boatloads of foreigners, surging onto the wharves of our ports and, seemingly, filling our cities' slums. We, their name said, are the *real* Americans.

At its peak, the American Party elected fifty-four congressmen and five US senators. Although Fillmore carried only one state as its standard bearer, he took 21 percent of the popular vote.

The party withered as rapidly as it sprang up. Immigration was a big issue, slavery a far bigger one. One contemporary compared the American Party's heyday to an infestation of locusts: "They came out of the dark ground, crawled up the sides of the trees, ate their foliage in the night, chattered with a croaking harshness, split open their backs and died."[1]

But concern over immigration lived on. During his 1858 Senate campaign, Lincoln expressed a vision of all Americans united by their devotion to its founding principles. "That old Declaration of Independence" was like an "electric cord . . . that links the hearts of liberty-loving men together," whether they were descended from the revolutionary generation or "men who have come from Europe."[2] This was idealistic and politic: Illinois was home to many men who had recently come from Europe (the Irish leaned Democratic, the Germans Republican). Privately, however, the Lincoln campaign worried that Irish railroad workers would ride the rails from town to town on election day, voting multiple times. Irish hearts were cordless.

The grinding tectonic plates of immigration produced an earthquake in New York City in July 1863. For three days, on the heels of the battle of Gettysburg, rioters kept the city in turmoil; order was restored only by Union troops clearing the avenues with howitzers. Hundreds of bystanders, rioters, police, and soldiers were killed. The proximate cause of the outbreak was hatred of conscription. The riot was also a class war (a rich man whose draft number came up could hire a substitute for $300). But most of the rioters were immigrant Irish, enraged at blacks (for whom the war was being fought) and their old stock upper-class sympathizers. The latter returned the hatred with interest. The "Irish anti-conscription Nigger-murdering mob," wrote one diarist, "must be put down by heroic doses of lead and steel."[3]

The Irish seemed particularly threatening because they were not only foreign but Catholic (unlike other Christian churches in America, Catholicism possessed a hierarchy headquartered abroad). They were also politically adept, trained in mass action by years of resistance to oppressive laws and landlords back home. German immigrants, equally numerous but religiously diverse and politically less active, escaped hostile notice, except when reformers tried to crack down on that cornerstone of their social life, the tavern; Elizabeth Cady Stanton and her fellow suffragists often doubled as temperance crusaders.

The flow of immigrants across the Atlantic increased and diversified as the nineteenth century went on. Irish and Germans were joined by Italians, Scandinavians, and Jews. There had been small numbers of all these ethnicities in America since colonial times. The best tavern in eighteenth-century Richmond was run by Serafina Formicola, former steward of Virginia's last royal governor. Peter Stuyvesant's dealings with Swedes and Jews have been mentioned. But immigration in massive numbers was new.

However unsettling their presence, immigrants were welcomed more often than not. Employers wanted their labor. Politicians wanted their votes. William Seward, Lincoln's rival turned partner, had been a notably pro-Irish governor of New York, in favor of public money for parochial schools. Tammany Hall, an urban Democratic Party machine founded originally by Aaron Burr, became a master at attracting and holding immigrant voters. Lincolnian, and sub-Lincolnian, rhetoric smoothed the process. At Tammany's Fourth of July celebrations, a participant reported, "As soon as the man on the platform starts off with, 'when in the course of human events,' word goes round that it's the Declaration of Independence, and a mighty roar goes up. The Declaration ain't a very short document and the crowd has heard it on every Fourth, but they give it just as fine a send-off as if it was brand new and awful excitin'."[4]

Immigrants themselves took pride in their new national status and used it to impress and assist later arrivals. They memorialized their contributions to the Civil War and other milestones in American history. Far more Irish fought for the Union than fought the draft; one of their storied regiments was nicknamed "The Fighting Irish." Italians boasted that Christopher Columbus, though he worked for Spain, came from Genoa. Ethnic social groups and aid societies tried to ease those more recently off the boat into American life.

One young member of the Hebrew Emigrant Aid Society in New York City was Emma Lazarus. Her family was well established in America—Sephardic Jews who had fled Portugal in the seventeenth century for the tolerant Dutch empire. Her father, Moses, made a fortune refining sugar;

helped found the Knickerbocker Club; and summered at
Newport, along with Astors, Belmonts, and Vanderbilts.
Emma, born in 1849, wrote poetry and journalism for publi-
cations both mainstream (*Scribner's*) and Jewish (*The American Hebrew*) and corresponded with literary lions (Emerson,
Henry James). Despite this hot-house upbringing, the woes
of the world, especially of Jews less fortunate than herself,
weighed on her—a burden "strangely heavy," wrote a friend,
for "the mind of a woman so young. . . . One never failed to
bring away from a talk with her an impulse to higher things."[5]

An 1882 article of hers in the *New York Times*, "Among
the Russian Jews," described a visit to a Jewish pauper's refuge.
The influx of poor immigrants was so great that an overflow
facility had been opened on Ward's Island in the East River,
by Hell Gate. The Jews there confronted their visitor with the
conundrum of identity. They were poor and unassimilated and
hence potentially an embarrassment to her and her upper-
crust family. *Is this what I really am?* But America had taken
them in. *This is what I am—a citizen of a saving country.* "Every
American," Lazarus wrote in the *Times*, "must feel a thrill of
pride and gratitude in the thought that this country is the
refuge of the oppressed. . . . However wretched be the material
offered to him by the refuse of other nations, he accepts it
with generous hospitality."[6] He, and she, accepted it.

In 1883, Lazarus got a chance to express these sentiments
again. For years a group of Frenchmen had been planning
and constructing a monumental gift to America, a gigantic statue of a torchbearing goddess. Two presidents, Ulysses
Grant and Rutherford B. Hayes, had formally accepted the
gift during each of their terms, and the site where it would

stand had been picked—Bedloe's Island, a tiny spot in New York's inner harbor. But the structure required an equally vast pedestal. Who would pay for it? Neither Congress nor the New York State government would vote to use public money. Private fund drives raised dribs and drabs. One money-raising scheme was to auction a leather-bound portfolio of original artwork and written items. Mark Twain, Bret Harte, and Chester Alan Arthur (who was the sitting president at the time and the third president connected with the project) contributed letters. Emma Lazarus was invited to submit a poem.

The poem she wrote was a grave and passionate sonnet. Sonnets in English follow Shakespeare or Petrarch. The Shakespearean rhyme scheme, three quatrains and a couplet (4 + 4 + 4 + 2), is inherently lopsided and a high risk. The concluding couplet is either a grand slam, bringing all the preceding lines home, or a swing and a miss. The Petrarchan pattern, two interlinked quatrains and a sestet (8 + 6), allows for the possibility of a more developed, two-step argument. This was what Lazarus achieved.

The title is "The New Colossus." The old colossus was the Colossus of Rhodes, one of the wonders of the ancient world, a bronze statue that reputedly bestrode the harbor mouth of that Greek island. (Archeologists believe it stood to one side, but that was not its posture in mythic memory.) It was built in the fourth century BC to commemorate a victory in the internecine wars that rent Alexander the Great's empire after his death. After fifty-two years it fell in an earthquake, its ruined form impressing sightseers for centuries more until it was melted by a Muslim caliph. That colossus had also been memorialized by a poem. "To thy very self, O Sun, did the people of Dorian Rhodes raise high this colossus" when "they crowned their country with the spoils of its foes."[7] Like the new colossus, the Colossus of Rhodes was an image of national pride: pride in conquest.

Lazarus begins by rebuking the Colossus of Rhodes.

> Not like the brazen giant of Greek fame
> With conquering limbs astride from land to land.
> Here at our sea-washed, sunset gates shall stand
> A mighty woman . . .

"Sunset gates"? New York harbor is on our east coast. But if you are fleeing Europe, it is the edge of the western world.

On the first page of his unfinished novel, *Amerika*, Franz Kafka describes the mighty woman, whom he had never seen, holding a sword. Where was his editor? What she holds is a torch.

> . . . [its] flame
> Is the imprisoned lightning, and her name
> Mother of Exiles. From her beacon-hand
> Glows world-wide welcome. Her mild eyes command
> The air-bridged harbor that twin cities frame.

The harbor is framed by "twin cities" because New York and Brooklyn were then separate municipalities. It is bridged by "air," not colossal legs, because the mighty woman is not marching out against the world but inviting a portion of it to come to her, here.

What portion of the world does the new colossus invite? Lazarus's quatrains set up the statue; her sestet delivered its message.

> "Keep, ancient lands, your storied pomp!" cries she
> With silent lips.

A statue cannot speak; it is not a living thing. Yet this one not only speaks; it cries out. The crying of "silent lips," heightened by the line break, is Lazarus's strongest writerly effect: the pressure of the message is so great it simply bursts out of her (poet and statue both). The statue's message is what Lazarus herself had seen on Ward's Island and written up for the *Times*, now recast in rhyme and meter.

> "Give me your tired, your poor,
> Your huddled masses yearning to breathe free,
> The wretched refuse of your teeming shore.
> Send them, the homeless, tempest-tost to me.
> I lift my lamp beside the golden door."

It is a coda to the Monroe Doctrine. Conquering limbs, storied pomp, and the corrupt, oppressive systems that generate them must stay away; the people they scorn and oppress may come.

This is important, but it is only half the story. The full meaning of Lazarus's poem depends on the identity of the subject. Who is the statue? "The New Colossus" calls her "Mother of Exiles," but she is much more than that.

The statue was offered as a binational transaction, France saluting America. But the original inspiration for the gift came from a very particular slice of the donor nation.

French attitudes toward America covered a gambit, as varied as French politics itself. Reactionaries disdained us as a toxic site of contaminating ideas; practitioners of realpolitik viewed us either as useful tools (backing the American Revolution to weaken Britain) or as rivals. Napoleon III, slipping an invading army and a monarch into Mexico while we were preoccupied by the Civil War, was both a reactionary and a would-be hemispheric competitor.

But from the American Revolution on, there were always sincere French friends of what the Marquis de Lafayette called "the most interesting of Republics," admiring our commitment to liberty, concerning themselves with our fate, and hoping that France might emulate our example.[8] Lafayette himself came to America in 1777 as a nineteen-year-old volunteer, named his youngest children Georges Washington and Virginie, and consulted with Thomas Jefferson at the dawn of the French Revolution on a French bill of rights. In the next generation, Alexis de Tocqueville toured America to study democracy in action and tried to apply what he learned as a legislator under the short-lived Second Republic.

Edouard Rene de Laboulaye, a law professor and belletrist a few years younger than Tocqueville, was a third specimen of the type, expressing his convictions in writing rather than action. As the Second Republic gave way to the Second Empire, he began a three-volume work on the political history of the United States, with the thought that foreign history would correct what domestic politics was producing. During the Civil War he published articles in French journals in support of the Union; French official policy, by contrast, was neutral, with a pull toward the Confederacy. He also wrote a fantasy novel, *Paris en Amerique*, in which a Yankee medium, Jonathan Dream, puts the narrator in a trance from which he wakes to find himself and his family transformed into Americans. He experiences a society free from the blemishes of the Second Empire: journalism without censorship, marriages contracted without dowries, and peaceful citizens uninterested in fighting duels (this, clearly, was America after Alexander Hamilton had been killed in one). He awakens from the trance a changed man. The Paris to which he returns, however, has not changed; he is found insane and locked up.[9]

For Laboulaye and other Frenchmen like him, writing and thinking about America was a safety valve and a goad, expressing hopes that were contrary to the reality of life around them, and possibly nudging their country in a better direction.

When the Civil War ended in a Union victory, Laboulaye founded an emancipation committee to raise money to help freedmen. He also expressed the hope, at an 1865 lunch in the garden of his country house, that the end of slavery in America might be commemorated by a colossal Franco-American sculpture.

The sculptor who caught Laboulaye's enthusiasm was one of his lunch guests, a younger acquaintance, Frederic Bartholdi. He had a typical artist's education in Paris: academic, governed by the study of models and the application of rules, embracing architecture and painting as well as sculpture. A trip to Egypt—where, unlike Rhodes, wonders of the ancient world still stood—showed him the possibilities of monumental design. The key, he wrote, was simplicity. "The details of the lines ought not to arrest the eye. . . . The surfaces should be broad and simple, defined by a bold and clear design, accentuated in important places. . . . [The work] should have a summarized character, such as one would give to a rapid sketch."[10] For the opening of the Suez Canal in 1869, he proposed a lighthouse at Port Said, the northern terminus, in the form of a gigantic robed torchbearer. This orientalism was too oriental for the Khedive of Egypt, who chose instead a plain tower of reinforced concrete.

Political upheaval brought the Franco-American statue a step closer to reality. Napoleon III abandoned his Mexican puppet monarch as soon as the Civil War ended; he would challenge America behind its distracted back, not to its reunited face. In 1870, however, he plunged into a war with Prussia. His defeat was total. The struggle to replace the Second Empire was long, sometimes bloody. A socialist commune ran Paris for two months before the French army crushed it. The first postwar elections to the national legislature returned a chamber filled with monarchists, but their claimant to the throne, a great-nephew of Louis XVI, imposed an impossible condition: he would reign only under the old royalist flag. The commander of the army, himself a monarchist, remarked that if the tricolor were replaced, the guns of his soldiers would fire themselves in protest. As a result, France became a republic once more.

Laboulaye and Bartholdi revived the idea of a Franco-American monument, this time in commemoration of the friendship between the two countries (or at least between America and French republicans). The approaching centennial of the Declaration of Independence gave the project a target date and an event to celebrate. Bartholdi began work on a model of the statue and visited America to promote it. As a warm-up, he sculpted an over-life-size bronze image of Lafayette at the moment of his first landing in America. The boat on which Bartholdi's Lafayette stands is symbolic, hardly larger than his feet. But the emotion with which he presses the hilt of his sword to his heart is very real.

The Lafayette statue was dedicated in Union Square in New York City in 1876, where it still stands; the colossal statue had years of work ahead of it yet. Pieces of it were exhibited as Bartholdi finished them—the arm and torch in Philadelphia, the head in Paris. These particular pieces were chosen for maximum public impact, since spectators could go inside them and look out. Gustave Eiffel, an engineer who was later to build a great monument of his own, was engaged to design and fabricate the statue's armature. Outside would be a copper sheath in the form of neoclassical robes; inside would be state-of-the-art iron struts and girders.

As the French people became accustomed to their new republic, and eager to display its artistic and technological achievements to the world, they raised money for the statue rapidly. By 1881 one hundred thousand Frenchmen had given enough to complete the mammoth. In America, however, fund-raising for the pedestal lagged. The portfolio for which Emma Lazarus had written her poem raised only $1,500 at auction, half what the organizers hoped.

The project was saved by a press lord. Joseph Pulitzer, a Hungarian Jewish immigrant who had fought for the Union in the Civil War and made a splash as a publisher in St. Louis, bought the *World*, a floundering New York newspaper, in 1883. He reinvented it as the modern tabloid, with smaller pages, bigger headlines, graphics, human interest, scandal, and crusades—the entire palette. One of his crusades, launched in March 1885, was to call on his readers to raise the money needed for the pedestal. "Let us not wait for the millionaires to give this money. [The statue] is not a gift from the millionaires of France to the millionaires of America" but a gift from one people to another. "The *World* is the people's paper, and it now appeals to the people to come forward."[11] Come forward they did, encouraged by the opportunity to behave better than their social betters and by the prospect of reading their names in the *World*, which daily listed all the new donors and the amounts of their contributions, however small. By August Pulitzer had raised $100,000, enough to give the colossus a place to stand.

The statue was dedicated on October 28, 1886, with speeches, fireworks, foghorns, and a twenty-one-gun salute, despite the rain. Grover Cleveland, the fourth president connected with the project, presided. Laboulaye was not there, having died three years earlier at age seventy-two. Neither was Emma Lazarus, who was in Europe nursing a bout of bad health. But Bartholdi was present to unveil the statue's face. Electric light blazed from the torch and the crown, as Lazarus had written it would.

Her name was Liberty. A French prospectus of 1875 explained it clearly. America was about to celebrate "the foundation of the great Republic," as France would recall its vital supporting role. "It is proposed to erect, as a memorial of the glorious anniversary, an exceptional monument. In the midst of the harbor of New York, upon an islet which belongs to the Union of States, in front of Long Island, where was poured out the first blood for independence, a colossal statue would rear its head. . . . It will represent 'Liberty Enlightening the World.' At night a resplendent aureole upon its brow will throw its beams far upon the vast sea."[12]

All the details of this statement were carefully chosen. Bedloe's Island, the "islet," was owned by the federal government; calling its owner "the Union of States" recalled the victorious conclusion of the Civil War. "Long Island, where was poured out the first blood for independence" refers to the first battle of the American Revolution after independence was declared, the Battle of Long Island, fought in what is now Brooklyn in August 1776. When installed, the statue's eyes would look across the harbor to the site, as anyone can verify by going to Prospect Park and returning its gaze. The brow bears a "resplendent aureole" because the statue is, among other things, literally a lighthouse (this feature of Bartholdi's Suez Canal plan survived the trip to New York). But the most important light it throws out is the message of liberty, symbolized both by its torch and by its seven-rayed crown. The Colossus of Rhodes had probably worn such a crown, since that was a symbol of the sun, the god to whom it was dedicated. The new colossus radiates the endowments of nature's God.

The prospectus did not mention it, but the statue's left arm cradles a tablet, inscribed July IV MDCCLXXVI. At its feet lie broken chains, recalling Laboulaye's first intention to commemorate emancipation.

Most of these details have slipped from popular memory, as they perhaps escaped notice at the time. Dedicatory rhetoric, like the spiels of park rangers, can cover too much. No one, except in circumstances requiring precision, now calls the statue Liberty Enlightening the World. But its identity and purpose survive even so. Everyone calls it the Statue of Liberty, or jocularly Lady Liberty. Bartholdi's monumental simplicity got—and gets—the message across.

Visual gestures that imprint themselves on the mind are sometimes called "iconic." This is not quite right. In Christian Orthodox theology, icons are subjects of meditation. Bartholdi's statue offers food for thought, as its prospectus suggests. But it is primarily, as he wrote, a sketch: something to be recognized and understood immediately. It is a logo— the logo of liberty.

Why is this important? It corrects Lazarus calling the new colossus Mother of Exiles. So she is. But America was not the only country in the Americas to harbor exiles.

Immigrants had been coming to Latin America from around the world, not just from the colonial powers as settlers or from Africa as slaves, for decades. Their traces can be found in the names of recent regional heads of state, from Alberto Fujimori (Peru) to Dilma Rousseff (Brazil). But the southern mother of exiles was Argentina.

In the late nineteenth and early twentieth centuries, a flood of immigrants poured into the mouth of the Rio de la Plata from mother Spain, but also from Italy, Germany, eastern Europe, and the Middle East. Since Argentina was a much less populous country than America, the proportion of the total they represented was that much greater. In America the percentage of the population that is foreign-born has peaked several times (1870, 1890, 1910) at or just below 15 percent (today it approaches that level). In Argentina in 1914 the proportion of foreign-born was almost 30 percent.

Argentina's immigrants became Argentinians. While John Quincy Adams's grim judgment that Latin Americans "have not the first elements of good or free government" may not be entirely correct, or forever fated, it is the case that Argentina's history in the twentieth century was a parade of demagogues and dictators. Argentina needed more than a Statue of Liberty; it needed the commitment to liberty that the statue expressed.

Immigrants stepping off the boat in New York, or Buenos Aires, were often fleeing particular evils—persecution, squalor—that could be abated by a simple change of venue. But American liberty is more than an absence of evils. It is a system of principles and conduct that keeps evils at bay. Maintaining it requires the devotion of Americans, native-born and newcomers alike.

The Statue of Liberty is a challenge as well as a welcome. *Come here, but be like us. I will show you the way.*

Lazarus died in 1887 of lymphoma. She had arranged her works for posthumous publication, putting "The New Colossus" at the head of the collection; when it appeared, edited by her sisters, the sonnet had been bucked to page 202.[13]

It was retrieved from obscurity by a friend and fellow bluestocking, Georgina Schuyler. Schuyler is an old Dutch New York name, but she had an immigrant in her family tree: her great-grandfather, Alexander Hamilton. In 1903, twenty years after "The New Colossus" was written, she arranged to have a plaque commemorating it and Lazarus installed on Bedloe's Island, in the pedestal of the Statue of Liberty.

chapter eleven

CROSS OF GOLD SPEECH
Economic Equality

W ILLIAM SEWARD'S GREAT SPEECH ON THE
"irrepressible conflict" embedded in the economic life of pre–Civil War America described
its competing systems as slave labor and free labor. The free
labor system, Seward declared, "conforms to the divine law
of equality." No person was property, even the humblest; all
were free agents. "Therefore" free labor "is always and everywhere beneficent."[1]

But was it? The nineteenth century saw changes in the
nature of work that left many Americans slighted or vulnerable. There had always been apprentices and farm laborers,
generally young, working for wages. But everyone hoped in
time to set up on his own. Increasingly, however, men worked,
in small shops or large factories, for wages lifelong.

Markets changed along with the workplace. Railroads
spanned the continent; steamships crossed the ocean. As

transportation costs dropped, crops and products competed with those grown or made in other states or on other continents. Your lifework became vulnerable to remote competitors.

There had always been rich Americans and the envy they excited. America's oldest political party, the Republicans of Thomas Jefferson and James Madison (later called Democrats), had been founded, in part, to combat "the opulent"—cronies of the rival Federalist Party, grown fat off its policies.[2] But after the Civil War, there seemed to be so many more rich. Some presided over tangible enterprises—Cornelius Vanderbilt owned railroads, John D. Rockefeller refined oil—but others—Jay Gould, Jim Fisk, Daniel Drew—made, or lost, fortunes by playing the stock market.

In the last decade of the nineteenth century, the suffering and the fearful focused their anxieties on the medium of exchange. The Civil War had been financed by printing paper money, which required all the skill of Treasury Secretary Salmon P. Chase not to be inflated into worthlessness, as had happened to the paper money printed during the American Revolution. In 1873 America went on the gold standard, backing the dollar with precious metal—historically stable in supply and not subject to political manipulation.

But silver was another precious metal; strikes in the American west had unearthed plenteous amounts of it. Supporters of bimetallism—a monetary system based on both silver and gold—hoped it would have an inflationary effect similar to printing money.

Debtors welcomed the chance to pay their obligations in cheaper dollars. As the century wound down, many farmers found themselves in that position. Between 1865 and

1890, the number of farms in America had almost doubled; increased production drove prices down, while payment on loans and mortgages still had to be met.

The Bible says that "the love of money is the root of all evil" (1 Timothy 6:10). Maybe the monetary system itself was.

The struggle over silver would convulse politics for a season and inspire a speech that made a timeless statement.

In 1890 a new party arose, the Populists, calling for inflation, whether via paper money or silver (the policy of coining unlimited amounts of the latter was called "free silver"). Its candidates won local races in the West and South and five seats in the House of Representatives.

One winning candidate, not a Populist but a Democrat who ran with their support, was a freshman congressman from Nebraska, William Jennings Bryan.

Bryan, born in 1860, had grown up in small-town southern Illinois, son of a local politician. Bryan's political idol was Thomas Jefferson; throughout his life, his favorite gift to celebrity acquaintances was a volume of Jefferson's aphorisms, arranged by topic. He moved to Nebraska in 1887, with the intention of practicing law and running for office.

He seems almost to have backed into silver as an issue. "The people of Nebraska are for free silver and I am for free silver," he explained early in his career. "I will look up the arguments later."[3] Once he had mastered the arguments, however, free silver became his cause, his signature, and his passion.

In addition to his duties as congressman, Bryan became editor in chief of the *Omaha World-Herald*, the state's highest-circulation daily. The actual editing was done by the publisher, and most of Bryan's copy was ghosted by the Washington correspondent, but the job gave him a platform and an opportunity to write whenever he chose.

His true verbal medium, however, was speech. His natural instrument was powerful, a necessity for orators in those unamplified days; his wife, Mary, sitting in their hotel room while he gave one out-of-town speech, heard him clearly from three blocks away. Yet his voice was not raucous or strident: listeners called it "melodious," "musical," "soothing."[4] Edward Everett brought a text to his lecterns but never looked at it; Bryan spoke without notes at all. He used minimal gestures and few elaborate rhetorical figures. He seemed to be communicating one-on-one, even to audiences that numbered hundreds or, as he became famous, thousands. One newspaper clipping early in his career identified the source of his power as an "entire lack of artfulness."[5]

Lack of artfulness took hard work. Bryan spoke so often that he had ample opportunity to test themes and applause lines. He practiced between appearances in front of a mirror, with his wife coaching; when she was in the audience, she would signal with nods or smiles when he was doing well.

These many tweaks, rehearsals, and prompts did not represent insincerity on his part. They were a form of exercise, of mental and physical training, the better to get his message across. The message itself was something that Bryan had come absolutely to believe. Imparting it—sharing it, when his listeners were disposed to agree with him—was his goal.

In 1892 the Populists ran James B. Weaver, a long-bearded Civil War veteran, for president; Bryan, despite running for reelection to Congress as a Democrat, backed him. Weaver won a million votes out of twelve million cast and carried five states, finishing a close second in Nebraska. Bryan won too, despite having been stuffed, via reapportionment, into a new, less congenial district.

It was a good showing for Populism, but a disaster a year later scrambled all political prospects. America, and the world, fell into a depression. Railroads and banks failed; unemployment soared. Economists and partisans trotted out pet theories to explain the debacle. Silverites blamed the gold standard, whose supporters blamed half measures that Congress had taken to placate silverites. Most blame stuck to the president, Grover Cleveland, a gold-standard Democrat. When the economy does well, the president takes the credit; when it crashes, he is the villain. Cleveland, and his allies in the Democratic Party, were doomed. But who would take their places?

The Republican Party held its 1896 convention in St. Louis in June. Its nominee was William McKinley, a fifty-three-year-old veteran of the Civil War and Ohio politics, as genial as he was shrewd. The Republican Party had been born out of a near-religious fervor to resist slavery, which carried other, less savory crusading impulses in its wake. McKinley took care to distance himself from bigots and moralists, hiring Catholics in state government, and soft-pedalling the issue of Prohibition. At the same time, he sharpened his stance on the currency, becoming a partisan of the gold standard, in part to offer a contrast to the man he expected the post-Cleveland Democrats to nominate, Missouri congressman Richard Bland. Bland, who would turn sixty-one in August, had been championing the silver cause so long and so devotedly that he had earned the nickname Silver Dick.

Bryan was determined that he should be the man the Democrats would nominate. In March 1895 he had turned thirty-five—the minimum age the Constitution requires for the presidency. That same month his congressional career had ended; he had hoped, after two terms in the House of Representatives, to represent Nebraska in the Senate, but the 1894 elections had given the state legislature, which made the choice, to the Republicans. Bryan spent his free time speaking and networking. He advised the Populist Party to hold its presidential convention after the two major parties did, so as to leave its choice open. He also declined an offer to be Nebraska's favorite son at the Democratic convention, urging prosilver states to endorse the cause, not local figures. He intended to be the favorite son of all the silverites at the convention.

The Democrats met in Chicago in July, in a coliseum built for a world's fair three years earlier. The hall could accommodate football games, or twenty thousand people, and was the largest indoor exhibition space in the world.

Charles Dawes, a young Republican operative who had lived in Nebraska and knew Bryan personally, warned McKinley that if Bryan got a chance to speak, he would win the Democratic nomination.

Everything conspired to give Bryan his chance. Bitter Cleveland supporters had backed a delegation of progold Democrats to represent Nebraska in Chicago. But the convention seated a slate of silver delegates, including Bryan, instead. When the platform committee produced a document calling for free silver, gold Democrats responded with a minority report, which meant there would be a debate on the floor. Five men were picked to speak—three for gold, two for silver, with the silver supporters going first and last. Bryan and South Carolina senator Benjamin Tillman were asked to speak for silver. Tillman wanted to close but said he would need a minimum of fifty minutes. Bryan told him their opponents would not accept a closing statement that long, and Tillman agreed to lead off. Bryan would have the last word.

The debate was scheduled for July 9, the convention's third day. Anticipation was high—scalpers charged $50 for a seat—but the confrontation got off to a bad start. Tillman looked wild and uncouth—like a "train robber," wrote one reporter.[6] He was in fact a murderer who had got his start in politics by killing black Republicans. His speech was bullying and vituperative, an accurate reflection of his character. "I am from South Carolina, the home of secession." Now it was time "to accomplish the emancipation of the white slaves."[7] He finished to a chorus of boos.

Senator David Hill of New York led off for gold with a speech that Bryan himself thought "very strong."[8] But he was followed by Senator William Vilas of Wisconsin and former Massachusetts governor William Russell. Vilas, bogging down in detail, was applauded only when he lost his voice; Russell could not be heard at all (he would die of heart failure a week later).

During this cavalcade of fustian, chaos, and boredom, so typical of great national conventions, a friendly journalist passed Bryan a note: "You can make the hit of your life." Bryan wrote back: "You will not be disappointed."[9]

Bryan had been preparing himself with speaker's tricks—eating a sandwich to settle his stomach, sucking a lemon to stimulate his vocal cords. When it was his turn to speak, he took the steps of the podium two at a time, looking, wrote the poet Edgar Lee Masters, like a "boxer."[10] In his forties Bryan would start to lose his hair, but now he still had a dark shock.

He spoke for twenty minutes. He began by poor-mouthing himself, an old speaker's gambit—Abraham Lincoln used it for years. "I would be presumptuous indeed to present myself against the distinguished gentlemen to whom you have listened if this were a mere measuring of abilities." But humility was particularly suited to this cause and this moment. "The individual is but an atom; he is born, he acts, he dies; but principles are eternal; and this has been a contest over a principle." Some individuals were not quite atoms, though, for Bryan and the silver men were Davids fighting a golden Goliath. "The humblest citizen in all the land, when clad in the armor of a righteous cause, is stronger than all the hosts of error."

At times Bryan seemed to relish the ideological upheaval that he was advocating. "In this contest brother has been arrayed against brother, father against son. The warmest ties of love, acquaintance and association have been disregarded; old leaders have been cast aside when they have refused to give expression to the sentiments of those whom they would lead, and new leaders"—like himself—"have sprung up to give direction to this cause of truth." Years later, the novelist Willa Cather, raised in Nebraska, would publish a story, "Two Friends," a remembrance of a young lawyer and an older rancher in a small western town who seemed to form a perfectly bonded yin and yang—the lawyer quick and ardent, the rancher sagacious and slow—until the election of 1896 and the crusade for free silver divided them politically and destroyed their comradeship. Bryan was describing the process in real time.

Elsewhere in his speech, he pulled back from incitement, wrapping himself in the familiar arguments of Thomas Jefferson and Andrew Jackson, the Democratic Party's founding heroes. Each man had opposed an incarnation of the Bank of the United States, the brainchild of Alexander Hamilton, a federally chartered institution that held the government's deposits and issued currency. In 1791 Jefferson had argued, in vain, that the First Bank of the United States was unconstitutional; in 1832 Jackson had killed the Second Bank of the United States by refusing to renew its charter.

The Banks of the United States, though created by the federal government, had been run as private enterprises. Hamilton had warned that letting politicians issue paper money would be "seducing and dangerous."[11] Bankers with a stake in the game would be guided by their sense of what the market would bear; politicians would be guided by what their constituents wanted. Bryan updated the counterarguments of his party's historic champions and applied them to the subject at hand. "Those who are opposed" to free silver "tell us . . . that the Government ought to go out of the banking business. I stand with Jefferson rather than with them, and tell them, as he did, that the issue of money is a function of government, and that the banks ought to go out of the governing business."

By recalling old party battles, Bryan sought to comfort, if not to convince, gold Democrats. But then he became aggressive again, spectacularly so. Hill and Russell represented eastern, urban states, and Bryan let them have it. "You come to us and tell us that the great cities are in favor of the gold standard; we reply that the great cities rest upon our broad and fertile prairies. Burn down your cities and leave our farms, and your cities will spring up again as if by magic, but destroy our farms and the grass will grow in the streets of every city in the country." The Democratic Party's most effective vote-getting machine was Tammany Hall of New York City; this apocalyptic imagery was not calculated to encourage its election-day efforts.

Bryan's peroration was the hit he had promised. "Having behind us the producing masses of this nation and the world, supported by the commercial interests, the laboring interests, and the toilers everywhere, we will answer [the Republican Party's] demand for a gold standard by saying to them: You shall not press down upon the brow of labor this crown of thorns, you shall not crucify mankind upon a cross of gold."

Bryan had said almost the same thing in a speech to Congress in December 1894: "The money centers"—the great cities and the bankers who inhabited them—demand "a universal gold standard. I, for one, will not yield to that demand. I will not help to crucify mankind upon a cross of gold. I will not aid them to press down upon the bleeding brow of labor this crown of thorns." Almost the same thing, but not quite. Bryan's first version was inferior in two ways. It reversed the Gospel chronology: Christ is crowned with thorns, then He is crucified. "And they clothed him with purple, and platted a crown of thorns, and put it on his head. ... And when they had mocked him, they took off the purple from him, and put his own clothes on him, and led him out to crucify him" (Mark 15:17, 20). Bryan in 1894 had also put the lesser torment at the climax: the crown of thorns is derisive and painful, but it is the crucifixion that kills. In Chicago, the ever-tinkering craftsman got the sequence and the drama right.

The man who seldom used gestures now also made two, to galvanizing effect. As he spoke of the crown of thorns, he drew his fingertips down his temples, like trickling blood; then he stepped back and stretched out his arms to mime the cross. Protestants (Bryan was a devout Presbyterian) are supposed to be iconoclasts, worshipping in churches unclut- tered by Catholic statuary. But here was a living Good Friday tableau.

This was the passage that gave his speech instant impact. The cross of gold would appear as a prop in political cartoons and is still the name by which the speech is known. Bryan, however, thought an earlier passage in his speech was better still, and he was right. It was no reworking of an old standby but a paragraph he had written fresh the night before, and it went beyond the money politics of the 1890s to make a point of permanent value. This passage took the form of a response to the progold debaters.

"We say to you that you have made the definition of a business man too limited in its application. The man who is employed for wages is as much a business man as his employer; the attorney in a country town is as much a busi- ness man as the corporation counsel in a great metropolis; the merchant at the cross-roads store is as much a business man as the merchant of New York; the farmer who goes forth in the morning and toils all day, who begins in spring and toils all summer, and who by the application of brain and muscle to the natural resources of the country creates wealth, is as much a business man as the man who goes upon the Board of Trade and bets upon the price of grain; the miners who go down a thousand feet into the earth, or climb two thousand feet upon the cliffs, and bring forth from their hiding places the precious metals to be poured into the channels of trade are as much business men as the few financial magnates who, in a back room, corner the money of the world. We come to speak of this broader class of business men."

The structure of this passage was parallelism, though Bryan shifted his categories halfway through. The small town/big city attorneys and merchants were in the same line of work, different only in scale and location. He might have paired the farmer and the miner with a rancher and a mining engineer, little guys and big guys working on the land and within it, respectively. But then he would have lost his geographic dichotomy, since farmers/ranchers and miners/engineers all worked the same countryside. By introducing urban crop and currency traders, he drew a distinction between producers and profiteers—an old distinction, though always somewhat bogus, for farmers and merchants, large and small, also make bets on future demand for their crops and goods as much as speculators at the wheat pit or the gold exchange.

Bryan's most important parallelism was his first: "the man who is employed for wages is as much a business man as his employer." This was applying the Declaration of

Independence to economics. All economic men are created equal, however much they earn, whether by wages or profits.

This simple statement rebuked socialism, the theory (most developed in Europe but already established in America) of irreconcilable class conflict. Socialist gradualists hoped that the underclass—Bryan's toilers—could overturn their oppressors peacefully, by democratic means. Victor Berger, a German-speaking immigrant from Transylvania, born the same year and month as Bryan, would build a socialist political organization in Milwaukee that, in the new century, would run the city government and send him to Congress (radicals would call him a slowcialist, or a sewer socialist, because he focused on issues like public utilities). Anarchists (revolutionary socialists) posited a violent overthrow of the existing order and hoped to bring it about by promiscuous acts of violence (the president of the United States would be murdered by an anarchist in 1901). Followers of Karl Marx, who had died in 1883, foresaw a more disciplined struggle (led by themselves).

Bryan was also contradicting the wilder flights of his hero Jefferson—and of William Jennings Bryan, class warriors both. Jefferson and the first Republican Party had railed against "the opulent." Bryan and the Democratic Party he hoped to lead invoked burned-out cities and grass-grown streets. But one problem with declaring a class war is the difficulty of drawing the battle lines. Where does virtue end and villainy begin? Jefferson was himself a man of opulent tastes—after serving a diplomatic posting in Paris he brought 288 bottles of wine back home with him—but because his wealth came from owning land and the people who worked it, it was, according to his peculiar calculus, more virtuous than the wealth of Hamilton's investor class. Bryan spoke of the crown of thorns pressing on the brow of labor, but his life experience little prepared him for addressing America's workers, who mostly labored in cities. The Bryan who wrote his favorite paragraph said instead that we are all in business together.

Bryan's credo makes a moral point; therefore, cynics might say, a useless one, for when have avarice and ambition ever paused before morality? But it offers a warning against economic stratification and the terrible arrogance that the very rich, and their hangers-on, can fall prey to. The marketplace—like the Jamestown General Assembly, the free world the Manumission Society wished to broaden, the electorate the Seneca Falls Convention asked to join—is a forum of equals. Some men and women do better than others—they make more money, win elections, see their ideals prevail. One idea that should never prevail in America is that success places them in a different order of being.

After Bryan finished speaking, there was silence. He feared for a moment that he had failed. Then the hall erupted. People who heard the sound compared it to Niagara Falls or artillery. Delegates and spectators laughed and wept, screamed and cursed, embraced, stood on chairs, threw hats, canes, and coats in the air. Silver delegations marched around the hall as the convention's band played "For He's a Jolly Good Fellow," carrying Bryan shoulder-high like a trophy or an idol. The pandemonium lasted half an hour, longer than the words that had set it off. John Peter Altgeld, governor of

Illinois and a supporter of Richard Bland, spoke for everyone when he exclaimed that it was "the greatest speech I have ever listened to."[12]

The convention picked its candidate the next day, July 10. In the nineteenth century, almost all political conventions were multiballot affairs, the tides of momentum that now play out in polls, caucuses, and primaries over weeks and months, then rising and falling on the convention floor. Bryan's tide carried him to victory fairly rapidly, on the fifth ballot. The Populist Party, meeting in St. Louis in mid-July, cross-endorsed him, as he had hoped.

He tried to win the election as he had his nomination, by speaking his way to victory. Traveling by train, he covered eighteen thousand miles, speaking over six hundred times, in halls, on platforms, or at stations wherever the train stopped. For two and a half months he bought his tickets himself, until his cash-strapped party finally provided him a private car, laughably named "The Idler."

The Republicans took the opposite tack, bringing audiences to their candidate. McKinley stayed at home in Canton, Ohio, where 750,000 supporters arrived by train in precisely scheduled delegations, marched to his house, heard him speak from his porch, then marched back to the station, their places taken by the next cohort. The Republicans also deluged the country with over two hundred million pamphlets, the equivalent of fourteen for every voter.

On election day Bryan's Herculean effort won him 6.5 million voters, a million more than any presidential candidate had ever gotten. But McKinley won over 7 million.

Bryan carried twenty-two states in the West and South; McKinley swept the Midwest, the Northeast, and the Electoral College.

One factor that hurt Bryan in the homestretch was a spike in wheat prices, caused by shortages in India, Russia, and Argentina. According to Bryan's theories about the deflationary curse of gold, this was not supposed to happen; the hard-eyed men in the back rooms of the great cities would not permit it. But McKinley had all but predicted it in one of his porch talks. "Free silver will not cure over-production nor under-consumption. . . . Free silver will not remove the competition of Russia, India and [the] Argentine Republic. . . . Free silver will not increase the demand for your wheat, nor make a single new consumer."[13] There was more in heaven and earth than was dreamed of in Bryan's economics. Worldwide gold strikes at the turn of the twentieth century would have a loosening effect on the money supply, further weakening the case for free silver.

Bryan would run for president twice more, in 1900 and 1908, losing again to McKinley (and thus ceding to him the distinction of being assassinated by an anarchist gunman), then to William Howard Taft. He would remain in public life for almost twenty years after he stopped running, as secretary of state and as a Chautauqua speaker, and though he would repeat the Cross of Gold speech for auld lang syne— recordings of it that are available online are of such reminiscent performances—free silver was never again his primary issue.

The Cross of Gold speech gave the wrong answer to an ancillary problem. But it remains noteworthy—not only for its best paragraph but for the myriad responses it and its author elicited. During the 1896 campaign, Bryan was deluged with gifts and mementoes. The most stirring were two bald eagles; the oddest was a fungus in the shape of his profile. Two sets of parents gave their triplets the names William, Jennings, and Bryan.

Bryan also got letters—two thousand a day, rising to three thousand in early November, a quarter million pieces of mail during the course of the campaign. (By contrast, McKinley as president got about a hundred letters a day.) Bryan and his wife threw most of them away—how could they have kept them?—but five thousand pieces survive. Four-fifths of them were from men, the rest from women and children.

"In all times of great peril to the people," wrote D. D. Hatfield, miner, "God has raised up a leader to save them from their errors and lead them . . . to a knowledge of their rights and duties."

"I have felt the pangs of hunger," wrote Willis N. Shaw, railroad brakeman, "and if humanity in the United States were as deeply interested in the welfare of this nation as I am you would be elected by the largest majority that any man ever received for any office. . . . May the God of the widow and the fatherless—the God of the poor and the oppressed—be with you and guide you."

"God has brought you forth," wrote W. B. McCormick, furniture salesman, " . . . to lead the people out of this state of oppression and despondency and into the Canaan of peace and prosperity."[14] Only one correspondent, of those whose letters survive, threatened violence if Bryan lost. The vast majority wrote to cheer him on.

He had acknowledged them as Americans, businessmen, equals. They returned the compliment. They are the equivalents of the Jamestown burgesses, the Zenger trial jurors, the Seneca Falls signers—the ordinary people who accompany the history-makers and make history happen. They are us.

chapter twelve

ARSENAL OF DEMOCRACY FIRESIDE CHAT

"The Great Arsenal of Democracy"

WILLIAM JENNINGS BRYAN WAS TAPPED BY Woodrow Wilson to be secretary of state in 1913. He quit two years later because he believed that Wilson was not doing enough to keep America out of the world war that had engulfed Europe in the summer of 1914. This war, and its sequel, would extend the territory of American liberty.

The reformist impulse, so allied to the religious impulse, embraced the hope that war itself might be done away with. The first woman in Congress, Jeannette Rankin of Montana, elected to the House even before the passage of the Nineteenth Amendment, was among the handful of representatives to vote no when the United States, after many provocations, declared war on Germany in April 1917.

Wilson led America into war, as Bryan had feared, but he hoped that it would be a war to end wars—a hope that was shared by virtually all Americans once peace returned.

Wilson wanted to secure peace by enlisting America in his brainchild, the League of Nations, a permanent assembly of the world's countries. Competing alliances had plunged the world into war; a grand ongoing counsel of all nations would forestall it. The Senate rejected Wilson's vision on the grounds that a strict adherence to the league's covenant might compel America to make war on future aggressors at the league's behest.

Other Americans blamed armaments, and those who made them, for causing wars. If there were fewer guns, they would be less likely to go off. In the early thirties a Senate committee headed by Gerald Nye grilled scions of the houses of Morgan and DuPont on their allegedly bloodstained profits.

Diplomacy offered a less sensational approach to disarmament. In 1921, America proposed that the leading naval powers of the world cut back their fleets and set a ratio of battleship tonnage of five tons for America, five for Britain, and three for Japan (America and Britain had Atlantic and Pacific fleets, while Japan had only the latter, hence the disparity). The Senate accepted this scheme. "The very angels sang in joy," said Sen. Samuel Shortridge when it passed.[1]

Not all men were angels. Great power politics reappeared, driven not by anything so old-fashioned as dynastic ambition but by totalitarian ideologies. Lenin, Trotsky, and

Stalin were too busy terrorizing their own country to lead the worldwide communist revolution they professed to seek, but Mussolini (who seized power in Italy in 1922), Hitler (who followed in Germany in 1933), and the Japanese military (which dominated Japan by 1936) readied their nations for war. By the midthirties, Italy had invaded Abyssinia, Germany had rebuilt its army, and Japan had repudiated the battleship tonnage ratio and established a puppet state in Manchuria.

Franklin D. Roosevelt was elected president in 1932 to deal with the Depression, not these matters. He was a Hudson River Valley aristocrat whose family had been in the New World since the days of Peter Stuyvesant and whose fifth cousin, Theodore, had followed William McKinley in the White House. Like Theodore, Franklin was a man of liberal inclinations; unlike him, he belonged to what was then the more liberal of the two major parties, the Democrats.

Domestic affairs consumed his first years in office. When he spoke of foreign policy, especially in election years, he echoed the American desire for peace. "We are not isolationist," he said in 1936, "except insofar as we seek to isolate ourselves completely from war."[2]

He had, however, a better-than-average background in world affairs for an American politician. One of his lifelong passions was stamp collecting—a child's introduction to geography and history embodied in bright bits of paper. Another, more serious obsession concerned anything to do with ships, particularly the ships of the US Navy. Partly this was in emulation of his famous cousin, who had served McKinley as assistant secretary of the navy from 1897 to

1898; Franklin served Wilson in the same role from 1913 to 1920. The younger Roosevelt dreamed of a fleet with forty-eight battleships, one for every state. He was not shy about using the ships he actually had, either. Unlike Bryan, he thought Wilson was too pacific, feeding Americans "a lot of soft mush about everlasting peace."[3]

America had to hope for everlasting peace, given the shrinkage of its postwar military. Although the navy remained one of the largest on earth, the army, according to Gen. Douglas MacArthur, could fit into Yankee Stadium.

In the summer of 1937, Japan attacked China directly, which got Roosevelt's attention. If "terror and international lawlessness" prevailed "in other parts of the world," he said in a speech in October, "let no one imagine that America will escape." The threat, as he saw it, went beyond conflict *per se* to defiance of the recognized laws of diplomacy and war. "Without a declaration of war, and without warning or justification of any kind, civilians, including vast numbers of women and children, are being ruthlessly murdered with bombs from the air."[4] But when a reporter asked him the next day if he contemplated any new policy to respond to these outrages, Roosevelt answered, "No; just the speech itself."[5]

Roosevelt was a master of mixed signals, crossed signals, and double talk. Nobody, one journalist testified, "showed greater capacity for avoiding a direct answer while giving the questioner a feeling he had been answered."[6] Some questioners felt they had not been answered. Roosevelt "does not follow easily a consecutive chain of thought," one of his own cabinet secretaries confided to his diary. Talking to him "is very much like chasing a vagrant beam of sunshine around a vacant room."[7]

His coyness and misdirection, often amounting to duplicity, stemmed from a need to keep his options open until the last possible moment: choosing forecloses the possibility of different choices. The need to keep his options open arose, in turn, from a need for control: once you choose, others will make their own choices in response. Roosevelt had lost the use of his legs to an attack of polio when he was thirty-nine years old, which no doubt stoked his need to exercise control over himself and his surroundings, but the impulse must have been present in his character years before.

His crabwise approach to rearmament was dictated most decisively by logistics and politics. Fitting the American military to face the threats of a darkening world would take an enormous shift in priorities and production, which could only happen after an equally great shift in popular sentiment. Congress and the voters would not pay for a buildup for which they saw no urgent need. Roosevelt had to plan, build, and convince.

Gradually Roosevelt assembled a competent team. In 1939 he appointed two relatively junior officers, Admiral Harold Stark and General George Marshall, chief of naval operations and chief of staff of the army, respectively. Both men had had early run-ins with him: Marshall disagreeing with one of his more vagrant suggestions during a White House planning session; Stark refusing as long ago as 1914 to let the assistant secretary of the navy take the helm of a destroyer Stark was commanding. In Roosevelt's mind, these encounters had proved their mettle. When Marshall was appointed chief of staff, he warned the president he would say what he thought, "and it would often be unpleasing."[8] Roosevelt was pleased.

In 1940 he put two Republicans in his cabinet. Henry Stimson, his new secretary of war, had served in Republican administrations for decades, most recently in that of Herbert Hoover, the man Roosevelt had replaced in the White House. Frank Knox, the new secretary of the navy, had been the running mate of Roosevelt's opponent in 1936. More important to Roosevelt than their party affiliation was their fighting spirit—both had seen active duty in the world war— and their agreement with his grim diagnosis of the current world situation.

Early in the postwar years, the army and the navy had developed hypothetical war plans in which every conceivable enemy (including Britain) was assigned a different color. The new team adopted rainbow plans, anticipating multicolored threats by multiple enemies. Rainbow 1, the most conservative plan, looked only to defend the Western Hemisphere, which was daunting enough: Iceland, Greenland, and Newfoundland formed a hop, skip, and a jump across the northern Atlantic, while the bulge of western Africa was only eighteen hundred miles from the easternmost tip of South America. Ideas could move even more easily than fleets and troops: Germany and Italy might encourage friendly coups in unstable South American republics. Roosevelt invoked the worries of James Monroe: "for the first time since the Holy Alliance," he told one cabinet meeting, America might be menaced in its own hemisphere, north and south.[9]

Roosevelt also appointed boards to oversee war production. These included executives (the chairman of U.S. Steel, the president of General Motors) and a labor leader (the vice president of the CIO, an alliance of unions) as well as government officials. They had a lot of work to do: new battleships and a new aircraft carrier were on the drawing boards, but the keels had yet to be laid; the aircraft industry had designed a new bomber with a range of two thousand miles, but the US Air Corps (then part of the army) had only seventeen of them.

Meanwhile events were in the saddle, and the dictators rode. Japan conquered northern China and drove inland up the country's rivers. Germany, after annexing several neighbors, invaded Poland in September 1939, igniting a second European world war. In May 1940 Germany struck west; France sued for peace the following month. Germany began bombing Britain in late summer and in September signed a Tripartite Pact with Italy and Japan in which each pledged to aid the others in the event of war with the United States.

In the midst of these storms, Roosevelt sought an unprecedented third term. At that time there was no legal requirement that a president serve only two, but George Washington had done so, a choice made into a custom by four of his near successors (Jefferson, Madison, Monroe, Jackson). The only president to seek a third term had been Ulysses Grant, but his party had dashed his hopes by denying him a third nomination. Roosevelt's campaign was a violation of republican norms, justifiable only (if it was) by the world crisis.

He won handily—a victory he was bound to justify by meeting the world crisis.

In October 1940, before the voters went to the polls, Admiral Stark prepared a twenty-six-page double-spaced memo that blandly described itself as outlining "steps we might take . . . should the United States enter war either alone or with allies."[10] Like all shrewd memo writers, Stark presented four carefully arranged options: barebones (Plan A—hemisphere defense only), two extremes (Plans B and C—all-out war in the Pacific, or in the Pacific and Europe simultaneously), and the option he favored (Plan D—holding the line in the Pacific while helping Britain with a "full national offensive": logistical, monetary, and, ultimately, military).

America had been pursuing a Pacific-forward policy for a century: taking California from Mexico, buying Alaska from Russia, annexing Hawaii, stripping the Philippines and Guam from Spain, sending missionaries to China. Stark instead looked east, identifying Europe as our primary concern and Germany as our most serious enemy. If Britain beat Germany, he had told Knox before he began to write, "we could win everywhere; but if she loses . . . while we might not *lose everywhere*, we might, possibly, not *win anywhere*."[11]

In the military's phonetic alphabet, used for radio and phone messages, the word for *D* was *dog*. Stark showed the Plan Dog memo to Marshall, then gave it to Knox and the president in November.

Roosevelt's response was to take a Caribbean vacation.

He loved being on ships as much as he loved studying them. In early December he boarded the USS *Tuscaloosa*, a navy cruiser, with a handful of male cronies, making a swing around the islands, fishing, drinking, playing cards, and

watching the latest Hollywood movies. It was relaxing—
and stimulating. "Use your imaginations," Roosevelt had
told his subordinates, who were struggling with war plans
and production problems, before leaving them to chase the
sun.[12] Away from Washington, he was able to use his own
imagination.

A bleak missive came to him when the *Tuscaloosa* lay
off Antigua, delivered by seaplane: a letter from Britain's
prime minister, Winston Churchill. The two men shared
certain qualities: each belonged to his country's upper crust
(Churchill's was uppermost: his mother had been a king's
mistress). Each was a naval man, Churchill having been first
lord of the admiralty in the run-up to, and first year of, the
last world war, and then again in 1939–1940. Churchill had
the stronger mind but held the weaker hand. The Royal Air
Force was winning the air war over Britain, but German sub-
marines were bleeding his island nation to death. If shipping
losses continued at current rates, she could hold out for only
six more months. On top of everything else, Britain, which
had been paying for American munitions, was nearly broke.
Churchill begged for ships, planes, and weapons. "We look
to the industrial energy of the Republic."[13]

When Roosevelt returned to Washington in mid-
December, he claimed not to have read a single report for-
warded to him while at sea. He had much to report himself.
In a press conference, he floated the idea of supplying Britain
by loan. "What I am trying to do," he explained, "is to elim-
inate the dollar sign." He compared his scheme to lending
a garden hose to a neighbor whose house was on fire. You
wouldn't charge him fifteen dollars for the use of your hose;

GIVE ME LIBERTY

you'd simply let him borrow it. Blaze over, he would return it or, if it was damaged, replace it. So long as "I get a nice garden hose back," Roosevelt concluded, "I am in pretty good shape."[14] Churchill later called this plan, so plainly described, "the most unsordid act in the whole of human history."[15]

Roosevelt's press conference outlined a policy. He justified it in a long statement to the nation by radio. William Jennings Bryan had spent decades crisscrossing America orating. Radio brought the podium into the living room. The speaker was now at the listener's elbow. Roosevelt, reflecting the new intimacy, called his presidential broadcasts fireside chats.

He had a musical tenor voice. His accent registered as posh—rolling and dropping terminal r's. Partly it was pseudo-British, an affectation of the rich and of actors. Partly it was an authentic legacy of r-dropping New England (his mother belonged to an old Massachusetts clan, and he had been educated at Groton and Harvard). He prepared his chats carefully, talking over martinis with his speechwriters—Sam Rosenman, a New York pol and judge, and Robert Sherwood, a Broadway playwright. He insisted that the written texts he spoke from use dashes rather than commas, as a bolder visual aid, and had them typed on limp paper so that the pages would not rattle when turned.[16] He spoke slowly, the better to be heard through static.

He read this fireside chat, the sixteenth of his presidency, in the White House diplomatic reception room on December 29, 1940, to an audience that included his cabinet, Hollywood stars Clark Gable and Carole Lombard, his mother, and, via the microphones on the desk before him, five hundred radio stations.

232

"My friends," he began: an old salutation. Washington's Farewell Address, in which he told America he would not serve a third term, had begun "Friends and fellow citizens."[17] "This is not a fireside chat on war [*waugh*]. It is a talk on national security." Roosevelt began with an evasion—one he had maintained for years, and which he would maintain throughout this chat and for months afterward: we are not at war, nor are we going to war. The evasion was politic: Americans were not yet ready to hear, or think, the whole truth. It was practical: Marshall had told him that, even rearming full speed ahead, America would not be ready to fight for another eighteen months. But Roosevelt's definition of national security would involve backing one belligerent to the utmost, and what neutral could do that and remain so indefinitely?

He invoked history. He began at the beginning. "Never before since Jamestown and Plymouth Rock"—the twin settlements of Virginia and Massachusetts—"has our American civilization been in such danger as now." He moved up to the preceding century. "One hundred and seventeen years ago, the Monroe Doctrine was conceived by our Government as a measure of defense in the face of a threat against this hemisphere by an alliance in Continental Europe." The Holy Alliance, as he had told his cabinet. But thanks to the Monroe Doctrine, "during the whole of this time the Western Hemisphere has remained free from aggression."

That interval of security was over. "The width of those oceans is not what it was in the days of clipper ships." He gave a geography lesson: Senegal (the western African colony of newly defeated France) was closer to Brazil than Washington,

DC, was to Denver. Former targets, once conquered, could become new staging areas. "Any South American country in Nazi hands would always constitute a jumping-off place for German attacks on any one of the other republics of this hemisphere."

He made pitches to two problematic American ethnic groups (both solidly Democratic). Irish Americans had no love for Britain. But if Britain went down, "could Ireland hold out? Would Irish freedom be permitted as an amazing pet exception in an unfree world?" Mussolini was one of Hitler's allies—a fact Roosevelt framed, with an eye to Italian Americans, as a personal aberration. "Even the people of Italy have been forced to become accomplices of the Nazis, but . . . they do not know how soon they will be embraced to death by their allies."

He turned to consider "evil forces." Some were "already within our gates." This skirted demagogy, branding anyone who disagreed with him as a tool, unwitting or witting, of dictators. He had in mind a witting tool, Charles Lindbergh, heroic pilot and eloquent opponent of war, who had toured Nazi Germany and been mesmerized by its seeming efficiency. Perhaps, Lindbergh believed, it and not America, with its partisanship and inane squabbles, was the wave of the future.

There was no demagogy, only description, in his metaphors for Germany, Italy, and Japan. "No man can tame a tiger into a kitten by stroking it. . . . There can be no reasoning with an incendiary bomb."

Just past the halfway point, he came close to telling the full truth about America's situation and his intentions. "If we are to be completely honest with ourselves, we must admit that there is risk in any course we may take." So national security might indeed entail war. He then backed away from what he had almost said. "The course that I advocate"—arming Britain—"involves the least risk." The British "do not ask us to do their fighting." Instead, with our help, they would do our fighting for us—"for their liberty and for our security." He threw in a flourish as colloquial as the garden hose. "You can, therefore, nail"—he repeated it—"nail any talk about sending armies to Europe as deliberate untruth."

He donned the protective garments of expertise. Aiding Britain "is not a matter of sentiment. . . . It is a matter of realistic, practical military policy, based on the advice of our military experts." They know what they are talking about; you should agree with them.

Yet his conclusion, and the sentence that gave the talk its name, circled back to honesty—and to sentiment. "We must be the great arsenal of democracy." As with many famous phrases, there was a fight over paternity. Rosenman later said that it had been coined by Jean Monnet, a French business-man, who had spoken it to Justice Felix Frankfurter. Frank-furter asked him not to repeat it so that Roosevelt could use it, as if new, himself. Sherwood claimed that another Roosevelt advisor, Harry Hopkins, had seen it in a newspaper article.[18]

Whoever coined it, the phrase was honest—for an arsenal is not a bank making loans, or a convoy carrying food, but a repository of weapons of war. If we were the arsenal of democracy, we were entering the war, whether we sent armies to Europe or not.

The phrase was laden with sentiment of the deepest kind, because it defined the war as being about more than aggression or the threat of it. It was about defending a system of life. The enemy stood for tyranny. "The shootings and the chains and the concentration camps are not simply transient tools but the very altars of modern dictatorships." Their means were their ends. In their world "there is no liberty, no religion, no hope." Roosevelt was a customary Christian—he was a vestryman of his local Episcopalian church, and he and Churchill would worship together when they first met on the deck of a battleship off Newfoundland—but he always included religion whenever he listed essential liberties. He was now asking America to defend liberty against a menace from Europe.

In a discussion of war production, he invoked the spirit of Bryan. He wanted there to be no strikes derailing assembly lines, but at the same time he wanted to assure labor that it would not be exploited. "The worker possesses the same human dignity and is entitled to the same security of position as the engineer or the manager or the owner. For the worker provides the human power that turns out the destroyers, and the planes, and the tanks." Unlike Bryan, Roosevelt had been helping labor unions (and been helped by them, at the polls) for years. Here he presented the equality of economic man in its purest form.

He ended with an upbeat throwaway. In his last meeting with his speechwriters, hours before he went on the air, they had asked him to add something optimistic. He added this: "I believe that the Axis powers are not going to win this war. I base that belief on the latest and best of information."

Sheer bluff; Stark and Marshall, Knox and Stimson, had told him nothing of the kind. In it went anyway.

Roosevelt had not asked Americans to defend liberty everywhere. He said nothing about liberty in Latin American countries, nominally democratic, which actually weren't (Argentina and Brazil had been racked by coups; Mexico was a one-party state); nothing about liberty in colonial empires, which he disliked (rather, he included the British Empire in his praise of Britain); nothing about liberty in the Soviet Union, at that moment an ally of Germany's, though soon to become a victim. He called on Americans to defend the liberty of America, of its neighbors and nearby oceans—and of the European countries that were fighting to roll the dictatorships back.

President Monroe had said that we cherished "sentiments the most friendly" to liberty on both sides of the Atlantic, though we would defend it only on ours, where we could. President Roosevelt now said that, the Atlantic having shrunk, we would defend it in western Europe too.

A Gallup poll taken shortly after the chat showed over two-thirds of Americans agreeing that "our country's future safety depends on England winning this war."[19] One quarter disagreed. This result was driven, in part, by intense and sympathetic coverage of the pounding Britain was taking in the air war; Germany could not control the skies, but it had rained destruction on the ground, which Americans saw in newsreels and wire photos.

Gallant resistance can inspire. But terror can also intimidate. The president's rhetoric helped shape the reactions of his listeners sitting by their radiators (if not their firesides).

America kept up the policy of no war/war for a year. Hitler labored to avoid provoking America, forbidding his naval forces in the Atlantic to fire at American ships, even in self-defense. In the end, it was Japan that tripped the wire, bombing the Pacific fleet on December 7, 1941, as it lay at anchor in Pearl Harbor. Roosevelt and his team had expected a Japanese attack but thought it would fall on Singapore and the oil-rich Dutch East Indies (the Japanese struck there too, of course). Jeannette Rankin, reelected to the House in 1940, voted once more against going to war, this time alone; afterward she had to be escorted to her office by a protective police guard. Germany and Italy fulfilled their treaty obligations by declaring war on us. America would fight a two-hemisphere war after all, but it still proceeded along the lines of Plan Dog, with Germany as the primary target.

When Churchill learned of Pearl Harbor, he was startled, determined—and jubilant. He knew instantly, he wrote in his war memoirs, that the United States would now be "in the war, up to the neck, and in to the death. So we had won after all! . . . Hitler's fate was sealed. Mussolini's fate was sealed. As for the Japanese, they would be ground to powder." He recalled something a fellow politician had told him years before. "The United States is like 'a gigantic boiler. Once the fire is lighted under it, there is no limit to the power it can generate' . . . I went to bed and slept the sleep of the saved and thankful."[20]

On the enemy side, Admiral Isoruku Yamamoto, commander in chief of Japan's Combined Fleet, shared Churchill's view of American industrial might. In the 1920s he had spent several years in the United States as a student and a military attaché, and he would tell his colleagues that "anyone who has seen the auto factories in Detroit and the oil fields in Texas knows that Japan lacks the national power for a naval race with America."[21] He placed his hopes, therefore, on a quick knockout blow.

Churchill and Yamamoto—and Roosevelt's planners and producers—were right. Free men cannot fight with bare hands. America's industrial heft virtually guaranteed victory (though without the administration's years of preparation, the struggle would have been far longer).

But materiel alone never wins wars. Men have to work and fight with a will, for a reason. Roosevelt had given one in his sixteenth fireside chat.

chapter thirteen

TEAR DOWN THIS WALL SPEECH

"Across Europe, This Wall Will Fall"

PLAN DOG IDENTIFIED GERMANY AS THE PRIMARY threat to America and to liberty (ours, everyone's) in World War II—rightly. Nazism's combination of science and superstition made that country the most powerful and most alluring of our enemies. Even though Japan had first attacked us, on our soil, our primary priority remained Germany's destruction. In May 1945, overwhelmed by Soviet, American, and British armies, Germany finally surrendered. Berlin would become the symbol of the next, cold world war.

Franklin Roosevelt had died in April 1945, after being elected to a fourth term. Like Wilson before him, he hoped his war would lead to a peaceful world. A week after his arsenal of democracy fireside chat, he had described in a State of the Union address the worldwide order that he hoped would prevail once the dictators were defeated. He called for "a worldwide reduction of armaments to such a point and in such a thorough fashion that no nation will be in a position to commit an act of physical aggression against any neighbor—anywhere in the world."[1]

His hope, like Wilson's, was disappointed. Not all the aggressors had been on the same side. The Soviet Union—Hitler's jackal, then his prey—found itself, after gigantic losses and immense efforts, the conqueror of half of Europe. Roosevelt had hoped to charm Stalin, as he had American voters and Winston Churchill. "You know," he told one cabinet secretary, "I really think the Russians will go along with me about having no spheres of influence."[2] Churchill, more realistic or more desperate, offered Stalin a frank deal—a Soviet sphere of influence encompassing most of the Balkans, with Britain retaining the upper hand in Greece. Churchill himself called his proposal "rather cynical."[3] Since the arrangement tracked the prospective course of Soviet armies, Stalin accepted it.

Hitler, Mussolini, and the Japanese leaders had been bold, even to rashness. The Soviets showed a patient indefatigableness. They developed the atomic bomb and the hydrogen bomb shortly after America did. They sponsored foreign clients following, or at least espousing, Communist doctrine; the first fifteen postwar years saw Communist revolutions in China, Vietnam, and Cuba. In countries the Soviets could not control, they made use of spies and sympathizers; in the United States they managed to penetrate the atomic bomb program, the Roosevelt administration, and Hollywood.

The Cold War was cold only in comparison with the hecatombs of World Wars I and II; local wars and revolutions, pro- and anti-Communist pogroms, flared across the globe. In the midst of this strife, Berlin remained a static point: stable because opposing forces had met, balanced, and locked there.

Postwar Germany had been divided into four zones of occupation, each assigned to one of the victors—the Soviet Union, Britain, France, and America. The former capital was similarly split, although it was located in the heart of the Soviet zone, the future East Germany. Tension flickered over these divisions like lightning. In 1948 the Soviets blocked rail and truck traffic into West Berlin; America and its allies supplied the city from the air. In 1961 the Communist East German government—successor rulers of the former Soviet zone—stanched a steady drain of refugees to the west by sealing East Berlin with a wall—twenty-seven miles of concrete through the middle of the city, overseen by watchtowers and backed by a cleared death-strip in which any unauthorized person was shot. In 1963 President Kennedy gave a censorious speech on the wall's western side: "Freedom has many difficulties and democracy is not perfect, but we have never had to put a wall up to keep our people in. . . . Two thousand years ago the proudest boast was *civis Romanus sum* [I am a Roman citizen]. Today, in the world of freedom, the proudest boast is *Ich bin ein Berliner* [I am a Berliner]."[4] The president's German tag became famous. Yet the city's divisions remained unchanged.

Berlin was simultaneously an ongoing experiment in comparative political systems and a frozen locker of Cold War policies. The free west flourished—pleasure boats dotted its small waterways—while the east was a gray barracks. In

Spandau Prison, Rudolf Hess, the last high-ranking Nazi war criminal, lived out his life sentence under a rotating, four-power guard. The site of the former British embassy, on the Wilhelmstrasse, was now a vacant lot in East Berlin. The British disdained to rebuild, as a sign of their disapproval of East Germany, but, because embassies have extraterritorial status, the East Germans could not touch the site without provoking an international incident. So it sat.

Postwar agreements, still honored, allowed the occupying powers to send military personnel into each other's zones. A passage through the wall on the Friedrichstrasse, known as Checkpoint Charlie (*Charlie* equals *C* in the military phonetic alphabet), was the scene of an ongoing Cold War ballet. When an American vehicle arrived at the checkpoint, it stopped, though it was not obliged to. East German soldiers paraded around it without boarding; members of the American military removed their name tags, since the East Germans had no right to know who they were. The inspection, which was unauthorized, was unacknowledged and frustrated by the inspected. Dance over, the vehicle moved on.[5]

As the Berlin Wall went up, Ronald Reagan was making the transition from entertainment to politics. Like William Jennings Bryan, he had been born in a small town in Illinois. A warm baritone voice, a winning personality, and good looks took him from college plays, to radio sportscasting, to Hollywood. In the mid-1950s, after his career as a star faded, he shifted to television and speaking, hosting a show sponsored by General Electric and acting as a corporate spokesman.

He had been interested in politics all along. He was a Roosevelt fan, doing an excellent impression of him. In

Hollywood he first encountered Communists, who maneuvered to control actors' civic groups. Olivia de Havilland, one of his fellow stars, recalled their tactics. If a Communist-backed motion at a meeting faltered, "Dalton Trumbo, a brilliant man, got up and spoke absolute nonsense to delay the vote, like Jimmy Stewart in *Mr. Smith Goes to Washington*." Once most of the people in attendance had drifted away, "the radicals untabled the motion and passed it, one-two-three."[6] Communists also sought to control the labor unions of those who worked on movie lots. Reagan, a leader in the Screen Actors Guild, opposed their efforts and received in return a phoned threat that his face would be fixed (i.e., with acid). His studio issued him a revolver and a personal guard.

Reagan read and was impressed by *Witness*, the bestselling memoir of Whitaker Chambers, journalist and former Soviet spy. One of the turning points of the book comes as Chambers watches his baby daughter in a high chair. "My eye came to rest on the delicate convolutions of her ear— those intricate, perfect ears. The thought passed through my mind: 'No, those ears were not created by any chance coming together of atoms in nature (the Communist view). They could have been created only by immense design.'"[7] Reagan could quote the passage years later, from memory.[8]

Away from the big screen he wrote his own material. As his most recent biographer put it, "Colleagues at every phase of his life would recall [him] immersed in his own private world with just a yellow tablet and fountain pen, undisturbed by his surroundings, writing umpteen drafts of speeches, radio broadcasts, and letters in longhand, even at times when others were hired to do his bidding."[9]

His work as a corporate pitchman, speaking in plant after plant, reimmersed him in ordinary life. "We saturated him in Middle America" was how one of his handlers put it.[10] When his anecdotes of Hollywood wore thin, he sensed and responded to the political concerns of his audiences.

In 1964 Reagan was recruited to give a televised fund-raising appeal for the floundering presidential campaign of Republican Barry Goldwater. Goldwater sank, but Reagan was a hit. He ran for office himself, in 1966 and 1970, winning two terms as governor of California.

The seventies saw the high-water mark of Soviet ambitions. America lost the Vietnam War—the longest we had fought from the American Revolution on; Cuban troops installed Communist regimes across Africa; the Soviet Union targeted western Europe with intermediate-range nuclear missiles and invaded Afghanistan. Republican and Democratic administrations alike seemed unable to stay the tide, much less reverse it.

Reagan sought the Republican presidential nomination in 1976, losing narrowly. Months later, he met with Richard Allen, a foreign policy expert eager to work for him on his second run for the job. "My idea of American policy toward the Soviet Union is simple, and some would say simplistic," Reagan told him. "It is this: We win and they lose. What do you think of that?"[11]

Reagan's victories in the 1980 and 1984 presidential elections gave him the chance to implement his policy. Far from being simple, it was a full-court press, as complex as Plan Dog. He called simultaneously for a defensive missile shield and disarmament talks. The first would outpace the technological capabilities of the Soviet Union; the second would give it a gracious line of retreat. He chipped away at recent Soviet gains by supporting anti-Communist insurgencies around the world and even undermined a very old acquisition by covertly supporting a free labor movement in Poland.

In early 1985 there was a jog, or a possible blink, in the Communist world. After a string of ailing gerontocrats, the Communist Party of the Soviet Union chose as its general secretary fifty-four-year-old Mikhail Gorbachev. Gorbachev's watchwords, *perestroika* (restructuring) and *glasnost* (openness), described modifications he wished to make in the Soviet status quo. Did they represent actual reforms or cosmetic changes only? Reagan and Gorbachev met in Iceland in 1986 to try to work out a nuclear weapons deal; they failed, but talks continued.

In June 1987 Reagan stopped in Berlin on the way home from an economic summit meeting in Venice. He had been to Berlin once before, in 1982, a visit that brought out thousands of left-wing protesters. (The international Left at that time regularly did the Soviet Union's bidding.) Berlin was marking its 750th anniversary in 1987; Reagan expected this occasion to be more peaceful and more productive.

He spoke before the Brandenburg Gate, a triumphal arch built by the Prussian monarchy at the end of the eighteenth century, which had served as a witness to the ups and downs of German history ever since. The charioteer at its summit was stolen by Napoleon and restored after his fall. The Nazis used the gate for parades and ceremonies. The Berlin Wall consigned it to the death-strip on the eastern side. Reagan stood on a podium, with his back to the gate and the barrier. He was seventy-six years old, the oldest man to serve in the White House; his voice had grown a bit husky, his body language a bit stiff. But he spoke with confidence, born of talent, practice, and conviction.

However much Reagan liked writing, the volume of a modern president's words is too great even for a Balzac to generate. Reagan's speechwriters were mostly young, conservative activists. The head of their team was Anthony Dolan, then thirty-eight; the Berlin speech itself was assigned to Peter Robinson, who had just turned thirty. But even as they churned out words for their boss, they channeled Reagan's voice. "His policies were plain," Robinson wrote, explaining the process. "He had been articulating them for decades—until he became President he wrote most of his material himself. [We] were never attempting to fabricate an image, just to produce work that measured up to the standard Reagan himself" had set. He had approved the draft of the Berlin speech in a meeting with his speechwriters in May.

The obvious model for any president speaking in Berlin was Kennedy's 1963 speech. The most famous line in it had been his German-language statement of identification. Reagan now used several German phrases himself: a tribute to Berlin's attractiveness lifted from a popular song, the local equivalent of "I Left My Heart in San Francisco," *Ich hab' noch einen koffer in Berlin* (I always have a suitcase in Berlin); and a backhanded tribute to the Berlin temperament, *Berliner herz, Berliner humor, ja, und Berliner schnauze* (Berlin heart, Berlin humor, yes, and Berlin snout, which equated to sass, rudeness, wiseass-ness). These Berlitz phrase-book bits were affectionate, corny, not stirring. Stirring would come later.

Reagan began with a discussion of Berlin as a symbol of the Cold War. "Behind me stands a wall . . . part of a vast system of barriers that divides the entire continent of Europe. From the Baltic, south, those barriers cut across Germany in a gash of barbed wire, concrete, dog runs, and guard towers. Farther south, there may be no visible, no obvious wall. But there remain armed guards and checkpoints all the same—still a restriction on the right to travel, still an instrument to impose upon ordinary men and women the will of a totalitarian state. Yet it is here in Berlin where the wall emerges most clearly."

The Berlin Wall was not a countryside frontier like Hadrian's Wall or the Great Wall of China. It was an antistreet in the heart of a city.

Its perverse closeness to ordinary urban life highlighted the deaths visited on those who tried to cross it. By the time Reagan spoke, 137 people had been shot, drowned, or otherwise killed making the attempt—from Ida Siekmann, a fifty-eight-year-old woman who had jumped over it to her death in August 1961, to Lutz Schmidt, a twenty-four-year-old man who had been shot helping a friend clamber across it in February 1987. This number of murders would have been a slow day's work in the Cambodian killing fields or the Ukrainian Holodomor, to say nothing of the Nazi extermination camps. But compiling such a tally in a great city—not by criminals but by officers of the state; not against bandits, rioters, or arsonists but against ordinary people trying to move a few miles or a few blocks—made each death at the wall peculiarly conspicuous and revolting.

Reagan quoted Richard von Weizsacker, president of West Germany, on the German question—when, if ever, the split country would be reunited: "The German question is open as long as the Brandenburg Gate is closed." Reagan went on: "As long . . . as this scar of a wall is permitted to stand, it is not the German question alone that remains open, but the question of freedom for all mankind."

This was darkly stirring. But Reagan had always been best, whether as an actor or a politician, as the good guy: recalling, perhaps, his upbeat youthful idol Roosevelt; reflecting certainly his own optimistic nature. So he pivoted. "Yet I do not come here to lament. For I find in Berlin a message of hope . . . a message of triumph."

Reagan surveyed the postwar world of western Europe and Japan. Its leaders, helped by America, "understood the practical importance of liberty—that just as truth can flourish only when the journalist is given freedom of speech, so prosperity can come about only when the farmer and the businessman enjoy economic freedom." West Germany's leaders "reduced tariffs, expanded free trade, lowered taxes. From 1950 to 1960 alone, the standard of living in West Germany and Berlin doubled." This was the free marketeer's version of Bryan's and Roosevelt's paeans to economic man: respect the farmer and the businessman as much as the magnate; respect them by giving them the opportunity to make their way.

Reagan zoomed in on Berlin. "Where four decades ago there was rubble, today in West Berlin there is the greatest industrial output of any city in Germany—busy office blocks, fine homes and apartments, proud avenues. . . . Where a city's culture seemed to have been destroyed"—first by Nazism, then by bombs—"today there are two great universities, orchestras and an opera, countless theaters, and museums. Where there was want, today there's abundance."

Though he continued to face ahead, his text turned behind him, to the east, beyond the wall. "In the Communist world, we see failure, technological backwardness, declining standards of health, even want of the most basic kind—too little food."

He addressed his opposite number, Mikhail Gorbachev. "And now the Soviets themselves may, in a limited way, be coming to understand the importance of freedom. We hear much from Moscow about a new policy of reform and openness. . . . Are these the beginnings of profound changes in the Soviet States? Or are they token gestures, intended . . . to strengthen the Soviet system without changing it?"

Reagan proposed a test. "There is one sign the Soviets can make that would advance dramatically the cause of freedom and peace."

His speech was only half done, but now came the intended climax, the rhetorical shot meant to be heard round the world's newscasts. Peter Robinson had first heard the prototype of the coming lines back in April, when he visited Berlin with the presidential advance team, sent ahead to scout out venues. (Poor Lincoln, training into Gettysburg, cold). Robinson had dinner with Berliners, who talked about the wall, the looming presence in their lives. "My sister lives twenty miles in that direction," said one. "I haven't seen her in more than two decades." Another described a guard tower he passed every morning on his way to work, and its attendant soldier. "That soldier and I speak the same language. . . . But one of us is a zookeeper and the other is an animal." The hostess was most vehement. "If this man Gorbachev is serious with his talk of *glasnost* and *perestroika* he can prove it. He can get rid of this wall."[12]

Robinson wrung the line through many versions: "bring down this wall," "take down this wall." Once he went full Kennedy: "*Herr Gorbachev, Machen Sie dieses Tor auf.*" "What did you do that for?" Dolan, the supervisor of all his drafts, asked. Robinson explained that since the crowd would be German, Reagan should give his big line in German. "When you're writing for the president of the United States," Dolan replied, "give him his big line in English."[13]

At the speechwriters' May meeting with Reagan, the president had singled out "that passage about tearing down the wall. That wall has to come down. That's what I'd like to say" to any East Germans who might be able to pick up his words via radio.[14]

The State Department and the National Security Council lobbied against the line as too confrontational, too insulting to Gorbachev, with whom there were hopes of progress on arms control, and submitted their own, more anodyne versions. Their objections went all the way to Reagan at least twice, the last time on the very morning of the day he was to speak, and he rebuffed them every time. In his limousine on the way to the Brandenburg Gate, Reagan told a senior aide he would deliver the line as written. "The boys at State are going to kill me, but it's the right thing to do."[15]

"General Secretary Gorbachev," Reagan said in his speech, "if you seek peace, if you seek prosperity for the

Soviet Union and Eastern Europe, if you seek liberalization: Come here to this gate! Mr. Gorbachev, open this gate! Mr. Gorbachev, tear down this wall!"

Reagan was not the first American to hope that the wall would fall. Kennedy in 1963 had looked forward "to that day when this city will be joined as one . . . in a peaceful and hopeful globe."[16] The advisors Reagan referred to as "the boys at State" had written in one of their alternative drafts, "One day, this ugly wall will disappear."[17] But these hopes were idealized, their timelines unspecific. Reagan took Gorbachev's own catchwords and challenged him to live up to them. Walls do not fall on their own (parts of Hadrian's are still standing after nineteen hundred years). What men build, men must dismantle. Reagan was inviting Gorbachev to do the job.

He went on to survey the ongoing arms control talks. "But," he said, "we must remember a crucial fact: East and West do not mistrust each other because we are armed; we are armed because we mistrust each other. And our differences are not about weapons but about liberty." Tyrants yearn to suppress it; free men will fight to defend it, if necessary.

He told an anecdote about eastern (Communist) tyranny. "The totalitarian world finds even symbols of love and worship an affront." In the sixties the East Germans built a sky-high television tower (*Fernsehturm*) in their half of Berlin—a twelve-hundred-foot-tall needle with a metallic spherical visitors' platform halfway up. "Ever since," Reagan said, "the authorities have been working to correct what they view as the tower's one major flaw, treating the glass sphere . . . with paints and chemicals." The flaw? "When the Sun strikes that sphere . . . the light makes the sign of the cross." *Berliner schnauze* called the effect "Pope's revenge."[18]

Reagan's churchgoing was genial and undogmatic. In this paragraph, there is not a Bible verse to be found; what would William Jennings Bryan or the Flushing remonstrators have thought? But like Roosevelt before him, Reagan was careful to keep God in his sights. Even in Berlin, he concluded, "symbols of worship cannot be suppressed."

His speech ended with a prediction. "Across Europe, this wall will fall. For it cannot withstand faith; it cannot withstand truth. The wall cannot withstand freedom." This was almost true. Walls cannot withstand free men, if they are resolved to remove them.

When Reagan left the White House at the end of his second term in January 1989, the wall still stood; three more people were yet to die trying to cross it—Ingolf Diederichs jumping from a train, Chris Gueffroy shot, Winfried Freudenberg killed in a balloon crash. Mr. Gorbachev never came to tear it down. But in the summer of 1989, he signaled that he would allow it to be destroyed.

Three times the people of Eastern Europe had risen against their Soviet-imposed governments—in East Germany in 1953, Hungary in 1956, Czechoslovakia in 1968—only to be suppressed by Soviet troops. In 1981 the Polish army itself had repressed Poland's Free Labor Movement (which was why the Reagan administration had needed to help the movement covertly). In July 1989, six months after Reagan left office, in a speech in France, Gorbachev renounced that option: "Any interference in domestic affairs and any attempts to restrict the sovereignty of states—friends, allies or any others—are inadmissible."[19]

But the Communist order in Eastern Europe was already crumbling. The Polish government had agreed in April to hold free elections. In May Hungary dismantled its border fence with Austria, and thousands of East Germans and Czechs streamed through the gap. In October Erich Honecker, who had built the Berlin Wall in the first place, was deposed as general secretary of the East German Communist Party; the following month, Berliners from both sides of the wall tore it down with chisels and hammers, as guards, suddenly without orders, stood by. In September 1990 former president Reagan returned to Berlin, where he did a photo-op, whacking with a hammer at a still-standing segment.

What effect had Reagan's words had on its destruction? None, according to his otherwise perceptive biographer: "[The wall] had 'fallen' in November 1989, not as a result of Reagan's plea, as some believe. . . . It was the German people themselves who took up sledgehammers and pickaxes to demolish the ugly scar."[20] This is blinkered. Reagan had envisioned victory over the Soviet Union for a decade. He pursued it with weapons, negotiations, little wars, secret ops, and words. His words at the Brandenburg Gate had told the subject peoples of Eastern Europe that their masters were hesitating and that America was on their side. Superpower negotiations would not distract us from the most important thing, which was liberty, including theirs. On Reagan's 1990 trip to Berlin, Sabine Bergmann-Pohl, the last head of the East German government, told him, "Mr. President, we have much to thank you for."[21] Sometimes eyewitnesses know what they have seen.

Reagan's peroration in 1987 had spoken only of "this wall . . . across Europe"—a prudent specification. As Eastern European tyrannies trembled in 1989, the government of Communist China seemed threatened by massive student demonstrations in Beijing. It responded by calling in the army and massacring the demonstrators—fewer than three hundred of them, according to Chinese officials; twenty-seven hundred, according to the Chinese Red Cross; ten thousand, according to a secret cable by the British ambassador.[22] No walls fell there.

Reagan did what he could, which was what he had planned to do. Roosevelt had extended the zone of our liberty to embattled Britain, aiding it as an arsenal, then as an ally. Reagan extended it to Eastern Europe, enough to undermine its Soviet masters.

In November 1990, when the two Germanys were reunited, I went to celebrate at a party at the German consulate (there were no geographical prefixes now) in New York City. All the guests were given souvenir chips of the wall, embedded in Lucite cubes, with a silhouette of the Brandenburg Gate on one face. My cube is on my desk as I write this.

CONCLUSION

THESE ARE THE DOCUMENTS THAT MADE THIS A country of liberty. A country where men and women, of all backgrounds, worship and think, write and speak, vote and aspire to office. A country that believes in rights that cannot be unmade because they were never made—only found to be aspects of our natures, put there by God. A country that is the partisan—sometimes active, always tacit—of liberty in the world.

The General Assembly of Jamestown set a precedent of elected representatives voting equally on matters of public importance. The Flushing Remonstrance declared religious liberty to be a matter of supreme importance. The trial of John Peter Zenger secured the freedom to publish even mockery of those who rule us, elected or not.

The Declaration of Independence set liberty, ordained by our Creator and inseparable from our equality, in black and white, at the top of our national birth certificate. The Constitution, among many other things, secured equality by forbidding kings and nobles and refusing to acknowledge slavery.

Glaring omissions had to be filled. The worst was slavery; silence was not enough. The New-York Manumission Society worked for the liberation of "our brethren." The Seneca Falls Declaration called for the vote to be given to our sisters.

The nineteenth century and the turn of the next saw restatements and iterations: we really mean it. In the midst of our worst tragedy, as grotesque as it was bloody, the Gettysburg Address embraced both Declaration of Independence and Constitution: we are better than this; we will prevail. The best lines of the Cross of Gold speech declared that no amount of money should create a belief in human inequality; Liberty Enlightening the World told all the world that came here that they were coming to a land of liberty.

What about the world that stays where it is but nevertheless concerns us? The Monroe Doctrine asserted that there should be no kings in this hemisphere; the "Arsenal of Democracy" fireside chat that there should be no Nazis in Britain; the "Tear Down This Wall" speech that Communists should not forever rule the heart of Europe. These were bold and definite statements, backed, as we became stronger, by years of planning and strenuous follow-through.

There could be a different set of thirteen documents. When twentieth-century historian Clinton Rossiter wrote about the Constitutional Convention, he devised as a thought experiment an alternate slate of delegates—different men from every state, but the same number from each, who could have done the job equally well. He thought

America in 1787 could have fielded a B team as well as an A team, and so it can, looking over its history, with liberty documents. (A few—the Declaration of Independence, the Gettysburg Address—would probably have to be on any list, just as Rossiter acknowledged that, of the actual delegates to the Constitutional Convention, George Washington and Benjamin Franklin were unique and irreplaceable.) That is a quality of a nation devoted to liberty—it declares itself, over and over. If I have omitted a favorite—where is the Mayflower Compact, "What to the Slave Is the Fourth of July?," the *Federalist Papers*, or "I Have a Dream"—it is there, in the wings, with brothers and sisters. More, we may hope, will come, repeatedly.

We may hope—but we cannot rest in the hope. Misunderstanding is always an option. The ignorant, the careless, the actively malicious are always with us. They may be us, if we are not careful. Maybe slavery was a positive good; maybe liberty, under the conditions of neoliberalism, is slavery. Maybe America is a collection of unmixable and mutually incomprehensible races; people of color have been held down long enough, time for them to switch places. Or maybe affirmative action has disadvantaged working-class whites, and it is time for them to push back. Or maybe race is a social construct, but so is truth; all truth claims are masks for power, so we should grab our own. Or maybe the system basically works (it must, since it has made us rich and powerful), so let us buy off whoever is buyable, or whoever we like, and not rock the boat by insisting on definitions. There are a million seductive exits from the highway of liberty (liberty itself, ironically, allows them).

A former president had an important conversation about liberty in the late nineteenth century. After serving two terms, Ulysses Grant took a world tour; a reporter from the *New York Herald*, John Russell Young, accompanied him and recorded his meetings and conversations. In the summer of 1878, he visited Berlin, where an international congress was meeting to settle frontiers in the Balkans (its arrangements would last thirty some years, a little less than Stalin's and Churchill's). While there, he met Prince Otto von Bismarck, the statesman who had united modern Germany only seven years earlier.

Here were two great nationalists of the modern era—one who had beaten the armies of secession in the world's largest republic and one who had, through shrewdness and carefully chosen wars against neighbors, forged a collection of kingdoms and statelets into an empire. The American came to Bismarck's palace on foot, tossing away a cigar before approaching the door. Bismarck, who had never fired a shot in battle, was in uniform; Grant, who had led thousands of men to their deaths, wore a suit.

Bismarck spoke English, well but a bit haltingly; when at a loss for words, wrote Young, he "seeks refuge in French."

Their talk moved, as conversation between strangers must, from the news to scattered points of contact. Bismarck uttered a few bland bulletins about the international congress—"I wish it were over, for Berlin is warm and I want to leave it." Grant asked after the emperor, Wilhelm I; Bismarck asked after an American officer he had met. Guest and host had a meeting of minds on the subject of assassins. Only a last-minute change of plan had kept Grant from being in

Lincoln's box at Ford's Theater the night he was murdered, and Bismarck himself had been shot at on two occasions.

"All you can do with such people," said Grant, "is to kill them."

"Precisely so," answered Bismarck.

Then their minds politely, but dramatically, diverged. The subject was the Civil War.

"What always seemed so sad to me about your last great war," Bismarck began, "was that you were fighting your own people. That is always so terrible in wars, so very hard."

"But it had to be done," said Grant.

"Yes, you had to save the Union just as we had to save Germany." Bismarck's wars of unification had involved the defeat and dissolution of several German states, some dating to the Middle Ages, holdouts against the new order; the countries that accepted it were allowed to maintain a shadowy pretend existence, like ghost territories scattered across the new German map. Bismarck assumed that Grant, and America, had been engaged in a similar process of consolidation.

"Not only save the Union," Grant corrected him, "but destroy slavery."

Bismarck tried to assimilate this new idea. "I suppose, however, the Union was the real sentiment, the dominant sentiment." Liberty is fine, but nationalism is what counts.

"In the beginning, yes," Grant agreed. "But as soon as slavery fired upon the flag, it was felt, we all felt, even those who did not object to slaves, that slavery must be destroyed." Grant was compressing events here: the idea that the nation—America—had to end slavery to save itself had taken a few years to sink in. The peace party in the North never accepted it. But the Lincoln administration did, and it won reelection with that goal in view and followed through on its intention.

Grant finished. "We felt that it was a stain to the Union that men should be bought and sold like cattle." A union in which denial of liberty was a permanent feature, not a stain to be deplored, contained, or eradicated, was not a union worth saving. It would not be America.

Bismarck was half right. Nationalism, including national unity, is the organizing principle of the modern world.

But Grant was entirely right. American nationalism embodies the principle of liberty. Without that, it is nothing. Without that, we are a more populous Canada or an efficient Mexico. Grant was not as eloquent as Lincoln at Gettysburg, but he had spoken for a new birth of freedom, soldier's version, all the same.

Bismarck ended the conversation graciously. "It was a long war, and a great work well done—and I suppose it means a long peace."

"I believe so," said Grant.[1]

It was, for black Americans, a long, bad peace. By 1878, despite Grant's best efforts, the federal government, no longer supported by voters weary of futility and expense, had given up trying to maintain the rights of freedmen. It would take decades to claw them back.

Liberty is never easy. You have to know what it is, believe that it is essential, and watch over and defend it. May these documents, and the men and women who wrote and endorsed them—settlers, villagers, jurors, farmers, advisors, speechwriters, politicians, statesmen—be an example for us.

ACKNOWLEDGMENTS

I would like to thank Susan Dunn and Nicole Seary for their invaluable assistance; my publisher, Lara Heimert; my editor, Roger Labrie; and my friend and agent for twenty-five years, Michael Carlisle.

My wife and fellow author, Jeanne Safer, gave me the idea for this book, heard every word, and believed in it all along.

BIBLIOGRAPHY

Adams, John Quincy. *The Diaries of John Quincy Adams*. Edited by David Waldstreicher. New York: Library of America, 2017.

————. *The Diary of John Quincy Adams*. Edited by Allan Nevins. New York: Longmans, Green, 1928.

————. *Memoirs of John Quincy Adams*. Philadelphia: J. B. Lippincott, 1874–1877.

Allen, Richard V. "The Man Who Won the Cold War." *Hoover Digest*, January 30, 2000.

Anbinder, Tyler. *City of Dreams*. Boston: Houghton Mifflin Harcourt, 2016.

Asada, Sadao. *From Mahan to Pearl Harbor*. Annapolis, MD: Naval Institute Press, 2006.

Bartholdi, Frederic Auguste. *The Statue of Liberty Enlightening the World*. New York: North American Review, 1885.

Basker, James G., ed. *American Anti-Slavery Writings*. New York: Library of America, 2012.

Bemiss, Samuel M. *Three Charters of the Virginia Colony of London*. Williamsburg, VA: 1957.

Billings, William M. *A Little Parliament*. Richmond: Library of Virginia, 2004.

Blackstone, William. *Commentaries on the Laws of England*. Philadelphia: J. B. Lippincott Co., 1893.

Blight, David W. *Frederick Douglass: Prophet of Freedom*. New York: Simon & Schuster, 2018.

Booth, Mary L., trans. *Paris in America*. New York: Charles Scribner, 1863.

Brogan, D. W. *The American Character*. New York: Vintage Press, 1956.

Brookhiser, Richard. *Alexander Hamilton, American*. New York: The Free Press, 1999.

————. *America's First Dynasty*. New York: The Free Press, 2002.

————. "Built to Last." *National Review*, December 18, 2013.

————. "Does Disarmament Work?" *American History*, September 29, 2015.

————. *Founders' Son*. New York: Basic Books, 2014.

———. *Founding Father*. New York: The Free Press, 1996.

———. *Gentleman Revolutionary*. New York: The Free Press, 2003.

———. "Jamestown." *Time*, May 7, 2007.

———. *Right Time, Right Place*. Basic Books, 2009.

———. *What Would the Founders Do?* New York: Basic Books, 2006.

Burns, Eric. *Infamous Scribblers*. New York: PublicAffairs, 2006.

Burrow, Edmund G., and Mike Wallace. *Gotham*. New York: Oxford University Press, 1999.

Burton, Alva Konkle. *The Life of Andrew Hamilton*. Philadelphia: National Publishing Co., 1941.

Chambers, Whittaker. *Witness*. Washington, DC: Regnery History, 2014.

Chateaubriand, Francois Rene de. *Memoirs from Beyond the Grave 1768–1800*. Translated by Alex Andriesse. New York: New York Review Books, 2018.

Chernow, Ron. *Alexander Hamilton*. New York: Penguin, 2004.

Cherny, Robert W. *A Righteous Cause: The Life of William Jennings Bryan*. Norman: University of Oklahoma Press, 1994.

Churchill, Winston S. *The Grand Alliance*. Boston: Houghton Mifflin, 1950.

———. *Their Finest Hour*. Boston: Houghton Mifflin, 1950.

———. *Triumph and Tragedy*. Boston: Houghton Mifflin, 1953.

Clay, Henry. *Speeches of Henry Clay*. Philadelphia: Cary & Lea, 1827.

Cross, Whitney R. *The Burned Over District*. Ithaca, NY: Cornell University Press, 1950.

Dangerfield, George. *The Era of Good Feelings*. Chicago: Elephant Paperbacks, 1985.

Dickinson, John. *An Address to the Committee of Correspondence in Barbados*. Philadelphia: William Bradford, 1766.

Douglass, Frederick. *The Portable Frederick Douglass*. New York: Penguin, 2016.

Dunn, Susan. *A Blueprint for War*. New Haven, CT: Yale University Press, 2018.

Dunn, Susan. *1940*. New Haven, CT: Yale University Press, 2013.

Eliott, J. H. *Empires of the Atlantic World*. New Haven, CT: Yale University Press, 2006.

Ellis, Joseph J. *Passionate Sage*. New York: W. W. Norton, 1993.

Ferling, John. *John Adams: A Life*. New York: Henry Holt, 1996.

Fernow, D. *Documents Relating to the Colonial History of the State of New York*. Albany, NY: Weed, Parsons and Company, 1883.

Fischer, David Hackett. *Albion's Seed*. New York: Oxford University Press, 1989.

Fowler, Robert. *A True Relation . . .* London: printed and sold at the Anchor & Mariner, 1659.

Garman, Tabetha. "Designed for the Good of All: The Flushing Remonstrance and Religious Freedom in America." MA thesis, East Tennessee State University, August 2006.

Gellman, David. *Emancipating New York*. Baton Rouge: Louisiana State University Press, 2006.

Ginzburg, Lori D. *Elizabeth Cady Stanton: An American Life*. New York: Hill & Wang, 2009.

Hamilton, Alexander. *Writings*. New York: Library of America, 2001.

Hamilton, William. *An Oration Delivered in the African Zion Church* . . . New York: Gray & Bunce, 1827.

Horn, James. *1619*. New York: Basic Books, 2018.

Irving, Washington. *Abbotsford and Newstead Abbey*. Philadelphia: Carey, Lea, Blanchard, 1835.

Jameson, J. Franklin. *Narrative of New Netherland*. New York: Charles Scribner and Sons, 1909.

Jay, John. *The Correspondence and Public Papers of John Jay*. New York: G. P. Putnam's Sons, 1890.

Jefferson, Thomas. *The Life and Selected Writings of Thomas Jefferson*. New York: Modern Library, 1944.

Journals of the House of Common 35. Reprinted by Order of the House of Commons, 1803.

Kaiser, David. *No End Save Victory*. New York: Basic Books, 2014.

Kammen, M. G. *Colonial New York: A History*. New York: Oxford University Press, 1996.

Katz, Stanley Nider, ed. *A Brief Narrative of the Case and Trial of John Peter Zenger*. Cambridge, MA: Harvard University Press, 1972.

Kazin, Michael. *A Godly Hero: William Jennings Bryan*. New York: Knopf, 2007.

Ketcham, Ralph. *James Madison: A Biography*. Charlottesville: University of Virginia Press, 1990.

Lamb, Mrs. Martha J. *History of the City of New York*. New York: A. S. Barnes, 1877.

Lazarus, Emma. *The Poems of Emma Lazarus*. Boston: Houghton, Mifflin, 1889.

Lehrman, Lewis. *Churchill, Roosevelt and Co*. Mechanicsburg, PA: Stackpole, 2017.

Lincoln, Abraham. *Collected Works*. Edited by Roy P. Basler. New Brunswick, NJ: Rutgers University Press, 1953.

Lincoln, Abraham. *Speeches and Writings*. New York: Library of America, 1999.

Lopate, Phillip, ed. *Writing New York*. New York: Library of America, 1998.

Madison, James. *Debates in the Federal Convention 1787*. Richmond, VA: James River Press, 1984.

Madison, James. *Writings*. New York: Library of America, 1999.

Maier, Pauline. *Ratification*. New York: Simon & Schuster, 2010.

Marshall, John. *Writings*. New York: Library of America, 2010.

May, Ernest R. *The Making of the Monroe Doctrine*. Cambridge, MA: Harvard University Press, 1975.

McGoldrick, Neal, and Margaret Crocco. *Reclaiming Lost Ground: The Struggle for Woman Suffrage in New Jersey*. New Jersey Historical Commission, 1994.

Minutes of the Manumission Society of New-York. New York: New-York Historical Society.

Moore, Frank, ed. *The Rebellion Record: A Diary of American Events, with Documents, Narratives, Illustrative Incidents, Poetry, etc.* New York: G. P. Putnam, 1864.

O'Callaghan, E. B. *The Documentary History of the State of New-York.* Albany: Weed, Parsons, 1849.

Paine, Thomas. *Collected Writings.* New York: Library of America, 1995.

Paton, W. R. *The Greek Anthology with an English Translation.* New York: G. P. Putnam's Sons, 1927.

Riordan, William L. *Plunkitt of Tammany Hall.* New York: McClure, Phillips, 1905.

Robinson, Peter. "Tear Down This Wall," *Prologue Magazine* 139, no. 2 (Summer 2007).

Rossiter, Clinton. *1787: The Grand Convention.* New York: Macmillan, 1966.

Schama, Simon. *Citizens.* New York: Random House, 1989.

Schor, Esther. *Emma Lazarus.* New York: Schocken Books, 2006.

Shorto, Russell. *Island at the Center of the World.* New York: Vintage, 2005.

Smith, Captain John. *Writings with Other Narratives of Roanoke, Jamestown, and the First English Settlement of America.* New York: Library of America, 2007.

Spitz, Bob. *Reagan: An American Journey.* New York: Penguin, 2018.

Stessin-Cohn, Susan, and Ashley Hurlburt-Biagini. *In Defiance.* Delmar, NY: Black Dome Press, 2016.

Thomas, Benjamin P. *Abraham Lincoln: A Biography.* Carbondale: Southern Illinois University Press, 1980.

Van Schreeven, William J., and George H. Reese, eds. *Proceedings of the General Assembly of Virginia July 30–August 4, 1619.* Jamestown Foundation of the Commonwealth of Virginia, 1969.

Warren, Charles. *The Supreme Court in United States History.* New York: Cosimo Classics, 2011.

Washington, George. *Writings.* New York: Library of America, 1997.

Wellman, Judith. *The Road to Seneca Falls.* Urbana: University of Illinois Press, 2004.

White, Shane. *Somewhat More Independent.* Athens: University of Georgia Press, 1991.

Widmer, Ted, ed. *American Speeches: Political Oratory from Abraham Lincoln to Bill Clinton.* New York: Library of America, 2006.

Widmer, Ted, ed. *American Speeches: Political Oratory from the Revolution to the Civil War.* New York: Library of America, 2006.

Williams, R. Hal. *Realigning America.* Lawrence: University Press of Kansas, 2010.

Wills, Garry. *Lincoln at Gettysburg.* New York: Touchstone, 1997.

Young, John Russell. *Around the World with General Grant.* New York: American News, 1879.

NOTES

INTRODUCTION

1. Jeremy Berke, "Here's President Donald Trump's Full Inauguration Speech," *Business Insider*, January 20, 2017.
2. Before the development of modern nations, people gave their loyalties to entities that were larger (empires) or smaller (Let 'em all go to hell, except Cave 76). But the principle of belonging to a geographic political body was the same.

   The only competing form of loyalty to nationalism and its analogues is religion—Christianity, Islam, Communism—but as a practical matter, politically incarnate religions break up into more tractable units.

   Much ink is spilled over the distinction between nationalism and patriotism. Those who insist that there is a real distinction generally prefer patriotism, which seems to mean nationalism they like, while nationalism means patriotism they dislike.
3. William Hamilton, 6.
4. Washington, 225.
5. Widmer, *American Speeches: Revolution*, 20–21.

CHAPTER ONE

1. Smith, 924.
2. Brookhiser, "Jamestown," 49–50.
3. Smith, 321.

4. Billings, 7.

5. *See* Horn, 121–154; Billings, 8–9.

6. Bemiss, 3.

7. Van Schreeven and Reese, 251.

8. Van Schreeven and Reese, 256.

9. Van Schreeven and Reese, 257.

10. *See* Fischer, 354–360; Brogan, 40–48.

11. Van Schreeven and Reese, 264.

12. Van Schreeven and Reese, 267.

13. Van Schreeven and Reese, 268.

14. Van Schreeven and Reese, 269.

15. Van Schreeven and Reese, 275.

16. Van Schreeven and Reese, 277.

17. Van Schreeven and Reese, 255.

18. Van Schreeven and Reese, 260.

19. Van Schreeven and Reese, 277.

20. Bemiss, 126.

21. Horn, 159.

22. Billings, 12.

23. Billings, 16.

24. Bemiss, 120.

25. Billings, 215, 227–228.

26. Eliott, 134.

CHAPTER TWO

1. *See* Shorto, 49–58.

2. Shorto, 147.

3. Burrow and Wallace, 43.

4. Burrow and Wallace, 46.

5. Shorto, 167.

6. Burrow and Wallace, 60.

7. Fowler.

8. Burrow and Wallace, 61.

9. Burrow and Wallace, 61.

10. Jameson, 397.

11. Jameson, 400.

12. Jameson, 401.
13. Jameson, 397.
14. O'Callaghan, I, 630.
15. Fernow, XIV, 402–403.
16. Madison, *Writings*, 297.
17. Fernow, XIV, 404.
18. Fernow, XIV, 404–405.
19. Fernow, XIV, 407.
20. Fernow, XIV, 408
21. Fernow, XIV, 408–409.
22. Fernow, XIV, 409.
23. Jameson, 400.
24. Fernow, XIV, 515.
25. Garman, 92.
26. Fernow, XIV, 526.
27. Fernow, XIV, 526.
28. Shorto, 304.
29. Kammen, 118–119.

CHAPTER THREE

1. Lamb, I, 541.
2. Brookhiser, *What Would the Founders Do?*, 18.
3. Burns, 32.
4. Burns, 102.
5. Katz, 41.
6. Burton, 15.
7. Warren, I, 48.
8. Katz, 58.
9. Katz, 150.
10. Katz, 62.
11. Katz, 65.
12. Katz, 66.
13. Katz, 65–66.
14. Katz, 70–71.
15. Katz, 93.
16. Katz, 81.

17. Katz, 87.
18. Katz, 98.
19. Katz, 87.
20. Katz, 99.
21. Katz, 99.
22. Katz, 101.
23. Burton, 69.
24. Burrow, 155.
25. Burton, 144.
26. Brookhiser, *Alexander Hamilton*, 206.
27. Brookhiser, *Gentleman Revolutionary*, 21.

CHAPTER FOUR

1. Katz, 79.
2. *Journals*, 398.
3. Paine, 52.
4. Ferling, 151.
5. Rossiter, 91–92.
6. Ferling, 150.
7. Jefferson, 311.
8. Ellis, 64.
9. Brookhiser, *Founding Father*, 177.
10. Jefferson, 178–179.
11. Blackstone, I, 41.
12. Jefferson, 719.
13. Dickinson, 5.
14. Brookhiser, *Alexander Hamilton*, 162.
15. Brookhiser, *Founders' Son*, 2.

CHAPTER FIVE

1. Horn, 87.
2. Horn, 113.
3. Basker, 2.
4. Basker, 35.
5. Washington, 158.
6. Washington, 1024.

7. Stessin-Cohn, 127.

8. Chernow, 53.

9. Gellman, 47.

10. Brookhiser, "Built to Last."

11. Brookhiser, *Gentleman Revolutionary*, 34.

12. Jay, I, 407.

13. White, 82.

14. *Minutes*, I, 16.

15. *Minutes*, I, 29–30.

16. *Minutes*, 39.

17. Burrow and Wallace, 286.

18. William Hamilton, 6–9.

CHAPTER SIX

1. Brookhiser, *Alexander Hamilton*, 54.

2. Brookhiser, *Founding Father*, 61.

3. Madison, *Debates*, 616.

4. Maier, 384.

5. Madison, *Debates*, 597.

6. *See* Irving, 39–40.

7. Washington, 1106.

8. Washington, 469.

9. Alexander Hamilton, 166.

10. Washington, 245.

11. Madison, *Debates*, 351.

12. Madison, *Debates*, 504.

13. Madison, *Debates*, 505.

14. Ketcham, 451.

CHAPTER SEVEN

1. Clay, 77–80.

2. Brookhiser, *America's First Dynasty*, 65.

3. Adams, *Diaries*, II, 4–5.

4. Chateaubriand, 218.

5. Chateaubriand, 274.

6. *See* May, 105.

7. Adams, *Diary*, 170.

8. May, 3.

9. Dangerfield, 293–294.

10. Jefferson, 324.

11. Dangerfield, 293–294.

12. Adams, *Diaries*, I, 581.

13. Adams, *Memoirs*, VI, 177.

14. Adams, *Memoirs*, VI, 179.

15. Adams, *Memoirs*, VI, 185.

16. Adams, *Memoirs*, 185–186.

17. Adams, *Memoirs*, 194–195.

18. Adams, *Memoirs*, 197–198.

19. I borrow this phrase from David Brooks, who used it in Michael Pack's film *Rediscovering Alexander Hamilton* (Manifold Productions, 2011).

20. Adams, *Memoirs*, VI, 197.

21. Lincoln, *Speeches and Writings*, I, 264.

22. Dangerfield, 304.

23. Dangerfield, 306.

24. Dangerfield, 204–205.

25. Adams, *Diaries*, II, 615.

CHAPTER EIGHT

1. Collection of the Gilder Lehrman Institute, Lucy Knox to Henry Knox, August 23, 1777.

2. Blackstone, I, 442–445.

3. *See* McGoldrick and Crocco.

4. Cross, 3, quoting Carl Carmer.

5. Adams, *Diaries*, I, 543.

6. Cross, 219.

7. Ginzburg, 31.

8. Ginzburg, 33.

9. Wellman, 60.

10. Ginzburg, 41.

11. Lincoln, *Speeches and Writings*, I, 111.

12. *See* Adams, *Diaries*, II, 555.

13. Wellman, 188–189.

14. Wellman, 48.
15. Blackstone, I, 41.
16. Wellman, 192.
17. *See* Ginzburg, 47.
18. Brookhiser, *Alexander Hamilton*, 134.
19. Wellman, 193.
20. Wellman, 195.
21. Wellman, 198.
22. Frederick Douglass, "The Rights of Women," *North Star*, July 28, 1848.
23. *See* Wellman, 205.
24. Wellman, 210.
25. Blight, 490–491.
26. *See* website of the Women's Rights National Historical Park, Seneca Falls, New York.

CHAPTER NINE

1. Widmer, *American Speeches: Revolution*, 646.
2. Lincoln, *Speeches and Writings*, I, 426.
3. Lincoln, *Speeches and Writings*, I, 677.
4. Lincoln, *Speeches and Writings*, II, 194.
5. Douglass, 460.
6. Brookhiser, *Founders' Son*, 222.
7. Brookhiser, *Founders' Son*, 220.
8. Lincoln, *Speeches and Writings*, II, 306.
9. Lincoln, *Speeches and Writings*, II, 353.
10. *See* Wills, 20–21.
11. Wills, 236.
12. Wills, 232.
13. Lewis Lehrman tells me it takes three hours and ten minutes to read aloud.
14. Moore, VI, 345.
15. Lincoln, *Speeches and Writings*, II, 433.
16. Wellman, 183.
17. Lincoln, II, 475–476.
18. Marshall, 415.
19. Widmer, *American Speeches: Revolution*, 233.
20. *See* Brookhiser, *Gentleman Revolutionary*, 84.

21. Told to me (at a Union League Club, appropriately enough) by an elderly man who heard it from his grandfather, who had been there as a child.
22. Lincoln, II, 749.
23. Lincoln, *Collected Works*, VII, 25.
24. George Kateb, "Abraham Lincoln and Statesmanship," lecture given at the James Madison Program (Princeton, NJ, May 17, 2016).
25. Widmer, *American Speeches: Abraham Lincoln*, 556.
26. *See* Brookhiser, *Founders' Son*, 151–165.
27. Lincoln, *Speeches and Writings*, II, 699.

CHAPTER TEN

1. Thomas, 170.
2. Lincoln, I, 456.
3. Lopate, 233.
4. Riordan, 129.
5. Anbinder, 298.
6. Anbinder, 299. It is not certain that Lazarus wrote the article, but given the similarity between it and her poem, she either wrote both or was a plagiarist.
7. Paton, I, 387.
8. Schama, 27.
9. *See* Booth.
10. Bartholdi, 42.
11. Anbinder, 302.
12. Bartholdi, 53.
13. *See* Lazarus, I, and Schor, 229–231, 247.

CHAPTER ELEVEN

1. Widmer, *American Speeches: Revolution*, 644.
2. *See* Madison, *Writings*, 531.
3. Cherny, 52–53.
4. Kazin, 48.
5. Kazin, 24.
6. Williams, 81.
7. Kazin, 57.
8. Williams, 82.
9. Kazin, 58.

10. Williams, 83.
11. Alexander Hamilton, 592.
12. Cherny, 60.
13. Williams, 140–141.
14. Kazin, 74–75, 323.

CHAPTER TWELVE

1. Brookhiser, "Does Disarmament Work?"
2. Dunn, *Blueprint*, 4.
3. Dunn, *Blueprint*, 3.
4. Kaiser, 31.
5. Kaiser, 33.
6. Dunn, *Blueprint*, 14.
7. Dunn, *Blueprint*, 34.
8. Dunn, *Blueprint*, 35.
9. Kaiser, 49.
10. Dunn, *Blueprint*, 46.
11. Dunn, *Blueprint*, 45.
12. Dunn, *Blueprint*, 52.
13. Dunn, *Blueprint*, 54.
14. Dunn, *Blueprint*, 68.
15. Churchill, *Finest*, 484.
16. *See* Dunn, *1940*, 210.
17. Washington, 962.
18. *See* Dunn, *Blueprint*, 85, 210.
19. Dunn, *Blueprint*, 89.
20. Churchill, *Alliance*, 511–512.
21. Asada, 183.

CHAPTER THIRTEEN

1. Widmer, *American Speeches: Abraham Lincoln*, 445.
2. Lehrman, 272.
3. Churchill, *Triumph*, 227.
4. Widmer, *American Speeches: Abraham Lincoln*, 554–555.
5. This is my memory of the scene. *See* Brookhiser, *Right Time*, 101–102.
6. Spitz, 213.

7. Chambers, xlv.
8. *See* Brookhiser, *Right Time*, 98.
9. Spitz, 84.
10. Spitz, 289.
11. Allen.
12. Robinson, "Tear Down This Wall."
13. Robinson, "Tear Down This Wall."
14. Robinson, "Tear Down This Wall."
15. Robinson, "Tear Down This Wall."
16. Widmer, *American Speeches: Abraham Lincoln*, 555.
17. Robinson, "Tear Down This Wall."
18. Lauren Oyler, "Letter of Recommendation: Berliner Fernsehturm," *New York Times Magazine*, April 6, 2017.
19. "Gorbachev Spurns Use of Force in Europe," *New York Times*, July 7, 1989.
20. Spitz, 744.
21. John Tagliabue, "Evolution in Europe," *New York Times*, September 13, 1990.
22. Adam Lushner, "At Least 10,000 People Died in Tiananmen Square Massacre," *Independent*, December 23, 2017.

CONCLUSION

1. Young, 408–417.

INDEX

Formicola, Serafina, 189
Fort Sumter, 168
Fowler, Robert, 34
France: as audience of Declaration of
    Independence, 76; fate of America
    in Civil War and, 178–179;
    invasion of Spain and, 131–132;
    liberty and, 3; Statue of Liberty
    and, 195–200
Franklin, Benjamin, 53, 65–66, 72,
    74–75, 86, 109–110
Franklin, James, 53
Franklin, Samuel, 94–95, 104
free press, 60–61, 119
free silver, 206–207, 209, 220. *See also*
    Cross of Gold speech
Free-Soil Party, 164
freedom of religion, 119, 257. *See also*
    Flushing Remonstrance
Fremont, John, 171
French and Indian War, 69
French Revolution, 127–128
fugitive slave law, 169

Garnett, Thomas, 20
Garrison, William Lloyd, 151–152
George III, King of England, 71,
    74–75, 79, 81
Georgia, 117
Germany, 225, 229, 239, 241.
    See also Berlin Wall; World War II
Gerry, Elbridge, 110, 115–116, 122
Gettysburg Address: continuation of
    theme of American liberty into the
    future and, 179–180, 258; economy
    of, 182; fate of the American
    experiment in the eyes of foreign

powers and, 176–177; military
    and, 175–176; recasting of history
    and, 183–184; role of the people in
    government and, 180–182. *See also*
    Civil War; Lincoln, Abraham
Gettysburg, Battle of, 173–174
Gilman, Nicholas, 109, 110
gold standard, 206, 209
Goldwater, Barry, 246
Gorbachev, Mikhail, 245, 247,
    252–255
Gordon, Nathaniel, 170
Gould, Jay, 206
Grant, Ulysses, 191, 229, 260–261
Greece, 128, 138

Haiti, 127–128, 145, 170
Hakluyt, Richard, 10
Hamilton, Alexander: adultery and,
    157–158; Bank of the United States
    and, 213; constitution of Haiti and,
    128; constitutional convention and,
    109, 112; on Creator as grantor of
    rights, 83; on free press, 65; idea of
    American king and, 120; New-
    York Manumission Society and,
    95–96, 104, 184; as supporter of US
    constitution, 116–117
Hamilton, Andrew: consequences of
    the Zenger defense by, 66–67; on
    Cosby, 58–59; Council's award of
    keys to city and, 64; death of, 65;
    defense of freedom of expression,
    62–63; defense of Zenger, 56–58;
    historical allusions and, 62, 78;
    invocations of liberty and, 61–62;
    on juries, 60; legal skills of, 58;

admiration for, 207; death of, 179; Declaration of Independence and, 73, 76–77; French Revolution and, 127–128; idea of American king and, 125; Lafayette and, 195; as member of Virginia Dynasty, 134; religious beliefs of, 81–82; signing of Declaration and, 83–84. *See also* Declaration of Independence

Johnson, Anthony, 90

Johnson, William Samuel, 111

Kateb, George, 183

Keese, John, 94, 104

Kennedy, John F., 243

King, Martin Luther, Jr., 184

King, Rufus, 112

Know-Nothing Party. *See* American Party

Knox, Frank, 228, 230

Knox, Henry, 121–122

Knox, Lucy, 147

Korean War, 93

Laboulaye, Edouard Rene de, 195–198, 201

Lafayette, Marquis de, 121, 195, 198

Langdon, John, 109

Lansing, John, Jr., 109

Lazarus, Emma: background of, 190–191; death of, 202; "The New Colossus," 192–194, 202–203, 258; unveiling of Statue of Liberty and, 199; vision of America and a saving country and, 191

League of Nations, 224

Lee, Arthur, 91

Lee, Richard Henry, 72, 74

legal culture, 51

legislation, Jamestown General Assembly and, 18

Letter Concerning Toleration (Locke), 39

Letters from a Pennsylvania Farmer (Dickinson), 83

Leutze, Emmanuel, 93

Liberia, 170

Liberty Enlightening the World. *See* Statue of Liberty

liberty of expression, British colonies and, 49

Liberty Party, 152

Lincoln, Abraham: approval of Butler's policy of not returning slaves, 169–170; black suffrage and, 185; on Clay, 141; colonization approach and, 171–172; compensated emancipation approach, 171; countermanding of Fremont's orders in Missouri, 171; Emancipation Proclamation of, 173; immigrants and, 188; on Liberty Party, 153; Nathaniel Gordon sentence and, 170; recognition of Haiti and Liberia, 170; Republican nomination and, 164, 168; Thirteenth Amendment and, 184. *See also* Gettysburg Address

Lindbergh, Charles, 234

Livingston, Robert R., 73, 93

Locke, John, 39, 80

London Company, 10, 12–14. *See also* Virginia Company

Lucius Junius Brutus, 62

INDEX

Poland, 247, 254–255
Polk, James, 144, 153
Poole, Robert, 21
Populist Party, 207–210, 219
Portugal, 89–90
Pory, John, 15, 17–18, 21–22, 26
Powell, William, 21
Powhatan tribe, 12–13, 17–18, 20–21
printing, 52
private property, 14
Privy Council, 72
Prohibition, 209
Prussia, 131
Pulitzer, Joseph, 199
Putin, Vladimir, 1

Quadruple Alliance (Britain, Prussia, Austria, Russia), 131
Quakers: abolitionism and, 151; Declaration of Independence and, 81; Declaration of Sentiments and, 157; in Flushing, 33–35; Manumission Society and, 94–96, 103; martyrdom in New England and, 43–44; schism is beliefs of, 151

race, 90. *See also* Civil War; slavery
Randolph, Edmund, 111, 115
Rankin, Jeannette, 223, 238
Read, George, 113
Reagan, Ronald: Communism and, 245; dismantling of the Berlin Wall and, 255; early career of, 244–246; election of as Governor of California, 246; policy toward Soviet Union of, 246–247,

255–256. *See also* Brandenburg Gate speech
religion: Anglicanism, 11; Catholicism, 11, 189; God as grantor of human rights and, 80–83; Irish immigrants and, 189; Jefferson's, 81–82; Miller and, 153; Mormonism, 149; New-York Manumission Society bylaws and, 96–98; use of in Brandenburg Gate speech of Reagan, 254; women and, 157; Zenger trial and, 58, 61–62. *See also* Flushing Remonstrance; Quakers
religious liberty, 38–41, 257
Republicans, 164, 209–210
revolutionary movements, 127–131
Rhode Island, 43, 47, 102, 109, 117
Robinson, Peter, 247, 251–252
Rockefeller, John D., 206
Rolfe, John, 13
Roosevelt, Franklin D.: Arsenal of Democracy fireside chat, 233–237, 258; background of, 225; call for disarmament after the war, 241–242; Depression and, 225; election for third term of, 229–230; fireside chats of, 232; habit of misdirection in speech, 226–227; Japan's attack on China, 226; lend-lease program, 231–232; letter from Churchill and, 231; military advisors of, 227–228; Pearl Harbor and, 238–239; planning for rearmament and, 227; professed antiwar sentiment of, 225; Stalin and, 242; war planning

and, 228, 230; war production and, 229
Roosevelt, Theodore, 225
Rosenman, Sam, 232, 235
Rossiter, Clinton, 258–259
Russell, William, 211, 214
Russia, 131, 143
Rutledge, Edward, 85

Schuyler, Georgina, 203
seditious libel, 54–55, 57–59, 65–66
Seneca Falls convention, 159–160. *See also* Declaration of Sentiments
Seward, William, 167–168, 173, 184, 190, 205
Shays Rebellion, 108
Shelley, Walter, 19
Sherman, Roger, 73–74, 118
Sherwood, Robert, 232, 235
Shortridge, Samuel, 224
silver standard, 206–207, 209
Simmons, John, 94
slave trade: Declaration of Independence and, 75, 89; history of in colonies, 89–91; sentence of Nathaniel Gordon and, 170; sentiment against, 91–92
slavery: Congressional advances against under Lincoln, 170; Connecticut and, 102; enslavement of free blacks and, 96–97, 101–102; Grant on, 261–262; John Jay and, 99–100; Lincoln on, 168–169; Lincoln's offer of compensated emancipation and, 171; Massachusetts and, 102; Missouri Compromise and, 150; New Hampshire and, 102; New York manumission act and, 102; Pennsylvania and, 102; political system and, 169; Rhode Island and, 102; Robert Troup and, 100; sentiment against, 91–92; in the US Constitution, 122–124; Vermont and, 102. *See also* abolitionism; New-York Manumission Society
Smith, Gerrit, 152–153
Smith, John, 12
Smith, Melancton, 95
Smith, William, 54–55, 65
socialism, 217
Society of the Cincinnati, 121–122
Somers Isles Company, 26
South Carolina, 117
Southard, Samuel, 135
Soviet Union, 242–243, 246
Spain, 10–11, 76, 89, 128–132
Spelman, Henry, 21
St. John, Henry, Viscount Bolingbroke, 119–120
St. John the Baptist, 90
Stalin, Joseph, 242
Stamp Act, 70, 72
Stanton, Elizabeth Cady: abolitionism and, 150–151; on black suffrage vs. women's, 164–165; call for women's suffrage and, 158–159; Declaration of Sentiments and, 155–158; development of women's convention and, 154–155; early life and marriage, 149–150; early life of, 149; references to immigration and, 159; temperance and, 189

Stanton, Henry, 150, 153, 159
Star Chamber, 59
Stark, Harold, 227–228, 230
Statue of Liberty, 199–201, 258
Stimson, Henry, 228
stock market, 206
Stockton, Richard, 84
Stuart, Charles Edward, 120
Stuyvesant, Peter: as addressee
   of Flushing Remonstrance, 4;
   background of, 31; death of, 46;
   Dutch West India Company
   response to Quakers and, 45;
   England of the Civil War and,
   45–46; Hodgson and, 35; policy on
   Quakers, 35–36; reforms in New
   Amsterdam and, 31–32; religious
   prejudice of, 32–33; response to the
   Flushing Remonstrance and, 41–42
Suu Kyi, Aung San, 1
Swedenborg, Emmanuel, 92

Tammany Hall, 190, 214
taxes, 111
"Tear Down This Wall" speech. *See*
   Brandenburg Gate speech
Texas, 153
Thirteenth Amendment, 184
Thompson, John, 75
Tillman, Benjamin, 211
tobacco, 13
Tocqueville, Alexis de, 195
Tripartite Pact, 229
Troup, Robert, 95, 98, 100–101, 104
Trump, Donald, nationalism and, 1
Tubman, Harriet, 167, 172
Twain, Mark, 192

US Constitution: addition of
   the Bill of Rights, 118–119;
   complexity of, 117–118; delegates
   to constitutional convention and,
   108–110; draft of, 111; election
   of executive and, 119; equality
   of Americans, 119; Fifteenth
   Amendment to, 185; Fourteenth
   Amendment to, 185; freedom of
   religion and, 119; freedom of the
   press and, 119; funding for debt
   and, 107–108; idea of American
   king and, 119–120, 124–126,
   258; Martin Luther King Jr. on,
   185; mechanics of convention to
   create, 110–111; national debate
   regarding, 115; nobility and, 120–
   122, 124; opponents of, 115–116;
   Pennsylvania's ratification of, 116;
   preamble of, 113, 181, 257–258;
   ratification process, 115–117; role
   of the people in government and,
   181–182; secrecy of convention
   and, 114–115; signers of,
   113–114; slavery and, 122–124,
   258; style committee for final
   rewrite of, 111–113; supporters of,
   116–117; Thirteenth Amendment
   to, 184
US Navy, 225–226

Van Buren, Martin, 151
Van Dam, Rip, 50–51
Vanderbilt, Cornelius, 206
Vermont, 102
Vietnam War, 246
Vilas, William, 211

CREDIT: LARA HEIMERT

Richard Brookhiser is a senior editor of *National Review*, columnist for *American History*, and the author of thirteen books, including *John Marshall: The Man Who Made the Supreme Court*, *Founder's Son: A Life of Abraham Lincoln*, and *James Madison*. He lives in New York City.